Here Comes the Bride

The Bride of Your Husband

The Bride of Christ

By Sue Angel

Copyright © 2010 by Sue Angel

Here Comes the Bride
The Bride of Your Husband
The Bride of Christ
by Sue Angel

Printed in the United States of America

ISBN 9781609573089

All rights reserved solely by the author. The author guarantees all contents are original and do not infringe upon the legal rights of any other person or work. No part of this book may be reproduced in any form without the permission of the author. The views expressed in this book are not necessarily those of the publisher.

Unless otherwise indicated, Bible quotations are taken from The *New American Standard Bible, Updated Edition* (NASU). Copyright © 1960, 1962, 1963, 1968, 1971, 1972, 1973, 1975, 1977, 1995 by The Lockman Foundation; The *Holy Bible, New International Version (*NIV*)*. Copyright © 1973, 1978, 1984 by International Bible Society; The King James Version (KJV); The *New King James Version* (NKJV). Copyright © 1993, 2000 by *Biblesoft PC Study Bible Complete Reference Library*; The *Revised Standard Version* (RSV). Copyright © 1993, 2000 by *Biblesoft PC Study Bible Complete Reference Library*; *The New Testament in Modern English, Revised Edition*. Copyright © 1947, 1955, 1957, 1958, 1960, 1972 by J.B. Phillips; *The Living Bible* (TLB). Copyright © 1993, 2000 by *Biblesoft PC Study Bible Complete Reference Library;* and *The NASB Interlinear Greek-English New Testament* (Marshall). Copyright © 1984 by Zondervan Corporation.

Greek and Hebrew definitions are from Biblesoft's *New Exhaustive Strong's Numbers and Concordance with Expanded Greek-Hebrew*

Dictionary. Copyright © 1994 by Biblesoft and International Bible Translators, Inc.

Information marked Wycliffe is from *The Wycliffe Bible Commentary, Electronic Database*. Copyright © 1962 by Moody Press.

Definitions marked Webster are from *Webster's New Twentieth Century Dictionary Unabridged*. Copyright © 1940, 1941, 1942, 1943, 1945, 1946, 1947, 1949, 1950, 1951, 1952, 1953, 1955, 1956, 1957, 1958, 1959, 1960, 1962 by The World Publishing Company.

Definitions marked M-W are from *Merriam-Webster's Reference Library* software. Copyright © 2001 by Merriam-Webster, Inc.

Definitions marked M-W Web Site are from www.m-w.com, Copyright © 2010 by Merriam-Webster, Inc.

www.xulonpress.com

This book is dedicated

to my wonderful husband Charles,

who demonstrates

the love of Christ to me

on a daily basis

Contents

❋❋❋

Acknowledgements ix
Foreword xi
Introduction xiii
Why God Created Marriage 15
Wedding Vows 22
Gender Differences 26
The Excellent Wife Is Trustworthy 34
Respect and Love 38
The Ring 48
The Husband's Name 53
Leadership 59
Provision 72
Protection 86
Embracing Passion 90
Defeating the Passion-killers 117
Looking Beautiful 125
Opening Your Heart 140
The Battle 154
A Forgiving Heart 181
Fulfilling Responsibilities 194
It's about Time 207
100-100 Marriage 218
Commitment 233
Rebuilding 243

Acknowledgements

✻✻✻

There are a number of people who did not sit at my keyboard, but who nevertheless played a role in the writing of this book. I want to offer my deep gratitude to them:

To my husband Charles who urged me to write this book. It would never have been published without your sacrifices, encouragement, prayer support, and wise counsel along the way.

To Anita Blanton, who has been my cherished faithful friend for almost forty years, and who worked with me in the *Here Comes the Bride* sessions. Your encouragement, spiritual insights, supportive prayers, and editorial advice have blessed my life and have influenced sections of this book.

To Linda Wear, my treasured friend whose consistent loyalty and love have never wavered throughout the four decades of our friendship. Your biblical insights, faithful prayers, and creative ideas have benefited me and have influenced portions of this book.

To Debbie Craft, my dear and loving friend for twenty years. As we worked together in women's ministry (first at church, and later in the *Here Comes the Bride* and *Woman to Woman* classes), your enthusiasm was infectious, your labor tireless, and your encouragement a blessing.

To Judy Andersen, a dear friend of great talent, creativity, and enthusiasm. Some of my fondest memories are of serving in women's ministry together with you: in church, in your home, and in the *Here Comes the Bride* and *Woman to Woman* meetings.

To the women who attended the *Here Comes the Bride* and *Woman to Woman* Bible studies. You will never know how much encouragement you have provided and continue to provide to me.

Foreword

❋❋❋

"Many women do noble things, but you surpass them all."
(Prov. 31:29 NIV)

It is my desire that our marriage is a proper reflection of the relationship between Jesus Christ and His bride, the church. Due to Sue's willingness to put into practice the teachings that she brings forth in this book, my responsibility as the husband (who should lead the family with integrity and faithfulness) is made much easier.

For 46 years, I have been the blessed husband of Sue, who makes my position in the family one of pleasure. Having been the long-time recipient of such a blessing, I can, without hesitation, recommend this work to any woman that is seeking to find completion in her life, while being the primary source of encouragement to her husband.

—Charles Angel

Introduction

❋❋❋

So that you will be warned about what to expect from this book, I will tell you first of all that I have made no effort to write something that is politically correct. In fact, you will find that the concepts on these pages are not at all compatible with contemporary American culture as it relates to the role of women. Nor have I written these words so that you will know how to always get your way about matters of disagreement with your husband. If either of those is the kind of book that you want to read, you will probably not find this one appealing.

It appears to me that marriage in today's society is failing at an alarming rate and that many members of the bride of Christ are way off course in their relationship to the Lord. My desire in writing this book is to help women to have successful marriages and to live godly lives. The best way to do that, it seems to me, is to see what the Word of God says. In following Scripture, we can become the wives and the bride that He has called us to be.

As you consider what God's Word has to say about these matters, you may be tempted to believe that His instructions are impossible to follow. You would be misled. Our Lord is not an unrighteous Judge. He doesn't require what we are unable to do.

Perhaps you think that I say these things because these behaviors came naturally to me. Again, you would be mistaken. By nature, I am fairly strong-willed. There are flaws in me that I still have not been able to totally eliminate. I am not a perfect Christian, and I am not a perfect wife. I do, however, yearn to be the Christian and the wife that God wants me to be. I have *learned* the importance of *striving* to follow His Word. My marriage and my spiritual life have improved greatly as I have learned and implemented these principles.

I first taught many of these lessons in women's groups called *Here Comes the Bride* and *Woman to Woman*. Although I've never known even one woman whose marriage or life grew worse because she implemented these changes, a number of ladies who put these principles into practice have told me that they saw dramatic turns for the better in their marriages and in their spiritual lives. It is my prayer that these concepts will be helpful to you as well.

Why God Created Marriage

✹✹✹

L et's consider a story about a couple (let's call them the Smiths) who went to visit some friends (the Johnsons, perhaps) in a nearby city and found that the Johnsons' house was extremely attractive. In fact, these houseguests were planning to build a house themselves, and they decided that they would like to replicate the house they were visiting.

The hostess in this beautiful dwelling told her guests that they were indeed fortunate, because her father was the architect who had designed this structure for her. "He would be happy to share the house plans with you," she said.

Without delay, Mr. and Mrs. Smith drove to the office of the architect to get the plans. Then with great excitement, they set out to build a house like the one that they had visited.

As soon as the structure was complete, Mrs. Johnson traveled to visit her former houseguests in their new home and found that they were not at all happy with the house. She could see why. Although the house was brand new, the roof sagged and there were numerous cracks in the ceilings and walls. The floor felt unstable.

Horrified, the architect's daughter called her father. "I can't imagine what happened," she said. "They had your plans."

Mrs. Johnson's father agreed to make a visit to check out the house and to try to determine what had gone wrong. Soon the architect arrived to examine the new house.

Here Comes the Bride

"I don't remember a tray ceiling in the plans for the master bedroom," he said.

"No, it wasn't in the plans," Mrs. Smith declared. "We liked the one in the living room, however, so we decided to put one in here too."

"The house wasn't designed for that," the architect explained. "Special supports must be in the attic for large tray ceilings like this."

"Where is the long wall between the living room and dining room?" queried the house designer.

"Oh, we wanted the area to be more open, so we left most of it out. It makes the house look bigger, and it will be easier for people to circulate when we have a party."

"That was a load-bearing wall!" the architect exclaimed in obvious exasperation. "It was necessary to the strength of the house."

Next, the architect looked under the house. He noticed that there was no footing under the concrete blocks; instead, the blocks just sat right on the top of the ground.

"Why didn't you dig a proper foundation under the house?" he inquired.

"That seemed like an unnecessary expense," Mrs. Smith replied.

The amazed architect asked, "How on earth did this place pass the city inspection?"

"Oh, we live outside the city limits," explained Mrs. Smith. "We had no city inspector."

There was nothing wrong with the house plans that the architect had designed. When his daughter and son-in-law followed those plans, the result was a beautiful and well-built house. The problem with the second structure was that it was not constructed according to the architect's design.

The Bible says,

"The wise woman builds her house,
But the foolish tears it down with her own hands." (Prov. 14:1)

The Hebrew word for *house* here can mean the physical structure, but it's usually used to mean *home* or *household*. *Strong's* defines the word this way: "a house (in the greatest variation of applications, especially family, etc.)" Examples of this word's being used in this sense are found in Gen. 7:1 when the Lord called Noah and his house (family) into the ark, and in Gen. 18:19 when God said that Abraham would teach his household. Thus, the Scriptures are saying that the wise woman builds her household, her marriage, her family...her home.

The architect in the preceding story provided good plans for the house, plans that were ignored with disastrous results. In fact, that poorly constructed house would soon collapse unless *extremely* expensive major repairs were made without delay.

Likewise, we have an Architect who has provided plans for building our marriages and lives. Just as the new homeowners made a horrible mistake when they deviated from the provided design, we are foolish if we decide that His plan for marriage and living isn't best and choose instead to follow our own ideas. We ignore the Designer's instructions to our own peril.

I have known women who said that they wanted to be godly wives with successful marriages, yet who—upon learning what our Architect has said about the matter—decided that it was too difficult. Like the house in our story, their marriages have been damaged as a result. Some of those "houses" have actually collapsed in divorce.

When a wife wants to *"build her house,"* she will need to depend upon the Lord's work within her if she wants to be successful. The wise woman will obey the Lord's instructions and therefore will build her house to endure. The foolish woman, who doesn't follow the Lord's plan, tears it down.

Obedience to Scripture is always the key, whether in our marriages or in our overall personal lives. Jesus said, *"Everyone who comes to Me and hears My words and acts on them, I will show you whom he is like: he is like a man building a house, who dug deep and laid a foundation on the rock; and when a flood occurred, the torrent burst against that house and could not shake it, because it had been well built. But the one who has heard and has not acted accordingly, is like a man who built a house on the ground without any foundation; and the torrent burst against it and immediately it collapsed, and the ruin of that house was great."* (Luke 6:47-49)

Have you ever wondered why marriage was traditionally set up the way it was? Have you considered why God's Word instructs us to assume certain postures in our marriages? For that matter, have you wondered why God created marriage in the first place? The apostle Paul gives us a clue in the fifth chapter of Ephesians:

"Wives, be subject to your own husbands, as to the Lord. For the husband is the head of the wife, as Christ also is the head of the church, He Himself being the Savior of the body. But as the church is subject to Christ, so also the wives ought to be to their husbands in everything...For this reason a man shall leave his father and mother, and shall be joined to his wife; and the two shall become one flesh. This mystery is great; but I am speaking with reference to Christ and the church. Nevertheless, each individual among you also is to love his own wife even as himself; and the wife must see to it that she respects her husband." (Eph. 5:22-24, 31-33)

Paul tells us in this passage that the marriage relationship is a picture of the union between Christ and His people, the church.

In the Old Testament as well, the Lord refers to His relationship with His people Israel as a marital relationship:

"The word of the LORD came to me: 'Go and proclaim in the hearing of Jerusalem: "I remember the devotion of your youth, how as a bride you loved me and followed me through the desert, through a land not sown."'" (Jer. 2:1-2 NIV)

Ladies, I don't believe that the Lord looked around at what He had made until He located something that resembled the relationship He desired to have with the saints and thought, "Now that would be a good illustration of what I want to convey. I'll use that." That's what *we* have to do when we choose a comparison, of course. We see a connection between something in creation and a point we desire to make; then we communicate the similarities between the two. God, however, isn't dependent upon what already exists. He is the Creator, after all. He made all things for a reason, and I believe that God created marriage for the express purpose of illustrating the union of Christ and His people.

Man and woman were both created in the image of God. (See Gen. 1:27.) According to Gal. 3:28, we are neither male nor female in Christ. There is, therefore, no difference in our relationship to the

Lord because of our gender. In the family, however, the Lord has placed men and women in differing roles to illustrate the relationship of the Son of God and His bride. (He has also called men and women to differing roles in the church as well as in the family. For example, see 1 Tim. 2:12.)

Let's look at some ways that marriage portrays the relationship of Christ and the church.

Obtaining a Bride

For the original marriage in the Garden of Eden, the Lord supernaturally anesthetized Adam. Then God opened the side of the sleeping man, removed a rib, and created for him a bride.

"Then the LORD God said, 'It is not good for the man to be alone; I will make him a helper suitable for him.' Out of the ground the LORD God formed every beast of the field and every bird of the sky, and brought them to the man to see what he would call them; and whatever the man called a living creature, that was its name. The man gave names to all the cattle, and to the birds of the sky, and to every beast of the field, but for Adam there was not found a helper suitable for him. So the LORD God caused a deep sleep to fall upon the man, and he slept; then He took one of his ribs and closed up the flesh at that place. The LORD God fashioned into a woman the rib which He had taken from the man, and brought her to the man. The man said,

"'This is now bone of my bones,
And flesh of my flesh;
She shall be called Woman,
Because she was taken out of Man.'

"For this reason a man shall leave his father and his mother, and be joined to his wife; and they shall become one flesh." (Gen. 2:18-24)

Since she was fashioned from his rib—meaning that part of Adam's own body had become this woman—Adam was afterward not completely whole without his wife. They were *"one flesh,"* or—so to speak—one person. Sexual union in marriage is a picture and symbol of this unity.

It's interesting that God put Adam to sleep for this procedure. Sometimes in the Bible, the word *sleep* is a metaphor for physical death. When Lazarus died, for example, Jesus told His disciples, *"Our friend Lazarus has fallen asleep; but I go, so that I may awaken him out of sleep."* (John 11:11) Paul wrote to comfort the Thessalonians about the Christians who had died, saying, *"But we do not want you to be uninformed, brethren, about those who are asleep, so that you will not grieve as do the rest who have no hope. For if we believe that Jesus died and rose again, even so God will bring with Him those who have fallen asleep in Jesus."* (1 Thess. 4:13-14) The euphemism is employed again in Acts 13:36: *"For David, after he had served the purpose of God in his own generation, fell asleep, and was laid among his fathers and underwent decay."*

God opened Adam's side to create Eve after the man was already asleep. Thus, Adam's side was riven while he slept. Likewise, Jesus—hanging from a Roman cross to purchase *His* bride—was already dead when His side was pierced.

"But when they came to Jesus and found that he was already dead, they did not break his legs. Instead, one of the soldiers pierced Jesus' side with a spear, bringing a sudden flow of blood and water." (John 19:33-34 NIV)

Thus, Adam's experience typified, or portrayed, the redemptive death of the Messiah. Adam's sleep as he obtained a wife was a picture of the death of Jesus Christ that made possible the creation of *His* bride, the church.

Paul wrote that we are the bride of Christ, but he also said that we are His body. *"Now you are Christ's body, and individually members of it."* (1 Cor. 12:27) This is also true in the natural marriage. The man and the woman become *"one flesh,"* just as we who belong to Christ as His bride become *"one spirit with Him."* (1 Cor. 6:17) You are not only your husband's bride, but in a sense you are his body as well because you have become one flesh with him. *"So husbands ought also to love their own wives **as their own bodies**. He who loves his own wife loves himself; for no one ever hated his own flesh, but nourishes and cherishes it, just as Christ also does the* *church—for we are members of His body."* (Eph. 5:28-30, emphasis mine)

In the following pages, we will consider numerous aspects of our marriages that should illustrate the relationship of the Son of God and His bride.

Wedding Vows

❊❊❊

My marriage began when my husband and I made some vows. I presume that yours started the same way.

Do you remember the vows you made on your wedding day? Most brides are so excited that they don't remember what they promised! I am grateful to my late uncle (the minister who officiated at our wedding back in 1964) because he gave us a little book containing the words that he spoke and those that we promised in our marriage ceremony.

If we say that someone has broken her wedding vows, we usually refer either to adultery or to divorce. The marriage vows do include the promises to be sexually faithful and to remain married until parted by death. There are a number of other vows, however, and it would probably benefit us all to occasionally remind ourselves of what we covenanted on that day.

Since I don't have a copy of your wedding vows, I will quote mine.

My uncle said, "Carolyn Sue, wilt thou have this man to be thy wedded husband, to live together in the holy estate of matrimony? Wilt thou love him, comfort him, honor, and keep him, in sickness and in health; and forsaking all others, keep thee only unto him so long as ye both shall live?"

I said, "I will."

Later, I said, "I, Carolyn Sue, take thee, Xury Charles, to be my wedded husband, to have and to hold from this day forward, for better, for worse, for richer, for poorer, in sickness and in health, to love and to cherish, until death us do part, according to God's holy ordinance; and thereto I plight thee my troth."

Still later, we exchanged rings. When we placed the wedding rings onto each other's fingers, we said, "In token and pledge of the vow between us made, with this ring I thee wed; in the name of the Father, and of the Son, and of the Holy Spirit. Amen."

Some of my marriage vows were in somewhat archaic language. Perhaps your vows were easier to understand. Perhaps not. Because weddings are filled with tradition, even modern ceremonies frequently use traditional language instead of contemporary terminology.

I must confess that when I first sat down to study my vows a few years ago, I was pretty unsure of what I'd promised on my wedding day.

"What on earth does it mean when it says, 'thereto I plight thee my troth'?" I wondered.

Other words in the vows are more familiar, but sometimes we still fail to realize exactly what they mean. Because of this, I would like for us to consider some definitions.

Vow

Let's begin with the word *vow*. My dictionary says that a vow is a solemn promise or statement, especially one that binds the person to an act, service, or condition. (M-W) The Hebrew word for vow is *neder*, which means *a solemn promise to God*.

It's a serious matter to make a vow. Repeatedly, the Bible tells us of the importance that God places on our keeping vows that we have made.

"Then Moses spoke to the heads of the tribes of the sons of Israel, saying, 'This is the word which the LORD has commanded. If a man makes a vow to the LORD, or takes an oath to bind himself with a binding obligation, he shall not violate his word; he shall do according to all that proceeds out of his mouth.'" (Num. 30:1-2) The passage goes on to say that the same is true of a woman who makes a vow, unless her father (if she is unmarried) or her husband

(if she is married) forbids her to keep the vow on the first day that he hears of it.

Consider these verses that also deal with vows:

"You shall be careful to perform what goes out from your lips, just as you have voluntarily vowed to the LORD your God, what you have promised." (Deut. 23:23)

"It is a trap for a man to dedicate something rashly and only later to consider his vows." (Prov. 20:25 NIV)

Do you get the idea that God expects us to keep our vows? I think these verses make it pretty clear that He considers keeping our covenants to be extremely important.

"Know therefore that the LORD your God is God; he is the faithful God, keeping his covenant of love to a thousand generations of those who love him and keep his commands." (Deut. 7:9 NIV)

The vows that you made on your wedding day were made not only to your husband, but also to the Lord. We serve a covenant-keeping God, and He wants us to be like Him.

According to God's Holy Ordinance

Notice that my wedding vows stated that my marriage should be lived according to God's holy ordinance. We are not free to set up our marriages any old way we choose. Marriage was God's idea. He created it, and He set the terms in His ordinance (or law) concerning marriage. My husband and I promised to live out our marriage according to God's instructions, which are clearly stated in the Bible.

In the Name of the Father, the Son, and the Holy Spirit

I made these vows in the name of the triune Lord. To vow in the name of God and then to break that vow is a most serious matter. It is probably at least part of what is meant by the commandment that forbids us to take the Lord's name in vain.

"You shall not take the name of the LORD your God in vain, for the LORD will not leave him unpunished who takes His name in vain." (Ex. 20:7)

Now in all likelihood, this commandment refers to blasphemy and to idle or irreverent use of His name as well as to breaking covenant. Nevertheless, we must remember to fulfill our vows. We are warned in the thirtieth chapter of Numbers that God regards breaking a vow as grave sin.

Perhaps you are thinking, "Yes, but I didn't realize some things about this man when I made that vow. I wouldn't have made the covenant if I'd realized how difficult it would be to live with him."

The Psalmist asked, *"...Who may dwell on Your holy hill?"* (Psa. 15:1) Then he wrote a list of qualifications for the one who could dwell there. One of these requirements was that if a person swears to his own hurt, he will not change; or as the NIV puts it, he is a person *"who keeps his oath even when it hurts."* (Psa. 15:4) The discovery that your husband has faults does not negate your responsibility to abide by your vows.

The Lord is our heavenly Bridegroom, and marriage was created to typify our relationship with Him. He keeps His covenant with His bride, although people frequently break covenant with Him. When we fail to keep our marriage vows, we illustrate a very serious offense: the breaking of our covenant with the Lord. Thus, this book will often refer to and define the vows that we made as brides and will remind us to be people who keep our covenants.

Sometimes a husband and wife will have a ceremony on their anniversary to renew their wedding vows. I would like to challenge you, ladies, to reaffirm in your hearts right now the vows of your marriage covenant. Perhaps you will also want to renew your spiritual "marriage vows" to the Lord Jesus.

Gender Differences

❊❊❊

Occasionally we hear someone say that the only difference between men and women is the plumbing.

That simply isn't true. Men and women are inherently different from each other. One thing that marriage illustrates is that while we are made in the *image* of God, we are still *different* from God.

"God created man **in His own image**, in the image of God He created him; male and female He created them." (Gen. 1:27, emphasis mine)

"Remember this, fix it in mind,
take it to heart, you rebels.
Remember the former things, those of long ago;
I am God, and there is no other;
*I am God, and **there is none like me**."* (Isa. 46:8-9 NIV, emphasis mine)

Throughout creation week, the Lord God repeatedly saw that His handiwork was good. God saw that the light was good. God separated the water from the land, and He saw that it was good. God caused the earth to bring forth plants and trees, and He saw that they were good. God saw that it was good when He created the sun, the moon, and the stars. He made the creatures that inhabited the waters and the birds that flew in the air, and He saw that they were good. On the sixth day of that week, He made the animals that lived on the land and again saw that His creation was good. (See Gen. 1:3-25.)

It was not until later on the sixth day that He first said that something was *not* good. He created the man from the dust of the earth. *"Then the LORD God said, 'It is **not good** for the man to be alone; I will make him a helper suitable for him.'"* (Gen. 2:18, emphasis mine)

The word that is translated *suitable* in that verse is interesting, because it literally means *opposite*. In one respect, that refers to standing opposite each other and facing each other. It means that they correspond to each other. The hen was opposite the rooster. The ewe was opposite the ram. The cow was opposite the bull.

Adam had no one opposite him, so God made him a helper to be opposite him. She was like him in many ways, made from his very body. (Gen. 2:21-23) Adam and Eve each had two arms, two legs, two ears, and one mouth. They both could think and walk and talk. Both of them were made in the image of God. (Gen. 1:27)

Yet in another sense, it is clear that she was not *exactly* like him. In many ways, the man and the woman were exactly *opposite* each other. That's why we say that we say that men are the *opposite* sex. We really are different from each other. Do you remember those Y-chromosomes? You have XX, but your husband has XY. Men and women are different from each other in every cell of their bodies.

Furthermore, a person's gender is not an accident.

"For You formed my inward parts;
You wove me in my mother's womb.
I will give thanks to You, for I am fearfully and wonderfully made;
Wonderful are Your works,
And my soul knows it very well.
My frame was not hidden from You,
When I was made in secret,
And skillfully wrought in the depths of the earth;
Your eyes have seen my unformed substance..." (Psa. 139:13-16)

In Gen. 1:27, quoted earlier, we see that God created the first two human beings male and female. Thus, the masculinity of Adam and femininity of Eve were God's choice. Furthermore, David in this Psalm indicates that God was also at work in forming *his* body before *he* was born. By implication, we are told that God formed each of us according to His will. It was not an accident of nature that I am a woman. My gender was the Lord's choice, just as Adam's and Eve's and David's were.

One major difference between men and women is this: The husband was designed to be the giver and the wife the receiver. This is because marriage pictures the union of Christ and the church. The Lord is the giver, and we are receivers. All that we have, we receive from Him.

"And he is not served by human hands, as if he needed anything, because he himself gives all men life and breath and everything else." (Acts 17:25 NIV)

We give Him ourselves. We give Him our hearts, our love, our praise, our reverence, and our service; but anything else that we give was His anyway. Perhaps one reason that women often find it easier to receive spiritual things than do men is that women are natural receivers. We were created and designed to receive from our husbands, and that helps us to spiritually receive. We will look at several areas in which husbands give and wives receive as we move through this book.

Gender differences are not merely the result of training and culture, as some would suggest. Although boys learn much about being men from observing their fathers and girls learn about womanhood from imitating their mothers, many of their traits and tendencies are inborn.

Just watch children at play. There are basic, natural differences between the way boys tend to play and the way girls do.

When our son was a child, he and his friends liked to build forts in our backyard. They were not doing this in order to have a fort. In fact, it was never a finished project. They were always working on it, changing it, and tearing it down to start over. If they were not working on the fort, they were playing sports, climbing trees, or riding bicycles. Physical activity was an important aspect of their time together. In fact, the action was more important than conversation in the boys' group.

Our daughter, on the other hand, often spent many hours in conversation with her friends. They may have set up a playhouse; but the primary purpose was to have a place to talk and pretend to be grown-up ladies, not to construct the playhouse. Regardless of what they might have been playing, the most important part of our daughter's playtime was the dialogue with her friend.

We don't need to teach boys and girls to be different from each other. In fact, people who want to do away with the distinctions must try to *train out* the differences and teach them to be alike—which I consider to be a bad idea, by the way.

Let's consider some of the differences between the male and female of the species. Perhaps it will help us to understand and accept our husbands better if we know that these things are as much a part of their personhood as our feminine ways are of ours.

As you doubtless have noticed, one physical difference between men and women is that men usually think about sex more often than their wives do, and they have a more intense desire for sexual relations than do their wives. This difference will be discussed at length in a future chapter.

There are numerous other physical differences, as well. One is that men are more muscular and are stronger than women are. This reminds us that our heavenly Bridegroom is strong, and we are weak. There are differences between a man's and a woman's skeletons and organs. The percentage of body fat differs according to gender.

Beyond physical differences, moreover, there are other basic distinctions between men and women. For example, women are more open about tender emotions than men are, and their emotions tend to fluctuate more than men's do. Women find it relatively easy to discuss their feelings; most men are much more hesitant to speak of their deepest emotions, hopes, fears, and anxieties.

A wife even views the home in a different way from the way her husband does, since it's her realm. (A husband usually views his job as his realm.)

For example, there is the atmosphere in the home. Most men's greatest desire for their homes is tranquility. Peace. A lack of stress and strife. A place of refuge from his workplace. The woman doesn't see it as a place of refuge from something, because the home itself is her realm.

When I was a young woman, my natural inclination was to unload any problem that had come up during the day as soon as Charles came into the house. That gave me immediate relief, because I knew that he could handle whatever it was and I could stop thinking about what to do.

Over the years, however, I learned that I should do everything I could to make our home into a haven—a place of refuge—for my husband. I learned that it was not a good idea to meet him after work with a list of complaints about the children's bad behavior, the broken faucet, or a financial need, except in a genuine emergency. While I did need to discuss these things with him—communication is vital to a successful marriage—I learned to greet him in such a way that he knew how glad I was to see him. I wanted to help him to make the transition from the stresses of work to the relative tranquility of home. Later, when he was more relaxed, I could discuss the children, the plumbing, and the finances—hopefully in a calm manner.

Men and women often have differing attitudes about the furnishings in the home. A number of years ago, my husband Charles and I went to purchase a new cabinet-model TV. (I'm showing my age here; this was long before flat-screened televisions came on the scene.) We located one that pleased us both and arranged to have it delivered on a certain date.

The delivery truck arrived at a time when Charles was at home but I was not. When the men brought the TV set into the living room and removed it from the crate, Charles took one look and told them they would need to take it back. It was not the set that we had purchased. The deliverymen checked the model number and realized that Charles was right, so they tried to persuade him to accept the model that they had brought. "After all," they said, "this is a more expensive television set than the one you bought."

Charles could have been satisfied with the substitution because it would perform and hold up at least as well as the one we had chosen, perhaps better. He wisely told them that they would need to bring the one we had selected, however, because he knew that I would not like the contemporary furniture style of the cabinet that they had brought.

This story reflects one difference in the way men and women see the home. When men consider a purchase, they are usually concerned primarily with how well an article will function, how much it costs, and how long it will last. Women, however, place great value on how it looks. Obviously, some men are more concerned about appearance than are other men are; and some women are more attentive to function, price, and durability than other women are. On the whole, however, women tend to place higher priority on the way it looks than do men, and men usually value how it performs and lasts more than women do.

Men and women usually even shop differently. Most women like to shop—although some of us are less enthusiastic about it. In fact, many ladies consider shopping to be entertainment; and they enjoy window-shopping even when they do not intend to purchase anything. Women—including those of us who do not consider shopping to be fun—will tend to look at white blouses in three or four stores, even if we wind up returning to purchase one of the first blouses we considered. It might take us two hours to buy one top.

A man, on the other hand, walks into one department store and finds the style, color, and size that he needs. Then he buys it. It takes a maximum of fifteen minutes.

Someone has observed that women shop, but men hunt. This is because God created men with different outlooks and different functions from those in the feminine gender. A man can decide about whether to buy a shirt without a long consideration.

This is similar to the male method of choosing a TV program. Have you ever wondered how a man can determine whether he wants to watch a television channel in the eighth of a second before he clicks again? I have. I believe that it's because men are more decisive than women are. Because he is the leader and protector, the husband needs to be able to make quick judgments.

The shopping difference may not be a big issue unless the two of you are shopping together. In that case, the man must be patient with his wife's indecisiveness; and the woman must consider how uncomfortable, boring, and tiring all of that back-and-forth shopping is to her husband.

I have found that if I am shopping for anything that requires very much thought, it is better if I do it when shopping alone. That way I don't feel rushed or pressured to make a speedy decision; and Charles is not forced to endure a long, drawn-out shopping trip.

On occasion, I need his input about a purchase—a piece of furniture, perhaps. We can handle those situations in one of two ways. For example, we can look for whatever we need in one or two stores per shopping day. It may take several trips before we can make the purchase, but he will not be wearied by the length of time involved if we were to visit every furniture store in one day. Another possibility is that I can do preliminary shopping alone first, then take him back when I have done all of the backtracking. Having eliminated many items, I can have the benefit of his presence as we consider two or three possibilities to purchase.

In all of these areas of difference, the wise woman will recognize that her husband is different from her and learn to accommodate him as much as possible. Don't you want him to understand that your femininity is the way that God made you? You wouldn't want him to expect you to think and act like a man, would you? Recognizing these differences as normal to men and women, the excellent wife will stop trying to make him to be like herself and begin to be more patient with him.

When the Greeks made up false gods, they envisioned them with the same attributes (including character flaws) that they themselves had. They "humanized" them. The trouble with a god made in our own image is that the god cannot meet the needs that only the true heavenly Bridegroom can fulfill.

In the same way, our husbands cannot function properly as husbands if they become feminized. Do you remember when Henry Higgins did the song in *My Fair Lady* that asked why women couldn't be more like men? We must guard against trying to make our husbands to be more like women! God made them different from us for a reason.

While these differences can be difficult in our relationships, they can also work to our advantage. Each spouse brings certain strengths to the marriage, and the balance of the two brings wholeness. While our husbands deserve the benefit of hearing our thoughts and insights, we must not try to force or manipulate our husbands into seeing everything the way we do. After all, God made them with these traits and gave the position of leadership to them.

Ladies, let us rejoice in the works of God. He knew what He was doing when He created your husband with different attributes from yours.

Perhaps you were once offended by these differences, thinking your husband to be difficult. Now you can realize that comparing men and women is in many ways comparing apples and oranges. Our functions in the family are not the same. Our responsibilities in the family are different. Husbands (who lead, protect, provide, and problem-solve) were created to depict Christ. Wives (who help their husbands, nurture the young, and follow their husbands' leadership) were designed to illustrate the church. Eve was created to be a suitable helper for Adam. God placed appropriate personality and physical traits in the two genders to enhance our roles in the family.

Thus, we are different from our husbands. Let us rejoice in our womanhood and strive to encourage our husbands in the masculine role in the family.

The Excellent Wife Is Trustworthy

✼✼✼

A concerned mother spoke the words of Proverbs 31 to her son, King Lemuel, which many scholars believe was another name for King Solomon. Since Solomon is designated at the beginning of the book to be the author of the Proverbs, I'm inclined to agree that the words in this chapter were spoken to King Solomon.

Proverbs 31 is made up of two parts. In the opening verses, the queen mother exhorts her son to maintain sexual purity, to avoid drunkenness, and to judge righteously the rights of others. She uses the remaining verses to advise her royal son concerning the kind of woman who makes a good wife.

You may recall that Solomon was the child of David and Bathsheba. As the story is told in the eleventh and twelfth chapters of 2 Samuel, King David saw the beautiful Bathsheba bathing as he walked on his rooftop. Although he was told that she was a married woman, he sent messengers to bring her to him. Bathsheba became pregnant as a result of their adulterous encounter.

To try to hide his sin, King David called Bathsheba's husband Uriah (a soldier away at the battlefield) back to the capital so that it would appear that Uriah was the father of Bathsheba's baby. David's scheme failed. Finally, he required his military commander to put Uriah into the most dangerous position in a battle so that he would be killed and David could take Bathsheba to be his wife.

David married the new widow, and a son was born to them. Nevertheless, David's sin was revealed. The Lord sent a prophet to tell the king that God was greatly displeased with his iniquity, and that the baby son of David and Bathsheba would die.

Soon Bathsheba was pregnant again, this time with the baby who would later become King Solomon.

In Prov. 31:2, the queen mother refers to the king as the *"son of my vows."* It appears that Solomon's mother had made some vows to the Lord concerning the upbringing of her royal son. Bathsheba had suffered a great loss when her first infant perished. Lemuel means *belonging to God,* and in 2 Sam. 12:25, Solomon is called Jedidiah, which means *beloved of God.* Perhaps, like Hannah, Bathsheba had made vows even before his birth. (See 1 Sam. 1:11.) Since Bathsheba's first child died because of David's sin with her, it would not be surprising that she might make vows before the Lord as she awaited the birth of her second son.

The queen mother taught her son this oracle in a manner that would help the wisdom of her words to remain with him. The verses concerning the qualities of an excellent wife are an acrostic passage. In the original language, these twenty-two verses begin with the twenty-two consecutive letters of the Hebrew alphabet—as do the verses of Psalms 25 and 34, and the sections of Psalm 119—to make memorization easier.

> 10 *An excellent wife, who can find?*
> *For her worth is far above jewels.*
> 11 *The heart of her husband trusts in her,*
> *And he will have no lack of gain.*
> 12 *She does him good and not evil*
> *All the days of her life.*
> 13 *She looks for wool and flax*
> *And works with her hands in delight.*
> 14 *She is like merchant ships;*
> *She brings her food from afar.*
> 15 *She rises also while it is still night*
> *And gives food to her household*
> *And portions to her maidens.*
> 16 *She considers a field and buys it;*
> *From her earnings she plants a vineyard.*

17 *She girds herself with strength*
And makes her arms strong.
18 *She senses that her gain is good;*
Her lamp does not go out at night.
19 *She stretches out her hands to the distaff,*
And her hands grasp the spindle.
20 *She extends her hand to the poor,*
And she stretches out her hands to the needy.
21 *She is not afraid of the snow for her household,*
For all her household are clothed with scarlet.
22 *She makes coverings for herself;*
Her clothing is fine linen and purple.
23 *Her husband is known in the gates,*
When he sits among the elders of the land.
24 *She makes linen garments and sells them,*
And supplies belts to the tradesmen.
25 *Strength and dignity are her clothing,*
And she smiles at the future.
26 *She opens her mouth in wisdom,*
And the teaching of kindness is on her tongue.
27 *She looks well to the ways of her household,*
And does not eat the bread of idleness.
28 *Her children rise up and bless her;*
Her husband also, and he praises her, saying:
29 *'Many daughters have done nobly,*
But you excel them all.'
30 *Charm is deceitful and beauty is vain,*
But a woman who fears the LORD, she shall be praised.
31 *Give her the product of her hands,*
And let her works praise her in the gates.
—Proverbs 31:10-31

Our husbands are not kings in royal palaces, but I think they too deserve "excellent" wives. Let's see how we measure up to the kind of woman this mother desired for her son.

The Hebrew word that is translated *excellent* in verse 10 includes the concept of literal or figurative strength. Presumably this passage refers primarily to strength of character, although her labors would contribute to physical strength as well. To locate a wife such as this, according to the queen mother, is to find a treasure worth more than jewels. Solomon would be wise to search for a woman of that great value. We women would be wise to *become* such wives to our husbands.

Verse 11 of Proverbs 31 says that the heart of the husband can trust his wife. In other words, the excellent wife is a trustworthy wife. Her husband can trust her to be the kind of wife that is described in those acrostic verses.

Our heavenly Bridegroom also desires that *His* bride will be trustworthy.

"In this case, moreover, it is required of stewards that one be found trustworthy." (1 Cor. 4:2)

"His master replied, 'Well done, good and faithful servant! You have been faithful with a few things; I will put you in charge of many things. Come and share your master's happiness!'" (Matt. 25:21 NIV)

Trustworthy and *faithful* in these verses are translated from the same Greek word. Our Lord is examining our hearts to see whether or not we are trustworthy.

"Every man's way is right in his own eyes,
But the LORD weighs the hearts." (Prov. 21:2)

"For this reason I also suffer these things, but I am not ashamed; for I know whom I have believed and I am convinced that He is able to guard what I have entrusted to Him until that day. Retain the standard of sound words which you have heard from me, in the faith and love which are in Christ Jesus. Guard, through the Holy Spirit who dwells in us, the treasure which has been entrusted to you." (2 Tim. 1:12-14)

The Lord is able and willing to guard what I've entrusted to Him: my heart and my very life. I must be careful to guard what He has entrusted to me, including the ability to make wise choices. Throughout this book, we will return to the concept of trustworthiness in our relationship to the Lord and to our husbands.

Respect and Love

❋❋❋

There are some dramatic gender differences between the deepest and most basic needs of a woman and those of her husband.

First, a woman's need to be loved is predominant. Her self-esteem depends upon feeling loved and cherished. A man, on the other hand, needs to be respected for his self-worth to flourish. He *wants* his wife's love, but his need for her respect is even greater.

A woman's supreme fear is that a man will merely use her instead of loving her. A man's greatest fear is that a woman will dominate him instead of respecting him. If a wife is disrespectful to her husband, she is attacking his manhood and self-worth.

The reason that your husband needs this honor and respect so much is that God made him that way. In fact, God has *commanded* us to respect our husbands. *"Wives, be subject to your own husbands, as to the Lord. For the husband is the head of the wife, as Christ also is the head of the church, He Himself being the Savior of the body. But as the church is subject to Christ, so also the wives ought to be to their husbands in everything. Husbands, love your wives, just as Christ also loved the church and gave Himself up for her...Nevertheless, each individual among you also is to love his own wife even as himself, and* **the wife must see to it that she respects her husband."** (Eph. 5:22-25, 33, emphasis mine)

Your husband has a God-given *need* for you to respect him. Man was created to picture Christ, you remember, and the woman was created to symbolize the church. The church *receives* much from

Here Comes the Bride

Christ, but she can *give* Him praise and honor. The Lord deeply desires reverence and praise from His bride; and He designed men (who symbolize Him) with a basic, innate need for honor, respect, and admiration to be earnestly and openly expressed by their wives.

In fact, the word that is translated as *respects* in Eph. 5:33 literally means *fear*. Although it is often used for ordinary fear, it is the also word that is used for fearing (or reverencing) God. For example, this is the Greek word that is used in Acts 10:35, Col. 3:22, Rev. 19:5, and other passages for fearing or reverencing the Lord.

We know that the instruction (in the Ephesians passage) to see to it that we fear our husbands refers to respect and honor rather than to regular fear because of the instructions in 1 Pet. 3:5-6: *"For in this way in former times the holy women also, who hoped in God, used to adorn themselves, being submissive to their own husbands; just as Sarah obeyed Abraham, calling him lord, and you have become her children if you do what is right **without being frightened by any fear**."* (Emphasis mine.)

As a symbol of Christ, your husband desires and needs your honor, respect, and esteem. If he took all that you do for him (sex, housework, meal preparation, and so forth) and didn't love you, you would feel used. In the same way, he will feel an attack on his manhood if you take what he does for you but fail to respect his leadership. I repeat: Men fear being dominated by a woman just as women fear being used by a man.

Perhaps you are thinking, "Well, that's all well and good, but what about my husband's responsibilities? If he treated me the way the Bible teaches, I might be more willing to do what I'm supposed to do for him."

Ladies, it is beyond the purpose of this book to instruct men. Someone else can teach your mate to be the kind of husband that God wants him to be. Nevertheless, it has to start somewhere if it's ever going to be the kind of marriage that God desires it to be. The husband should indeed take the lead in bringing his marriage to biblical standards, just as Christ loved us first. Even if your husband isn't fulfilling his role as he should, however, he might be led to do so when he sees you become a woman who obeys God in her marriage. I can't guarantee it, but it often happens.

The Excellent Wife Brings Honor to Her Husband

I even made a vow in my wedding ceremony to *honor* my husband. It's likely that you did, as well.

Our actions and words influence others to either honor or dishonor our husbands. We should behave in a dignified (not raucous, rowdy, or boisterous) manner so as to avoid bringing shame or embarrassment to our husbands. Speaking of the true beauty of a godly wife, Peter says, *"but let it be the hidden person of the heart, with the imperishable quality of a gentle and quiet spirit, which is precious in the sight of God."* (1 Pet. 3:4)

The other men, particularly the leaders, respected the husband of the Proverbs 31 wife.

"Her husband is respected at the city gate,
where he takes his seat among the elders of the land." (Prov. 31:23 NIV)

In those days, the leaders of the city assembled at the city gate; and we are told that the elders respected this husband. Since that fact is included in the passage about the excellent *wife*, we can presume that the wife had a part in bringing about this respect for her husband. Her lifestyle brought honor to her husband. Neither her behavior nor her words embarrassed him.

"An excellent wife is the crown of her husband,
But she who shames him is like rottenness in his bones." (Prov. 12:4)

Wouldn't you rather that the Lord would see you as an excellent wife than as corrupt decay in your husband's bones? Wouldn't you prefer that *your husband* see you as a beautiful crown than as rottenness?

Paul instructs that elders in the church should be men who manage their households well and that they must be men who practice hospitality. (Tit. 1:6-8, 1 Tim. 3:2-4) Obviously, these requirements would be difficult for a man to fulfill if his wife didn't follow his leadership in rearing the children or if she resisted his desire to invite people into their home. A man's ministry is restricted or released by the way his wife lives.

Our choices and behavior bring either respect or disrespect to our husbands. Are you an asset to your husband's reputation, or are you a liability? Do you ever sense that he is embarrassed by your behavior?

Another way that you can increase or decrease other people's regard for your husband is in your conversations with these people. If you ridicule him in the hearing of others, will that bring honor to him? Of course not! If you frequently criticize him and rehearse his shortcomings to your friends, will this not diminish their opinions of him? Tell others about the things you *appreciate* in your husband. Not only will this promote in your acquaintances a higher opinion of your husband, it probably will also encourage your mate to love and honor you more.

"...Her husband...praises her, saying,
'Many daughters have done nobly,
But you excel them all.'" (Prov. 31:28-29)

Honoring your husband is not merely an inner respect for him; it's praise. It's telling him and telling others what you admire and appreciate about him. When I vowed to honor my husband, I promised to extol his good qualities.

Although a man's need for respect is greater than his need for love, he nevertheless desires the love of his wife as well. It is true that the primary responsibility for love in the marriage is the husband's, because love originates with the Lord and not with the church. Christ's love invites ours. *"We love, because He first loved us."* (1 John 4:19)

Yet the Lord still expects us to love Him. He wants—and in fact commands—our love in addition to our reverential fear of Him. *"You shall love the LORD your God with all your heart, with all your soul, and with all your mind."* (Matt. 22:37 NKJV) Similarly, wives are also to love their husbands as well as to respect them and to submit to them. (Tit. 2:4)

Love thinks of the *beloved's* benefit rather than doing the lover's personal preference. Doesn't the Lord express His love to us by meeting *our* needs? (See John 3:16 and John 16:23-27.) How do we express our love to Him? Is it not by doing the things that please *Him?* Jesus said, *"If you love Me, you will keep My com-*

mandments." (John 14:15) In the same way, you express your devotion to your husband by thinking about *his* needs before your own. *"Love...is not self-seeking..."* (1 Cor. 13:4-5 NIV) That is to say, love thinks of the other person rather than oneself.

Thus, another vow that I made in my wedding was to love my husband. If this love were to be defined as much of the world defines it, then it would not be appropriate for a woman to vow to love her husband. After all, we can't *choose* to have goose bumps when we think of someone! Most people think love is nothing more than romantic feelings or physical attraction, and that it is something that happens *to* us. How often we hear the words, "I fell in love," or "I fell out of love," as though it were a pit!

That's not the way that the Bible describes love, however. First, we are told to have an affectionate, familial love (a love similar to the love we feel for other family members or friends) for our husbands. This is the word for love that appears in Tit. 2:4, where the Bible exhorts older women to live godly lives so that they can *"admonish the young women to love their husbands..."* (NKJV)

How does a woman learn to have fond, affectionate, feelings toward her husband? We cultivate this attitude in the same way that we develop any attitude. Attitudes are the result of repeatedly thinking a certain way over a period of time. They are habitual thoughts. Thus, the wife who continually rehearses her husband's good qualities to herself begins to think affectionately of him. On the contrary, a woman who incessantly dwells on her husband's faults will develop an unfavorable attitude toward him. God does not require of us what we cannot do. If He commands us to learn to have affectionate love toward our husbands, then we are able to do that.

Now cultivating this kind of love for your husband is not a one-time deal. Because it is contrary to the fleshly nature, we must constantly be on guard lest we return to selfishness, criticism, and bitterness. We must continue the process of rehearsing his endearing qualities so that we remain in a loving attitude.

You might try the exercise that I asked the ladies in my women's ministry groups to do a few times. To encourage them to focus on their husbands' good attributes, I placed a page in their notebooks that had each day's date for the coming month with a line next to the date. Each woman was to think of a quality about which to speak praise to her husband for every date in that month, and she was to think of a new trait for each day. She could repeat a compliment that she had spoken on a previous day, but it didn't count for that day's praise line in her notebook.

In an earlier chapter, we compared our homes and marriages to houses. Have you ever moved into a brand new house? It was really an exciting moment when you found that perfect house. It was just what you had always wanted, and everything was in pristine condition.

Before long, however, it ceased to be "perfect," and became "just a house" to you. A little more time passed, and you began to see a few things that needed improvement. There was a scratch on the finish of the cabinet. The laundry room was too small. The floor squeaked when you stepped in a certain place. You tried to learn to live with these problems, but you were unhappy about them.

Then you needed to buy some new living room furniture, and the walls were no longer the right color. When you painted the walls, you were really pleased with the result; but then it was quite obvious that the carpet needed replacing and the window coverings were all wrong. The new hardwood that replaced the carpet was adjacent to the old kitchen flooring, so the kitchen floor began to look dated to you. Somehow, the "perfect house" began to seem like a "dump."

What happened there? It was the same house. Obviously, some things deteriorated along the way. Other defects were there all along, but you hadn't noticed them before. Some imperfections became more obvious as *you* made changes. The biggest problem was that you began to dwell on the things that *didn't* please you and to ignore all the things that you loved about the house. Eventually, perhaps, you no longer wanted to live there.

This is a picture of what too many women do in their marriages. Consider this scenario: On her wedding day, the new bride thought, "This guy is *perfect!*" The honeymoon was a delight, and she was even more convinced that he had no faults.

It wasn't too long, however, before she noticed that he did have a couple of *teeny* little flaws.

She began to nag him a little to change. If he didn't correct the problem, she nagged him a *lot*. If he did change, she was very happy with the "new" him...for a while.

When the whiskers in the sink ceased to be a problem, however, she noticed that he dropped his clothes in the floor, left dirty dishes sitting around, or spent too much time in front of the TV. Unsatisfied again, she set off to fix that too. Soon she was so focused on his faults that she forgot about the wonderful qualities that had attracted her to him in the first place; and *he* wondered if it were possible to *ever* please this woman! Unfortunately, the next thought in both their minds might be, "Why on earth did I marry this horrible person? How did I manage to get into a marriage like *this*?"

I vowed on my wedding day to cherish my husband. My dictionary says that to cherish is to hold dear, to treat with care and affection, and to keep deeply in mind. (M-W) In other words, I attribute great value and worth to him. I treasure him. We can and must choose to do this, so it behooves us to remind ourselves of our spouses' desirable attributes. If we focus on the negative aspects of our husbands, it will tend to lead us *away* from this familial affection.

Then there is *agape* love, the kind of love all Christians are exhorted to exhibit toward other people. If we are to love our neighbors (Matt. 22:39), our fellow Christians (John 13:34), and even our enemies (Matt. 5:44) with *agape* love, should we not love our husbands this way even more? This kind of love puts the good of the beloved before the good of the lover. It's the kind of love that God demonstrated toward us when He gave His Son for us.

The New Testament describes *agape* love this way: *"Love is patient and kind; love is not jealous or boastful; it is not arrogant or rude. Love does not insist on its own way; it is not irritable or resentful; it does not rejoice at wrong, but rejoices in the right. Love bears all things, believes all things, hopes all things, endures all things. Love never ends..."* (1 Cor. 13:4-8 RSV) These are choices that we can make. Love is not an emotion; it's an act of your will.

Love is a spiral. We *agape* love because God first *agape* loved us. (1 John 4:19) The Bible says in John 16:27 that the Father Himself *phileo* (fondly and affectionately) loves you, *because* you have *phileo* loved Christ and you have believed that He came forth from the Father. *Agape* always begins with God, and His *agape* is perfect. As we saw in John 16:27, however, our showing familial, affectionate love (*phileo*) toward Him increases His *phileo* affection toward us.

The same thing can happen in marriage. One spouse loves, which encourages the other partner to love. When the second spouse responds to that love, it usually increases the first one's love.

Furthermore, the Bible tells us that love edifies (or builds up) the beloved. (1 Cor. 8:1) Actually, the word for *edifies* in that verse is the Greek word for building a house.

Everyone has emotional down times. When we are discouraged or weary, we need someone to build us up. We need someone to give us courage to go on and to help us believe that the future will be better.

Our husbands need that too, and we as wives can fill that role. One of the best ways that a wife can accomplish this is to be her husband's best friend and to encourage her husband in God as Jonathan did for his dear friend David. (See 1 Sam. 23:16.) When your husband is hurting, he needs someone to show compassion toward him, to care about his pain, and to remind him to turn to the Lord in his trials.

Have you ever wondered why Satan left Job's wife alive when he killed their children? I believe it was because she was not a woman who was likely to encourage her husband to trust God. Instead, she said, *"Do you still hold fast your integrity? Curse God and die!"* (Job 2:9) May we never be like Job's wife. Rather, may we always edify and encourage our husbands.

In my wedding vows, I also promised to comfort my husband. What does that mean? My dictionary indicates that to comfort him means that I will give strength and hope to him, that I will console him. (M-W) The Bible says that love gives consolation. (Phil. 2:1) Thus if I love him, I will also comfort and console him when he is discouraged.

Obviously, if I am to provide that kind of consolation, comfort, and edification to my husband, I must make every effort to avoid *dis*couraging him. I cannot encourage if I am actually bringing dejection and despair.

One of the most important functions of husbands and wives toward each other is the ministry of encouragement. *"So then we pursue the things which make for peace and the building up of one another."* (Rom. 14:19) We need to encourage everyone that we can, but this is especially true of our husbands. No one can encourage *or* discourage a husband to the degree that his wife can because spouses value each other's opinions so highly, because they know each other's strengths and weaknesses so thoroughly, and because they relate to each other so intimately.

How does this apply to our relationship to the Lord? The Lord doesn't get discouraged the way our natural husbands do, but our sinful attitudes and our complacency toward pleasing Him do cause Him sorrow and grief. Mark 3:5 says that Jesus was grieved by hard hearts. Paul exhorts us, *"Do not grieve the Holy Spirit of God..."* (Eph. 4:30) We can offer comfort to our heavenly Bridegroom by our repentance.

We humans, however, *do* fall into depression and despondency; and our Bridegroom has given us the Holy Spirit (sometimes called the Comforter or Helper) to encourage us. Jesus said, *"Nevertheless I tell you the truth; It is expedient for you that I go away: for if I go not away, the Comforter will not come unto you; but if I depart, I will send him unto you."* (John 16:7 KJV)

Our heavenly Bridegroom wants us to love Him supremely. In fact, He wants us to love Him more than we love anyone else. The Lord has commanded, *"Love the Lord your God with all your heart and with all your soul and with all your mind and with all your strength."* (Mark 12:30 NIV) He wants us to place Him in the position of supremacy in our hearts. We are to put no one before Him.

It's entirely possible for us to become so involved with *the Lord's* children that we neglect growing our love for *Him*, just as careless wives sometimes ignore their human husbands to focus on the kids. The result of this spiritual error is the same as that of neglecting spouses to place all our attention on natural children: Our love for the Bridegroom will wane.

Remember, ladies, the marriage relationship is a type (picture or symbol) of the relationship of Christ and the church.

Have you ever known a couple who divorced after twenty-five years of marriage, to the shock and surprise of all of their friends? Everyone considered them to be the perfect couple, and now *this!* What on earth has happened? There may be a number of contributing factors to such divorces, of course, but one problem may be that the children have been the focus—to the detriment of the marriage relationship.

A friend once told me that when her first child was born, her mother-in-law spoke some wise words to her. "Remember," the older woman said, "you had your husband before you had your son." She could also have added, "You want to still have a thriving relationship with your husband when your son is no longer living under your roof"—for I'm certain that was the message that she wanted to convey.

Your children will grow up and leave the nest. You and your husband are presumably striving to train them so that they will one day no longer depend upon you in the same way that they do now. Will you be ready? Or will your life have so exclusively centered on your children that you don't know how to live as a couple when the kids form their own families? Some husbands and wives find that they don't really know each other anymore and that they have little in common when the children are no longer under their daily care.

I urge you to love the Lord supremely and to love your husband second only to Him. You will be better able to minister to God's children if you place priority on loving the Lord, and devotion to your husband will be a blessing to your children as well as to your spouse. It will give the kids a sense of security while they are growing up, and it will save them much grief that would follow the surprising divorce of their parents when they reach adulthood.

May you always show reverence toward the Bridegroom and respect toward your husband, both in word and deed. May your love for Christ and for your husband grow stronger day by day.

The Ring

✻✻✻

We've been talking about husbands as givers and wives as receivers. One of the first things that we see a husband give is the ring. I don't think I have ever known a woman who balked about receiving a bridal ring. In fact, all of the brides of my acquaintance have been thrilled and joyful to receive their rings.

In a sense, the ring "seals" the marriage pact. Jewish weddings are two-part ceremonies today, but originally the two sections took place on two different occasions with a period of time in between the two. According to Jewish tradition, the couple is fully married when the betrothal (first part) takes place, even though the wedding ceremony is not complete. It is during the betrothal part of the ceremony that the bridegroom places the ring on his bride's hand and pronounces her to be betrothed to him.

This reminds me of the story of Joseph and Mary. They were betrothed, but not yet authorized for cohabitation. Nonetheless, when Joseph learned about Mary's pregnancy and considered ending the relationship, he would have needed to divorce her to do so.

"Because Joseph her husband was a righteous man and did not want to expose her to public disgrace, he had in mind to divorce her quietly. But after he had considered this, an angel of the Lord appeared to him in a dream and said, 'Joseph son of David, do not be afraid to take Mary home as your wife, because what is conceived in her is from the Holy Spirit.'" (Matt. 1:18-20 NIV)

The Greek word that is employed in Matt. 1:18, Luke 1:27, and Luke 2:5 to communicate that they were engaged indicates that she had received a betrothal gift or souvenir. This would be comparable to the betrothal ring.

Even Rebekah received a betrothal ring. (It was a nose ring, however.) Abraham had sent a trusted servant to find a bride for Isaac, and the servant gave her the ring.

*"Now Rebekah had a brother whose name was Laban; and Laban ran outside to the man at the spring. When he saw the **ring** and the bracelets on his sister's wrists, and when he heard the words of Rebekah his sister, saying, 'This is what the man said to me,' he went to the man; and behold, he was standing by the camels at the spring."*

Later, as the servant told the story, he included these words: *"Then I asked her, and said, 'Whose daughter are you?' And she said, 'The daughter of Bethuel, Nahor's son, whom Milcah bore to him;' **and I put the ring on her nose...**"* (Gen. 24:29-30, 47, emphasis mine)

While the giving of rings in weddings today is often reciprocal, in the original custom it was only the husband who gave his bride a ring to signify that she was marrying him. This reminds me that the Lord gave us the Holy Spirit when we entered into covenant with Him. The ring—like the Holy Spirit—is a seal of the union. The Bible says, *"And you also were included in Christ when you heard the word of truth, the gospel of your salvation. Having believed, you were marked in him with a seal, the promised Holy Spirit, who is a deposit guaranteeing our inheritance until the redemption of those who are God's possession—to the praise of his glory."* (Eph. 1:13-14 NIV) *"...And if anyone does not have the Spirit of Christ, he does not belong to Christ."* (Rom. 8:9 NIV)

Like Jewish brides, we receive our "Ring" at conversion—at betrothal as it were—and do not have to wait until we go to heaven and the wedding is complete.

My wedding vows included these words: "I, Carolyn Sue, take thee, Xury Charles, to be my wedded husband, to have and to hold from this day forward, for better, for worse, for richer, for poorer, in sickness and in health, to love and to cherish, until death us do

Here Comes the Bride

part, according to God's holy ordinance; and thereto I plight thee my troth." Charles likewise had made the same vow to me.

According to my dictionary, to plight one's troth is to put or give in pledge as a promise to be faithful; pledging means that something is given as security for the promise. (M-W) I understand that this pledge in our weddings refers to the wedding ring. After Charles and I made these vows, we exchanged wedding rings, saying, "In token and pledge of the vow between us made, with this ring I thee wed..." In other words, the ring was an emblem and earnest of the vows that had been made, just God has given us the Holy Spirit *"as a pledge of our inheritance."*

With the giving and receiving of the rings, we "wedded" each other. The word *wed* means *pledge*. (M-W Web Site) A pledge, as I said before, involves a promise with something given as security for the promise.

Have you ever noticed that when a woman wants to denounce her marriage, she is quick to remove the ring? It's because that ring is the symbol for the promises made at the wedding and, in fact, for the marriage itself. Even if she removes the ring merely because she's angry and wants to punish her husband, this action will demonstrate to him that she does not value the marriage. It has devastating effects on her husband and on their relationship. (Obviously, I'm not talking about removing a ring to take a shower or work in the yard. I'm referring to the time when a woman conveys the message that she rejects the marriage, whether or not she really means it.)

"Now He who establishes us with you in Christ and anointed us is God, who also sealed us and gave us the Spirit in our hearts as a pledge." (2 Cor. 1:21-22) *"Now He who prepared us for this very purpose is God, who gave to us the Spirit as a pledge."* (2 Cor. 5:5)

We dare not turn against the Spirit who is represented by the ring. God's attitude toward defiant sin and blasphemy was evident in the Old Testament: *"But anyone who sins defiantly, whether native-born or alien, blasphemes the LORD, and that person must be cut off from his people. Because he has despised the LORD's word and broken his commands, that person must surely be cut off; his guilt remains on him."* (Num. 15:30-31 NIV)

It was not only under the Law that God demonstrated this attitude, however. The Lord does not change, and He expressed the same thing in the New Testament: *"Whoever speaks a word against the Son of Man, it shall be forgiven him; but whoever speaks against the Holy Spirit, it shall not be forgiven him, either in this age or in the age to come."* (Matt. 12:32) *"For if we go on sinning willfully after receiving the knowledge of the truth, there no longer remains a sacrifice for sins, but a terrifying expectation of judgment and THE FURY OF A FIRE WHICH WILL CONSUME THE ADVERSARIES. Anyone who has set aside the Law of Moses dies without mercy on the testimony of two or three witnesses. How much severer punishment do you think he will deserve who has trampled under foot the Son of God, and has regarded as unclean the blood of the covenant by which he was sanctified, and **has insulted the Spirit of grace?"*** (Heb. 10:26-29, emphasis mine)

That *He* has made a pledge doesn't mean that *you* won't turn away from *Him*. It's His pledge and He is faithful, but *you* can still choose to forfeit. Hebrews 10:26-29 (quoted above) is not a warning for unbelievers. It refers to the person who had once been sanctified (made holy) but later trampled the Savior under foot, despised the blood of Christ, and insulted the Holy Spirit.

Please understand, my sisters, that it is not my purpose to create terror or despair in you. I don't believe that a Christian is condemned every time she fails. God is not watching for opportunities to doom us.

"But if we walk in the light, as he is in the light, we have fellowship with one another, and the blood of Jesus, his Son, purifies us from all sin." (1 John 1:7 NIV) *"…God's kindness leads you toward repentance…"* (Rom. 2:4 NIV) He longs for close communion with us. As we walk in the light of His presence, we walk in continual cleansing when we err.

Walking in the light means that we are walking close to Him, for He is the Light.

"Then Jesus again spoke to them, saying, 'I am the Light of the world; he who follows Me will not walk in the darkness, but will have the Light of life.'" (John 8:12)

It also means that we are exposing our failures to the Light through contrition before Him and confession of our sins to Him. (1 John 1:7)

We must be on the alert and repent quickly when we sin. Sin deceives and hardens our hearts. (See Heb. 3:12-13.) Eventually, the unrepentant person will no longer hear the Lord's gracious call to repentance.

No one else—not another human being, not a demon, not the devil himself—can snatch a Christian from the Father's hand. (See John 10:28-29.) Only *you* can abandon your position in Him. You must, however, guard your heart. Allowing sin to harden your heart toward your "Ring," the Holy Spirit who is the pledge given to you, is placing yourself in grave spiritual peril.

The Husband's Name

❋❋❋

We who are part of the bride of Christ have received our Bridegroom's name. The name *Christian*—obviously derived from the word *Christ*—identifies us as belonging to Jesus Christ. James 2:7 refers to our being called by His fair name, and John tells us that one day Christ's name will be inscribed upon our foreheads. (See Rev. 3:12 and 22:4.)

Asaph sang a song of thanksgiving because the Lord's name is near.

"We give thanks to You, O God, we give thanks,
For Your name is near…" (Psa. 75:1)

Inherited family surnames such as we have today were not common in Biblical times. The name of a man's father or of his city was sometimes added to his name to identify *which* Joshua or Judah. Joshua the son of Nun is one example. (Deut. 31:23) Jesus was often called Jesus of Nazareth. (John 1:45) Virgins' names were sometimes followed by "daughter of so-and so," as was the case with Rachel the daughter of Laban. (Gen. 29:10) This designation was also given to identify whom a man had married. *"Isaac was forty years old when he took Rebekah, the daughter of Bethuel…to be his wife."* (Gen. 25:20)

Otherwise, however, a married woman's name sometimes included an appendage to identify her as the *wife* of a certain man. For example, Bathsheba was called both "the daughter of Eliam" and "the wife of Uriah the Hittite." (2 Sam. 11:3) Deborah was called the wife of Lappidoth. (Judg. 4:4)

Even the very first wife received her husband's name.

"This is the book of the generations of Adam. In the day when God created man, He made him in the likeness of God. He created them male and female, and He blessed them and named them Man in the day when they were created." (Gen. 5:1-2)

The King James Version gives a rendering to this passage that is more faithful to the Hebrew. It says, *"This is the book of the generations of Adam. In the day that God created man, in the likeness of God made he him; male and female created he them; and blessed them, and **called their name Adam**, in the day when they were created."* (Emphasis mine)

In modern weddings, as soon as the pastor pronounces a man and woman to be a married couple, he usually says to the congregation, "Ladies and gentlemen, I present to you Mr. and Mrs. John Doe." One of the first things we notice that a married woman has received, therefore, is her husband's name.

When a woman receives her husband's name, it symbolizes the union of the bride and groom into one flesh. It typifies, as well, that the bride of Christ receives the name of her divine Bridegroom.

Would you not find it strange if a professing believer found it offensive to be called Christian? In the same way, I can think of no reason why a woman who loves her husband would prefer not to be called by her husband's name. Is she ashamed to be known by his name? Does she believe that she must remain independent of him and retain an identity apart from his? God's idea for marriage is the joining of two into one.

Perhaps you think that the name has little significance, but I believe that it has importance. It's more than taking the name; it's what taking the name symbolizes.

Consider the women who have been first ladies of the United States. Now, many of these may have been women of talent, intelligence, and character themselves. In spite of that, they would not have received the honor, respect, and protection that they enjoyed if their husbands had not been elected President. The position of the first lady's *husband* affords her those things.

As first lady, of course, she would have Secret Service protection even if she had retained her maiden name and had not called herself by her husband's name. It's the relationship that brings his benefits to her. Just remember, however, that *Mrs.* means *wife of.* Taking his name signifies the relationship that affords all of the rights, privileges, provisions, and protections.

What if *you* decided to assume the name of a President of the United States as if you were the first lady? Would that give you access to the President's assets or provide you the Secret Service protection that is available to the woman who is truly his wife? Of course not! Those benefits belong to the woman who genuinely has the right to be called by his name.

Likewise, merely *calling* yourself by the name of Christ would not give you the advantages that are available to those who have the relationship with Him. Some men in the book of Acts found that out:

"But also some of the Jewish exorcists, who went from place to place, attempted to name over those who had the evil spirits the name of the Lord Jesus, saying, 'I adjure you by Jesus whom Paul preaches.' Seven sons of one Sceva, a Jewish chief priest, were doing this. And the evil spirit answered and said to them, 'I recognize Jesus, and I know about Paul, but who are you?' And the man, in whom was the evil spirit, leaped on them and subdued all of them and overpowered them, so that they fled out of that house naked and wounded." (Acts 19:13-16)

"In His name" indicates that it is done in submission to His authority. Asking and receiving in His name are tied to being under His authority and being in right relationship with Him.

We are the bride of Christ, and we are called by His name. Protection and safety come to us in the name of the Lord:

"But let all who take refuge in you be glad;
let them ever sing for joy.
Spread your protection over them,
that those who love your name may rejoice in you." (Psa. 5:11 NIV)

"I will remain in the world no longer, but they are still in the world, and I am coming to you. Holy Father, protect them by the

power of your name—the name you gave me—so that they may be one as we are one." (John 17:11 NIV)

"The name of the LORD is a strong tower;
The righteous runs into it and is safe." (Prov. 18:10)

"Our help is in the name of the LORD,
Who made heaven and earth." (Psa. 124:8)

"Until now you have asked for nothing in My name; ask and you will receive, so that your joy may be made full." (John 16:24)

"Is anyone among you sick? Then he must call for the elders of the church and they are to pray over him, anointing him with oil in the name of the Lord; and the prayer offered in faith will restore the one who is sick, and the Lord will raise him up, and if he has committed sins, they will be forgiven him." (Jas. 5:14-15)

"Now after this the Lord appointed seventy others, and sent them in pairs ahead of Him to every city and place where He Himself was going to come...The seventy returned with joy, saying, 'Lord, even the demons are subject to us in Your name.'" (Luke 10:1, 17)

Salvation and forgiveness are ours only through His name:

"And there is salvation in no one else; for there is no other name under heaven that has been given among men by which we must be saved." (Acts 4:12)

"But as many as received Him, to them He gave the right to become children of God, even to those who believe in His name..." (John 1:12)

"...Everyone who calls on the name of the Lord will be saved." (Rom. 10:13 NIV)

"Of Him all the prophets bear witness that through His name everyone who believes in Him receives forgiveness of sins." (Acts 10:43)

"I write to you, dear children, because your sins have been forgiven on account of his name." (1 John 2:12 NIV)

"But when he had considered this, behold, an angel of the Lord appeared to him in a dream, saying, 'Joseph, son of David, do not be afraid to take Mary as your wife; for the Child who has been conceived in her is of the Holy Spirit. She will bear a Son; and you shall call His name Jesus, for He will save His people from their sins'" (Matt. 1:20-21)

Here Comes the Bride

The name *Jesus*, given to our Lord, comes to us from the Greek version of the Hebrew name that in the Old Testament is rendered as *Joshua*. The literal meaning of this name is *Yahweh Saves*, or *Yahweh delivers*. His name tells us that He is our Savior and Deliverer. His name describes who He is. It is through His name that we have life. (John 20:31)

When we assemble in His name with other believers, we are in His presence as well: *"For where two or three have gathered together in My name, I am there in their midst."* (Matt. 18:20)

We are instructed to praise and thank God's name, because it represents all that He is and does. *"Through Him then, let us continually offer up a sacrifice of praise to God, that is, the fruit of lips that give thanks to His name."* (Heb. 13:15)

Jesus taught us to pray this way: *"Father, hallowed be Your name..."* (Luke 11:2) The word *hallowed* means that we would consider His name holy, that we would venerate it and revere it.

In the Bible, God shows great concern for His name. Repeatedly, He tells what He will do when we call on His name. We are exhorted to rely on His name and to praise His name. He abhors the taking of His name in vain. We must beware of bringing shame to His name through evil behavior and hypocrisy. (See Rom. 2:24 and Amos 2:7, for example.)

We are to live our lives—in everything we do or say—in His name: *"Whatever you do in word or deed, do all in the name of the Lord Jesus, giving thanks through Him to God the Father."* (Col. 3:17)

The lovely name of Jesus is continually attacked in our society. *"If you are insulted because of the name of Christ, you are blessed, for the Spirit of glory and of God rests on you...However, if you suffer as a Christian, do not be ashamed, but praise God that you bear that name."* (1 Pet. 4:14, 16 NIV) To refuse to be called by His name or to be ashamed of His name is to spurn Him, for His name represents all that He is.

Occasionally, a man is unjustly shamed. If he has a devoted wife, she will continue to love being called by his name, knowing that her husband doesn't deserve the dishonor hurled at him. To refuse to be called by her husband's name indicates that she regards herself as independent of him rather than joined to him.

May you always recognize that you are no longer a single individual, but you have been united into one with your husband.

Leadership

❈ ❈ ❈

The next thing that the husband is to give to his wife is leadership, as indicated in the passage that we have read in Ephesians:

"Wives, be subject to your own husbands, as to the Lord. For the husband is the head of the wife, as Christ also is the head of the church, He Himself being the Savior of the body. But as the church is subject to Christ, so also the wives ought to be to their husbands in everything…For this reason a man shall leave his father and mother, and shall be joined to his wife; and the two shall become one flesh. This mystery is great; but I am speaking with reference to Christ and the church. Nevertheless, each individual among you also is to love his own wife even as himself; and the wife must see to it that she respects her husband." (5:22-24, 31-33)

Some ministers include the word *submit* or the word *obey* in the bride's vows. My wedding did not include one of those words. When I covenanted to take Charles as my husband, however, I promised to receive him as the master of our house—for that is what a husband is. (More on that later in this chapter.)

This is in agreement with the instructions of the Bible for our marriages. Paul wrote, *"Wives, submit to your husbands, as is fitting in the Lord."* (Col. 3:18 NIV) It is fitting. That is to say, it is proper and appropriate. Why is it appropriate? Because the husband represents Christ, and the wife symbolizes the church.

Peter instructs even a woman whose spouse does not follow God's Word to regard her husband as lord of the household. *"In the same way, you wives, be submissive to your own husbands so that even if any of them are disobedient to the word, they may be won without a word by the behavior of their wives, as they observe your chaste and respectful behavior."* (1 Pet. 3:1-2) Peter goes on to say that such behavior gives a woman beauty. *"For this is the way the holy women of the past who put their hope in God used to make themselves beautiful. They were submissive to their own husbands, like Sarah, who obeyed Abraham and called him her master..."* (1 Pet. 3:5-6 NIV)

Now, let me be clear. I am not suggesting that you sin. If doing what your husband asks you to do would violate Scripture, you must *respectfully* decline. *"...We must obey God rather than men."* (Acts 5:29) Disobeying a husband's instructions to steal is choosing to obey the Lord and avoid sin.

This is an altogether different situation from the woman who decides, "God doesn't want us to buy a new car," or believes, "God wants us to move to a better school district." Believing that her husband is making an unwise decision is not the same as seeing that he is asking her to sin. Unless her husband asks her to disobey Scripture, she is in rebellion when she disregards his decision.

The Greek word that is rendered *submit* in Colossians and *submissive* in the above passage in 1 Peter means *to subordinate oneself* or *to obey*. Literally, it means *to arrange one's self under*. Phillips paraphrases Peter's words as *"...you married women should adapt yourselves to your husbands..."* In other words, the wife who follows the Lord's command in this area arranges herself under her husband's authority.

Some women, when they hear Paul's words, will say, "I'm not going to be my husband's slave!" They think that if they yield to their husbands' leadership, it will enslave them. The difference between submission and slavery, ladies, is origin. Slavery occurs when one person forces obedience from another. Submission is an act of the submitter, not of the one in authority. It is a willing choice to yield.

This pictures the submission of the bride of Christ. There will come a day when *"...at the name of Jesus EVERY KNEE WILL BOW, of those who are in heaven and on earth and under the earth, and that every tongue will confess that Jesus Christ is Lord, to the glory of God the Father."* (Phil. 2:10-11) On that day, even those who do not desire to do so will surrender to Him, for they will have no choice—but their submission will be too late to yield benefits to them. For now, however, no one is forced to obey Him. He *invites* us to yield to His will, but we choose whether or not we will do so. This is illustrated by the willing submission of wives.

Women who are unwilling to hear these instructions have even said, "Well, I think Paul just hated women. I want to listen to Jesus, but not to Paul." Remember, ladies, that the Bible was not composed according to the whim of the men who actually wrote it down. God *inspired* them when they wrote. The New International Version of the New Testament gives an accurate rendering of 2 Tim. 3:16: *"All Scripture is God-breathed..."* The Holy Spirit breathed into Paul the teaching that he wrote in his epistles.

Occasionally, I hear a woman say that Paul's instructions in Eph. 5:22-24 refer to husbands and wives mutually submitting themselves to each other. The wife is to submit herself to her husband, and the husband is to submit himself to his wife. They base this interpretation on the preceding verse, which says, *"Submit to one another out of reverence for Christ."* (Eph. 5:21 NIV)

In the first place, that interpretation won't work. Two people *can* choose to bless each other. One can choose to give up one's own desires to give happiness to the other. In the area of authority, however, only one can have the final word. As a good friend used to say, "If two people are riding a horse, one of them has to ride in front." Only one of the two can be in authority.

If we look at the literal translation of this passage, moreover, it becomes evident that the above interpretation of mutual submission is based on faulty reasoning. According to my interlinear New Testament, verses 21-22 literally say, *"...being subject to one another in (the) fear of Christ: The wives to (their) own husbands as to the Lord."* (Marshall) Paul then goes on to discuss marriage and its portrayal of the relationship of Christ and the church before he adds two other instances in which submission is required. He commands children to obey their parents in Eph. 6:1 and slaves to subject themselves to their masters in Eph. 6:5.

After each command to subject oneself, he discusses the responsibilities of the one in authority to serve and bless the one under authority. Wives have a responsibility to submit, but husbands have a responsibility to love. He commands children to obey their parents; fathers must forsake provoking their children to anger and must bring up their children in the discipline and instruction of the Lord. Slaves are to obey their masters as though serving the Lord, even when no one is looking; masters are to do good to their servants—avoiding threats—because they too have a Master in heaven.

In other words, the basic thrust of these verses would be something like this: Submit yourselves one to another in the fear of Christ
- Wives to husbands
- Children to parents
- Slaves to masters

In none of these instances is Paul instructing the one in authority to submit to the choices of the one under authority. We readily recognize that parents must lovingly serve and bless the child, but that doesn't mean that they are to yield to the child's leadership! The idea is that those who are under authority should willingly choose to surrender to that authority.

Other women who read Paul's words would say, "Well, that was for the culture of that time, not for today." Paul's words are indeed contrary to contemporary American custom, but they were not written for a specific culture.

I'm loathe to say that something was for then and not for now unless Scripture indicates that it is no longer in force. Christ fulfilled ceremonial law, so we don't make animal sacrifices today. Paul asked Timothy to bring him some scrolls and a cloak that he had left somewhere. I don't think I'm supposed to be looking for parchments to take to Paul. If it isn't *obviously* for then and not for now, however, I'm going to presume that it's written to us today. Otherwise, who gets to decide what's still in force and what is not?

In fact, Paul quoted (in Eph. 5:31) a passage from Gen. 2:24 that immediately followed the creation of the very first wife—indicating that this teaching is God's will for wives of all times. This is how He intends for marriage to be. These words in Ephesians were given to tell women in every nation and culture how to function as the wives God desires them to be. We will be happiest when we perform in the way that our Creator designed us to operate.

Even before the fall, woman was to be subject to her husband. When God created Eve, He intended for her to be a suitable *helper* for Adam. (Gen. 2:18) Adam was not created for her, but she was made for her husband. *"For man does not originate from woman, but woman from man; for indeed man was not created for the woman's sake, but woman for the man's sake..."* (1 Cor. 11:8-9) Who can question that this pictures our relationship with the Lord? Is the Lord not the leader and authority? Were we not created to serve and please Him?

Most brides include a symbol of submission in their weddings, often without realizing what they are doing. If you wore a veil at your wedding, you wore a symbol of submission. A veil represents submission to the husband's authority, which in turn pictures the submission to the authority of Christ. (See 1 Cor. 11:10.)

There is an interesting story involving a veil and a bride in the Old Testament. *"Rebekah lifted up her eyes, and when she saw Isaac she dismounted from the camel. She said to the servant, 'Who is that man walking in the field to meet us?' And the servant said, 'He is my master.' Then she took her veil and covered herself. The servant told Isaac all the things that he had done. Then Isaac brought her into his mother Sarah's tent, and he took Rebekah, and she became his wife, and he loved her; thus Isaac was comforted after his mother's death."* (Gen. 24:64-67)

Rebekah was coming to marry a man whom she had never seen. When she first realized that she was looking at the man who would be her husband, she veiled herself. In Jewish weddings today, the bridegroom himself places the veil over his bride before the wedding, and the bride submits to this rite.

Even the bride who covers *herself* with the veil—as did Rebekah—symbolizes her willingness to submit to her husband's authority. Rebekah wasn't covering her head merely because it was customary to be veiled in the presence of just any man. She was traveling in the company of several men. (Gen. 24:59) Furthermore, she didn't veil herself when she saw Isaac approaching until she realized that this man would be her bridegroom.

Although most Christian brides wear veils in their weddings, many are unwilling to yield to their husbands' authority.

After Adam and Eve ate the forbidden fruit, the Lord told the woman, *"...Yet your desire will be for your husband, and he will rule over you."* (Gen. 3:16) On first reading, some people might think that the Lord refers to sexual desire, since it follows a mention of childbirth. That, I believe, is unlikely to be an appropriate interpretation. In most cases, it is the man—not the woman—who has more sexual desire.

Others who read this passage perhaps think that it means that a woman's natural desire is to please her husband (even though that is not what we usually observe in human nature).

A closer look, however, indicates that the opposite is true. In the very next chapter, Cain was angry because God had not accepted his offering. The Lord warned him to beware of sin. *"If you do well, will not your countenance be lifted up? And if you do not do well, sin is crouching at the door; and **its desire is for you**, but you must master it."* (Gen. 4:7, emphasis mine)

There's that word *desire* again. The Hebrew word that is translated *desire* in both Gen. 3:16 and Gen. 4:7 means *to stretch out*. It comes from a root word that means *to run over* or *run after*, or *to overflow*.

The Lord told Eve that her desire was for her husband and he must rule her. He told Cain that sin's desire was for him, but he must master it. He was warning Cain that sin's desire was to control him, but that he must instead master the sin.

Since the fall, women have had a desire to rule their husbands. They have stretched out their hands to control their husbands. They want to overrun their proper place of submission to their husbands and usurp the authority of their husbands. God's will, both before the fall and since, is that the husband should be the leader *because he symbolizes Christ*. The woman is to help, follow, and submit to him, *because she represents the church*.

Satan's fall was because he wanted to usurp God's place:
"How you have fallen from heaven,

O star of the morning, son of the dawn!
You have been cut down to the earth,
You who have weakened the nations!
But you said in your heart,
'I will ascend to heaven;
I will raise my throne above the stars of God,
And I will sit on the mount of assembly
In the recesses of the north.
I will ascend above the heights of the clouds;
I will make myself like the Most High.'" (Isa. 14:12-14)

Yes, Lucifer's desire was to usurp God's authority. In the Garden of Eden, he then deceived Eve and led her to become a usurper as well. She was led away from devotion of following her husband and followed the serpent instead. Adam was not deceived. *"And it was not Adam who was deceived, but the woman being deceived, fell into transgression."* (1 Tim. 2:14) When we defy God's delegated authority in our husbands, *we* choose to follow Satan as well.

How different their lives would have been if Eve had chosen to follow Adam (who was not deceived) instead of following the serpent's leadership and barging headlong into the deception of sin!

There's a lesson here for husbands, as well, although this book is aimed at wives. We have no record that Adam tried to stop Eve, even though Gen. 3:6 implies that he was with her when she sinned. While he himself was not deceived, moreover, Adam chose to abdicate and follow his wife into sin. Let us not—whether by nagging, by manipulation, or by raging—tempt our husbands to follow Adam's error and abandon the role of leader.

In our relationship to the heavenly Bridegroom, we likewise have the responsibility to submit to His leadership. Thus, Paul wrote, *"...I am jealous for you with a godly jealousy; for I betrothed you to one husband, so that to Christ I might present you as a pure virgin. But I am afraid that, as the serpent deceived Eve by his craftiness, your minds will be led astray from the simplicity and purity of devotion to Christ."* (2 Cor. 11:2-3) Jesus said, *"If anyone wishes to come after Me, he must deny himself, and take up his cross daily and follow Me."* (Luke 9:23) The follower of Christ must choose to submit to Him. We must daily choose to deny our own selfish desires and the tendency to please ourselves, so that we can please the Lord our Bridegroom.

Wedded Husband

On the day of my marriage, I vowed to take Charles as my wedded husband. I looked up the words *wed* and *wedded*. They come from the Old English *wedd*, meaning *pledge*. (M-W Web Site) In other words, I pledged to take him as my husband.

Originally, the English word *wife* didn't mean *married woman*, but simply *woman*. (M-W Web Site) If a man said, "my wife," he was saying, "my woman."

The word *husband*, on the other hand, does *not* merely mean *man*. This word comes originally from an Old Norse word *husbondi*, which meant *householder*. (M-W) It later evolved into the Anglo Saxon word *husbonda*, which meant *master of the house*. (Webster)

Eventually, the word *husbandman* came into being. We see this word in the King James Version of Gen. 9:20, 2 Tim. 2:6, and Jas. 5:7. It's an old-fashioned word for *gardener* or *farmer*. Do you remember the King James rendering of John 15:1? It says, *"I am the true vine, and my Father is the husbandman."* The husbandman tended the plants.

Charles became my "gardener" (husbandman) when he became my husband. That is, he tends to me. He cultivates me. He helps me to grow and be all I can be. He cannot fulfill this function if I do not yield to his leadership.

The word *husbandry* refers to the activities of a caretaker, one who controls or makes judicious use of resources. (M-W) Have you heard of animal husbandry? It's the care of farm animals. Just so, God calls our husbands to care for us. He wants the husband to be the manager, guardian, and caretaker.

Charles is my caretaker. He is my protector and provider. He is responsible for my well being, just as a man who works at animal husbandry is responsible for the welfare of the animals. Obviously, if I don't regard him as the master of the household (the leader), then he will not be able to protect and provide for me. More on that in later chapters.

We laugh about the fact that our husbands always want to hold the remote control for the television. Men in general like to be the one with the remote. Why is that? Is it not because the husband wants to set the direction? There's a reason for that, ladies. God made him that way! God created the husband to be the leader, because the husband symbolizes Christ.

Remember, my sisters, we are to be trustworthy wives. Can your husband trust you to follow his leadership in all areas? What about the children? Can your husband trust you with the children? Do you refrain from criticizing your husband to the children? Do you train the children according to their father's leadership even when he is not present? Does your husband know that when he is not at home, you still require what you would expect if he were there? Do your children know that it is useless to ask you to override their father's decision? If he tells the children to do their chores *before* playtime, do you see that they obey?

The Bible teaches that the husband is the head of the wife as Christ is head of the church. It instructs wives to submit to their husbands as to the Lord. (See Eph. 5:22-23.) It does *not* say, "Wives, be subject to your own husbands when you think they are making wise decisions." Nor does it say, "Wives, be subject to your own husbands except when you think they are too strict (or too lenient) with the children."

If you submit only when you think he is right, you have not submitted at all. You are merely doing what you wanted to do anyway. You are doing what you would have done if you were the leader or if you had no husband. It takes no submission to do that.

I know of no area in which it is more difficult to submit than when you differ about something that affects the children. If you disagree, appeal to him privately. He deserves to have the benefit of your insights. Notice that I said to appeal to him and present your thinking, but then you must allow *him* to make the decision. (This is not the same thing as haranguing him until he does what you want him to do.) Then you must support—especially in front of the children—his final decision.

In a sense, we have an obligation to rear the children of the Lord as well. Can the heavenly Bridegroom trust you to lead women who are younger in the Lord than you are?

"Older women likewise are to be reverent in their behavior, not malicious gossips nor enslaved to much wine, teaching what is good, so that they may encourage the young women to love their husbands, to love their children, to be sensible, pure, workers at home, kind, being subject to their own husbands, so that the word of God will not be dishonored." (Tit. 2:3-5)

Now, you may think, "I'm only 30 years old, so I don't have to worry about those requirements for older women." Let me encourage you to think again. When the apostle gives these instructions, he refers to the younger women with a Greek word that literally means *new*, and by implication is used to mean *youthful*. It seems to me that if this word means *new*, the instructions would include women who are older in the Lord leading those who have not known the Lord as long. Besides, even in chronological age, every woman is older than some other woman or girl is.

We older women have a responsibility to teach what is good. You know, we are *always* teaching *something* by our behavior, by our words, and by our attitudes. We are either teaching what God desires, or (by our example, if not by our words) we teach what is displeasing to the Lord. Does your life teach what is good to those who are coming behind you? Do you demonstrate submission to the heavenly Bridegroom? If the younger women follow your example, will they learn to please the Lord?

It's significant that the *older women* are to train the younger women in these areas. Paul did *not* tell Titus to train the younger women. In the first place, a man who personally trains a young woman who is not his wife is flirting with temptation. (Now, I'm warning against personal discipleship training in a one-on-one setting, not public teaching in a group setting.) Secondly, a man cannot set the example of how to be a good wife!

When Paul wrote, *"so that they may encourage the young women,"* he used the Greek word (here rendered as *encourage*) that means *to make of sound mind,* or (figuratively) *to discipline* or *to correct* them. It comes from a root that includes the concepts of safety, deliverance, protection, and self-control. When we older women encourage these things in our children or in younger women, we are bringing correction and protection to their lives; we are helping them to find safety. This Greek word (translated as *encourage* in Tit. 2:4) is also related to the word that is rendered in various translations as *sensible, discreet, sober-minded,* or *self-controlled* in verse 5.

Now self-control is not something that you could impose on another woman or even on your child. If you were to attempt that and be successful, it would not be *self*-control. So how can you help them to find this safety and deliverance from an unsound mind? How can you help them to develop this self-control? How can you encourage a younger woman—whether your daughter or another young woman—to learn to be a good wife or a good mother? How do you help them to be kind and pure?

One of the best ways is through praying and interceding for the younger women as well as our natural children. We can engage in spiritual warfare on their behalf for their protection from the enemy of their souls.

When Paul wrote to the Ephesian Christians about the warfare in the spiritual realm, he included these words: *"For our struggle is not against flesh and blood, but against the rulers, against the powers, against the world forces of this darkness, against the spiritual forces of wickedness in the heavenly places. Therefore, take up the full armor of God, so that you will be able to resist in the evil day, and having done everything, to stand firm...With all prayer and petition pray at all times in the Spirit, and with this in view, be on the alert with all perseverance and petition for all the saints..."* (Eph. 6:12-13, 18)

Intercession is especially important when we see that a young sister is failing to obey God: *"If anyone sees his brother committing a sin not leading to death, he shall ask and God will for him give life to those who commit sin not leading to death..."* (1 John 5:16) *"Therefore, confess your sins to one another, and pray for one another so that you may be healed. The effective prayer of a righteous man can accomplish much."* (Jas. 5:16)

Furthermore, you can lead other women to develop this sensible attitude and soundness of mind through your example. A young woman can learn this way of life by following the example of one who has it. We must strive to lead lives that are worthy to be followed. Then, like Paul, we can say, *"Follow my example, as I follow the example of Christ."* (1 Cor. 11:1 NIV)

Do you exercise self-control in your daily life? Self-control is listed with the fruit of the Spirit. If you want to bear this fruit, you must die to your flesh and walk in the power of the Holy Spirit. As those who come behind observe this, they can follow your example.

Another way that you lead your natural and spiritual children to be sensible or self-controlled is by encouragement and exhortation. *"We urge you, brethren, admonish the unruly, encourage the fainthearted, help the weak, be patient with everyone."* (1 Thess. 5:14)

To assist these children and younger women in becoming sensible, we must hold them accountable; but in order to truly help them and also to make sure that we ourselves are walking in sensibility, we must keep an eye on our own hearts, lives, and attitudes as well. *"Brethren, even if anyone is caught in any trespass,* **you who are spiritual***, restore such a one* **in a spirit of gentleness***; each one* **looking to yourself***, so that you too will not be tempted."* (Gal. 6:1, emphasis mine) When we are *"full of goodness, filled with all knowledge,"* we will be *"able also to admonish one another."* (Rom. 15:14)

Still another way that you can encourage younger women and your children to be godly is by reminding them to read the Bible and apply it to their lives. We never progress in any area of our spiritual lives without spending time in the Word of God. Without knowledge of the Bible, we don't recognize what needs to be reined in and what should be encouraged.

Suppose a girl is brought up in a home totally without Christ. No one teaches the Scriptures to her. If she is born again as a young adult, she knows absolutely nothing of what the Bible says. Even if she is passionately in love with Jesus, grateful for His forgiveness, and earnestly longs to please Him, she will really mess up without knowledge of His will. Perhaps she hears someone teach that Christians should love everyone, so she has sex with all of the men she dates, thinking that she is "showing love" to them! She wouldn't be doing this in rebellion toward the Lord; in fact, she would be trying to *please* the Lord!

This is why Paul tells us to *"...try to **learn** what is pleasing to the Lord."* (Eph. 5:10 NIV, emphasis mine) We cannot follow the leadership of the heavenly Bridegroom if we don't know what He wants us to do.

When the tempter comes to us, he doesn't say, "I am a demon, and I have come to lead you into sin." No, the Bible says, *"...Satan himself masquerades as an angel of light. It is not surprising, then, if his servants masquerade as servants of righteousness..."* (2 Cor. 11:14-15 NIV) Thus when Satan or a demon comes to us, he will often pretend that what he leads us to do is right.

In order to avoid deception, each of us must know what the Word of God says. The Holy Spirit authored the Bible, and He *never* contradicts Himself. If we hear an inner voice that says *anything* that contradicts the Scriptures, we will know that it is not the voice of the Holy Spirit. But how can we determine that if we are not familiar with Scripture? Without this knowledge of the Bible, we will be vulnerable to either follow our natural desires or to be led by Satan's kingdom. Thus, we must encourage those who follow us to increase their knowledge of the Word of God.

Do those who come behind have in you an example of holy living? Do they see the importance of obeying Christ? By your own discretion, sensibility, sober-mindedness, and self-control, you can lead your natural children and the younger women. You can demonstrate to them by example how to have these qualities in themselves.

What kind of attitude do you manifest toward your husband? Do you submit to his authority in the family? If your daughter or younger friend watches your life, will she learn to love her husband and follow his leadership? Will she cultivate affectionate, fond attitudes toward him, or will she constantly criticize him? Will she look for ways to serve him, or will she always think of things that he should do for her? May we always encourage the younger women (by words *and* by example) to follow the leadership of their husbands.

Provision

❊❊❊

The book of Ruth speaks of finding rest in the house of one's husband. Ladies, I think I can just imagine what you're saying:

"Rest? In the house of my husband? When? There's the laundry, the ironing, the cooking, the dishes, the vacuuming, the dusting, the scrubbing, the children...it never ends. Haven't you ever heard that old rhyme? 'Man's work is from sun to sun. Woman's work is never done.' Rest in the house of my husband? You've got to be kidding!"

So let's go back to what Naomi said to her two daughters-in-law when she was ready to return to Bethlehem. Naomi's husband and two sons had died, and her sons' widows indicated that they would follow her back to Israel.

Naomi tried to dissuade them. *"...Go, return each of you to her mother's house. May the LORD deal kindly with you as you have dealt with the dead and with me. May the LORD grant that you may **find rest, each in the house of her husband**..."* (Ruth 1:8-9, emphasis mine) What do you think she meant by "finding rest"?

Eventually Orpah did kiss Naomi good-bye and return to her own people, but Ruth steadfastly clung to Naomi and insisted that she would accompany her mother-in-law to Israel.

You know the story. Ruth gleaned in the field of Boaz to support herself and her mother-in-law. When Boaz came to the fields from his home in Bethlehem, he noticed Ruth. *"'Boaz asked the foreman of his harvesters, 'Whose young woman is that?' The foreman replied,*

'She is the Moabitess who came back from Moab with Naomi. She said, "Please let me glean and gather among the sheaves behind the harvesters." She went into the field and has worked steadily from morning till now, except for a short rest in the shelter.' (Ruth 2:5-7 NIV)

Boaz apparently provided a shelter in the fields so his servants could take rest breaks there. Since there was such a shelter available, it was in all likelihood the location of the meal Boaz provided for Ruth: *"At mealtime Boaz said to her, 'Come here, that you may eat of the bread and dip your piece of bread in the vinegar.' So she sat beside the reapers; and he served her roasted grain, and she ate and was satisfied and had some left."* (Ruth 2:14)

Naomi was pleased when she heard where Ruth had gleaned, because Boaz was a near kinsman. He could be their redeemer. Naomi urged Ruth to glean in no other field but his. *"Then Naomi her mother-in-law said to her, 'My daughter, shall I not seek security for you, that it may be well with you? Now is not Boaz our kinsman, with whose maids you were?...'"* (Ruth 3:1-2)

The word that is translated *security* in the above verse comes from a root word that means *rest*. Naomi said that she would seek *rest* for Ruth. Now Ruth had already experienced some rest in the field structure of Boaz, but Naomi clearly is not speaking of that. The near kinsman, or redeemer, had the responsibility to redeem the property of his dead childless brother or close relative, and to take the widow for his own wife in order to raise up a child in his brother's name. (See Deut. 25:5-6.)

In Ruth 3:3-4, Naomi sent Ruth to Boaz at his threshing floor with instructions about what she should do. When Ruth returned, Naomi asked how it went, and Ruth gave a report: There was a relative closer than Boaz. Although Boaz desired to redeem and marry Ruth, he must first speak to the other man. Then Naomi said, *"Wait, my daughter, until you know how the matter turns out; for the man will not rest until he has settled it today."* (Ruth 3:18) Ruth could rest, because Boaz would *not* rest until he had settled the matter.

The society in which Ruth lived was not like ours. Life was very hard for women without husbands, fathers, brothers, or grown sons to provide for them. Physically weaker, women lacked the strength to do many of the jobs that men did. The laborsaving devices available to us were unknown to them. Besides, there was so much to do that one person could not do all of the work. The children needed care. The food must be prepared while the man worked in the fields. The man had all he could do, and the wife did as well.

Furthermore, daughters in Israel did not inherit lands from their fathers as the sons did. Only if there were no sons did the daughters inherit their father's property. (See Num. 27:1-8.) Women of that day inherited no land on which to plant or property on which to build a house. Throughout the Bible, therefore, God instructed His people to care for the widows and the fatherless. (See Deut. 14:28-29, Deut. 24:19, 1 Tim. 5:3-4, and Jas. 1:27.) Today many women work in the same kinds of jobs as men do and can more easily support themselves. In Ruth's day, it was quite difficult.

For a woman who had a husband, however, provision came from him. He *did* inherit *his* father's property. A woman usually inherited lands through her *husband's* inheritance. What her husband inherited was available to her as well, since she was his wife.

The meaning of the word *security* in Ruth 3:1 is related to the word rendered *rest* in Ruth 1:9 and means *a place to settle down in quietness*. It comes from a root word that means *to rest* or *to settle down*.

The rest found in the husband's house didn't mean that she had no work to do. It meant that she no longer had to provide for herself. When she had a husband—a provider—she could settle down in peace. She didn't go out to glean in someone else's field to bring home some food. Her husband provided for her needs. As his wife, she served him in the home, yielded submissively to him, and bore and nurtured his little ones.

Women instinctively want security. They really want their husbands to provide for them. I have known many men who prefer that their wives do not work outside the home. Other husbands don't have a preference about that. While many women choose to work for pay, I have known only one woman who was ambivalent about whether or not her husband also had a job. Women usually want their husbands to be willing to work to earn money and provide security for the family.

Moreover, being out of work is extremely hard on the self-image of most men. God made men with this instinct to be the breadwinner, because He calls husbands to provide for their families. *"If anyone does not provide for his relatives, and especially for his immediate family, he has denied the faith and is worse than an unbeliever."* (1 Tim. 5:8 NIV)

I am not saying that a married woman should never have a job outside the home; sometimes circumstances dictate that she must. I am saying, rather, that her husband is the one who is *responsible* for the provision.

Since that is true, I would certainly say that a man who is able to do so should work to provide financially for his family. Sometimes that might not be possible. For example, he might lose his job and have trouble finding another one. He might be a college student, and his wife is earning her Ph.T. (putting hubby through). He might be doing the preliminary work to start his own business or to start a ministry, and he needs for his wife to temporarily be the breadwinner. He might lose his health and be unable to work. He might work hard every day, but his salary is so low that it would not be possible for the family to live on it. When possible, however, the husband has the responsibility to provide for his family's financial needs.

Although the husband is primarily responsible for providing the family's material needs, the wife still has responsibilities about finances even if she doesn't have an outside job. Verses 16 and 24 of Proverbs 31 indicate that the excellent wife sensibly spends the household money at her disposal, and sometimes she is able to make more money for the family.

"She considers a field and buys it;
From her earnings she plants a vineyard." (Prov. 31:16)

Notice that she *considered* the field before she bought it. This was not an impulse purchase. She gave it some thought before she decided whether it was worth the money. The purchase was part of a plan. Take note also that she didn't purchase it for a frivolous or selfish reason, but for the purpose of planting a vineyard to help the entire family.

Suppose you give allowances to your two children each Saturday morning. By the following Friday afternoon, one child still has a little money left. The second one complains incessantly all week about insufficient funds. When you ask why this child is always out of money, he replies that he usually spends all of his money on junk food or arcade games the first day he has it. Then he doesn't have any funds for the remainder of the week.

Is that very different from the woman who doesn't have enough money for groceries and household expenses because she frequently purchases expensive jewelry and makes weekly trips to the spa? Is it different from the woman who doesn't spend a lot of money in any one purchase, but constantly buys a myriad of useless or unneeded trinkets? Is it different from the person who squanders the family finances on gambling? The result is the same: When the time comes to buy necessities, she has no money. We would say that such a woman has wasted her money. She had a set amount, and she didn't use it wisely.

Poor women in Biblical times, particularly widows, often gleaned in the fields of others. This was the case, as you recall, with Ruth. The Proverbs 31 woman would make clothing and belts to sell. Our great-grandmothers sold extra eggs or butter. Sometimes we also must do something to increase the family income.

My personal conviction is that it is better that wives do not work away from the home *when that is possible*. I would add that a woman probably should not work in a job away from home if her husband does not want her to do that or if the outside job hampers her ministry to her own family.

You might be surprised at how much less money your family would need if you were not working outside the home. Work-related expenses (commuting expenses, office clothing purchases, child-care, meals eaten out and/or convenience foods for meals at home, etc.) consume a large percentage of the working wife's salary. The higher tax bracket that her earnings bring is a surprisingly significant factor.

Perhaps you would be willing to stay at home if you thought you could afford it. If that's the case, I suggest that you try the following: In the coming months, faithfully record every single expense that you would not have if you were not working outside the home, including but not limited to the list in the previous paragraph. For example, you would also want to include any food expenses for office parties, gifts for workplace exchanges, dry cleaning for your office clothes, and so forth. If you pay someone to help with your housecleaning, write that down. If you send out your husband's dress shirts because you don't have time to iron them, list that. Be sure to include the part of your gasoline that would not be used if you were not commuting to work, and try to guess the percentage of your automobile wear-and-tear and repairs.

At income tax time, compute your family's taxes twice—once using both of your salaries, and once as if you had not earned anything—in order to see what taxes are added because of your own salary. Then subtract from your own income all of your work-related expenses and the extra income tax that you owed because of your salary. (If you have not kept the records of job-related expenses for an entire year, find the average monthly amount that you spent over the period of several months that you recorded and then multiply by twelve.) Only then will you see how much you have truly earned by giving up such a large portion of your time to work in another man's "field."

Sometimes a woman will say, "But we couldn't live in a house this large and nice if I didn't have an outside job." That may or may not be true, depending upon what her bottom line is after she has subtracted her working expenses and taxes. Even if it is true, however, I wonder how much she gets to enjoy her lovely house if she must leave early in the morning and only return in time to get food on the table, help the children with their homework, do a load of laundry, and then get everyone into bed. Even her weekends are not times of rest, because she must catch up on all of the shopping, housecleaning, laundry, and errands that were not accomplished while she was at the office.

I am not saying that it is always wrong for a married woman to work outside the home, but that I believe staying home is a worthy goal. In fact, it might be preferable for the husband to take a second job before the wife begins to work outside the home. *Any* wife who takes an outside job is taking a "second job," because the home responsibilities are still there. When the husband takes the second employment, he is more likely than a "working wife" is to realize that it needs to be a temporary situation. I asked my husband about that, and he agreed that it's better for the husband to take a second job, *provided that the wife is making the home a place of refuge for him and is ministering to his needs.*

Obviously, a second income is truly essential in some families. Note that I said, "when that is possible" when I indicated my opinion about the wisdom of staying at home. Often a woman who needs to earn money can determine a way to make her home to be the base for some kind of self-employment without most of those work-related expenses.

Regardless of whether or not you have an outside job, part of your husband's provision would include his authority over finances and how money is spent. When he asks you not to spend any extra money this month, how do you respond? Perhaps for one reason or another he has asked you to write the checks and balance the account each month. Special care must be taken in this case that he does not have to ask your permission to spend money. While you would need to let him know what your financial situation is when he is contemplating a purchase, he is still the one in authority and he must be free to make the decision.

Boaz was attracted to Ruth because she was *"a woman of excellence,"* or as the NIV renders it, *"a woman of noble character."* The Hebrew word that Boaz used to describe Ruth in Ruth 3:11 is the same word that refers to the wife in Prov. 31:10. Do you remember the description of the excellent wife of noble character in Proverbs 31? One of the first things we learn about her is that she is trustworthy. The queen mother said this about the wife she desires for her son:

"The heart of her husband trusts in her,
And he will have no lack of gain." (Verse 11)

If we are to be excellent wives, we must be worthy of the trust of our husbands. A wife must be like a treasure chest that protects what her husband entrusts to her. Can your husband trust you? Can he trust you with the checkbook or charge cards? A woman who spends money with abandon is likely to have a husband who *does* have a lack of gain.

I have heard women tell wild stories about the creative ways that they deceived their husbands concerning money. For example, one woman who balanced the family checkbook laughed about writing checks at an expensive department store for perfume and other costly items but entering the amounts in the check register as if she had written the checks at the supermarket. If her husband looked into the checkbook, he presumed that she had written those checks for food. Was she a trustworthy wife?

The trustworthy woman doesn't write checks for more than the grocery bill in order to have cash to spend on something that her husband doesn't want her to purchase. She doesn't hide new clothes for a few weeks and then feel justified in telling her husband, "No, this isn't a new outfit. I've had it awhile." She doesn't tell him that she spent a certain amount of money on shoes for the kids to hide the fact that part of the sum was for some other purchase, of which he would not approve. She doesn't lie about what things cost. The excellent wife doesn't deceive her husband—period. She is trustworthy.

You may be thinking, "What difference does it make if I deceive him? What he doesn't know won't hurt him, and he's too tight with the money." Ladies, a woman who is dishonest with her husband concerning money is not trustworthy. A woman who cannot be trusted is not *"an excellent wife."* The Bible says, *"...it is better to be a poor man than a liar."* (Prov. 19:22)

Some wives spend money recklessly to comfort themselves when they feel neglected by their husbands, when they are depressed, or when they are angry with their husbands. This may feel good at the moment, but it is a very unwise course of action. If the husband of such a wife finds out what she has done, his trust in her will be diminished. Financial problems will add stress to a marriage, moreover, which can greatly decrease the couple's patience with one another. If the wife spends money in a way that she cannot afford to spend it, the anxiety about meeting financial obligations can trigger significant arguments about other things. The pleasure that she gained in the short run will be temporary, and the eventual result will be negative.

Furthermore, spending the money because you are angry is actually a form of seeking revenge; the Scriptures do not permit you to do this.

*"Do not say, 'I'll do to him as he has done to me;
I'll pay that man back for what he did.'"* (Prov. 24:29 NIV)

"Never pay back evil for evil to anyone. Respect what is right in the sight of all men." (Rom. 12:17)

Many times the true reason that we think we need more money is that we are not content with what we have, although it is in reality adequate. Regardless of how much we have, we will not feel rich until we are satisfied with what we possess.

"But godliness actually is a means of great gain, when accompanied by contentment. For we have brought nothing into the world, so we cannot take anything out of it either. If we have food and covering, with these we shall be content. But those who want to get rich fall into temptation and a snare and many foolish and harmful desires which plunge men into ruin and destruction." (1 Tim. 6:6-9)

Beware of developing an attitude of "keeping up with the Joneses" that will lead you to discontentment with what you have. The apostle Paul warns that this is a perilous attitude.

Certainly, we *always* have a responsibility to try to live within our means, to spend our money appropriately, and to avoid waste. We can do this in countless ways.

For example, with few exceptions, cooking from scratch will usually give you the same or better meals for less money. Boneless chicken breast is much more expensive than the kind that includes the bone. You can stock up when bone-in chicken breast is on sale. Cut it all off the bone when you get home, wrap the pieces in wax paper, and freeze them in plastic bags. (That way you can remove from the freezer only the number of pieces that you need.) Boil the bones, cool, and remove the cooked meat that clings to the bones. You can freeze these pre-cooked chunks for quick meals requiring chopped, cooked chicken. Freeze the broth for gravies, dumplings, soup, and so forth.

Remember that time is money. Either you pay someone else to do something for you (cutting the meat off the bone, for example), or you save the money by doing it yourself. If you are staying at home, you have the time to do such money-saving activities.

Coupons are another way to save money. One year we had to buy a new dishwasher, and my husband figured up that I had saved enough on coupons that year to pay for the dishwasher. Just remember that it won't save money if you use every coupon that comes your way. In fact, buying unneeded items simply because you have a coupon may result in your spending *more* than you need to spend. Using the coupons on items that you need to purchase anyway, however, will help your budget. Don't be afraid to try store brands, though. Many are as good as the national brands, and they often cost less than the name-brand price even with coupon savings.

Cooking and shopping are not the only ways to save money. A woman who sews can save by making and/or repairing her family's clothing, and perhaps she can earn extra money by sewing or mending for others who cannot sew. Some ladies baby-sit for other women's children. Try to conserve gasoline by combining errands and planning the least mileage in doing them. Be creative. Look for ways to save and/or earn money.

One other characteristic of the excellent wife's use of money is that she is kind to the poor.

"*She extends her hand to the poor,*
And she stretches out her hands to the needy." (Prov. 31:20)

According to the margin of my Bible, the Hebrew literally says, "*She spreads out her palm to the poor.*" She gives with an open hand to those less fortunate. She is compassionate, unselfish, and generous.

"*One who is gracious to a poor man lends to the LORD,*
And He will repay him for his good deed." (Prov. 19:17)

The apostle Paul tells us that our income is ours in order to give us something to share with others, as well as to provide for our own needs. (Eph. 4:28)

The Lord's Provision

Once again, I remind you that marriage is a picture of the relationship of Christ and the church, with our husbands representing

Christ and we wives representing the church. How does finding rest and provision in the house of one's husband illustrate the relationship of Christ and the church?

The Lord tells us that we must be trustworthy in the way we manage what He gives to us, whether it is in the realm of possessions, spiritual gifts, talents, our time, or anything else. Paul wrote, *"...it is required of stewards that one be found trustworthy."* (1 Cor. 4:2)

A considerable amount of Scripture discusses money and how we handle it. Jesus said, *"Whoever can be trusted with very little can also be trusted with much, and whoever is dishonest with very little will also be dishonest with much. So if you have not been trustworthy in handling worldly wealth, who will trust you with true riches?"* (Luke 16:10-11 NIV) In other words, if you are not worthy of your natural husband's trust in the way that you handle money, your heavenly Bridegroom cannot trust you with true (spiritual) riches. Most of us have heard about ministries that were destroyed because the minister was not trustworthy with money.

The Lord our Bridegroom is the provider of all our needs; we cannot provide for ourselves. Even what our natural husbands provide depends upon the Lord's enabling.

Receiving provision from the heavenly Bridegroom demonstrates that the bride of Christ is feminine. Perhaps you are familiar with the following words from Psalms:

"Delight yourself in the LORD;
And He will give you the desires of your heart." (Psa. 37:4)

The Hebrew word that is rendered as *delight* in this verse is a primitive root that means *to be soft or pliable, to be effeminate,* or *to be luxurious.* We often hear the word *effeminate* used negatively today to describe men who have womanly characteristics, but my dictionary says that it literally means *marked by qualities more typical of women than of men.* (M-W) In other words, it can merely mean *feminine.*

The bride of Christ is feminine, and the Lord is masculine. We are to be soft and pliable toward the Lord, yielding to His leadership and finding joy in Him. We are to look to Him to be our provider.

He can safely give us the desires of our hearts when we are soft and pliable toward Him, because we then have godly desires.

Boaz was a type (symbol or picture) of Christ. Boaz was even from Bethlehem, the town where our Lord was born. I think that the current provision for us (the rest that we now have in the Lord Jesus) is perhaps like Ruth's rest and provision in chapter two of the book that bears her name. She worked in the field belonging to Boaz, and then rested in his shelter for a while before she worked again. (Ruth 2:7)

Boaz provided drink for Ruth's thirst. As she labored in his field, he told her, *"...When you are thirsty, go to the water jars and drink from what the servants draw."* (Ruth 2:9) Jesus has said that we can come to Him and drink the water of the Holy Spirit. *"Now on the last day, the great day of the feast, Jesus stood and cried out, saying, 'If anyone is thirsty, let him come to Me and drink. He who believes in Me, as the Scripture said, "From his innermost being will flow rivers of living water."' But this He spoke of the Spirit, whom those who believed in Him were to receive; for the Spirit was not yet given, because Jesus was not yet glorified."* (John 7:37-39)

Furthermore, Boaz provided the meal for Ruth, as I noted earlier in this chapter. *"At mealtime Boaz said to her, 'Come over here. Have some bread and dip it in the wine vinegar.' When she sat down with the harvesters, he offered her some roasted grain. She ate all she wanted and had some left over."* (Ruth 2:14 NIV) He provided more than enough, just as Christ our heavenly Bridegroom provides for us with abundance. *"And my God will supply all your needs according to His riches in glory in Christ Jesus."* (Phil. 4:19) Ruth shared the leftover food with her mother-in-law. (Ruth 2:18) The Lord provides us with abundance so that we can share with others, as well. *"And God is able to make all grace abound to you, so that always having all sufficiency in everything, you may have an abundance for every good deed."* (2 Cor. 9:8)

The Law commanded, *"When you reap the harvest of your land, do not reap to the very edges of your field or gather the gleanings of your harvest. Do not go over your vineyard a second time or pick up the grapes that have fallen. Leave them for the poor and the alien. I am the LORD your God."* (Lev. 19:9-10 NIV) *"When you are harvesting in your field and you overlook a sheaf, do not go back to get it. Leave it for the alien, the fatherless and the widow, so that the LORD your God may bless you in all the work of your hands."* (Deut. 24:19 NIV)

Boaz went beyond that ordinance, however, for he instructed his servants to actually pull out some sheaves and drop them on purpose for Ruth to glean. *"As she got up to glean, Boaz gave orders to his men, 'Even if she gathers among the sheaves, don't embarrass her. Rather, pull out some stalks for her from the bundles and leave them for her to pick up, and don't rebuke her.'"* (Ruth 2:15-16 NIV)

As Boaz made Ruth's labors easier, thus giving her a measure of rest, so also Christ invites us to come to Him for rest from our labors. *"Come to me, all you who are weary and burdened, and I will give you rest. Take my yoke upon you and learn from me, for I am gentle and humble in heart, and you will find rest for your souls. For my yoke is easy and my burden is light."* (Matt. 11:28-30 NIV)

This rest comes when we cease from our own labors and allow His power to anoint us for service: His work in and through us. *"There remains, then, a Sabbath-rest for the people of God; for **anyone who enters God's rest also rests from his own work**, just as God did from his."* (Heb. 4:9-10 NIV, emphasis mine)

Boaz continually provided for Ruth. Even when she left the threshing floor after the nighttime encounter with him, Boaz provided for her. *"He also said, 'Bring me the shawl you are wearing and hold it out.' When she did so, he poured into it six measures of barley and put it on her..."* (Ruth 3:15 NIV)

Eventually, Boaz did indeed redeem Ruth and she became his bride just as Naomi had hoped. (Ruth 4:13) Ruth no longer merely gleaned in his field for provision, but she came to live in his home with access to all of his abundance and all that bearing his name afforded.

Likewise, Christ has redeemed us, and we are His bride. We serve Him. We submit to His will. We bear children (lead others to Christ) and train them. Yes, even now we are in His household. *"So then you are no longer strangers and aliens, but you are fellow citizens with the saints, and are of God's household."* (Eph. 2:19)

"For thus the Lord GOD, the Holy One of Israel, has said,

*'In repentance and rest you will be saved,
In quietness and trust is your strength...'"* (Isa. 30:15)

There is, however, a sense in which we are not yet totally in that dwelling place of quiet rest. Jesus said, *"In My Father's house are many dwelling places; if it were not so, I would have told you; for I go to prepare a place for you. If I go and prepare a place for you, I will come again and receive you to Myself, that where I am, there you may be also."* (John 14:2-3) Someday we will celebrate a wedding feast and will at last be totally at rest in the house of our heavenly Husband. Hallelujah!

Christ is the heir of His Father. *"God, after He spoke long ago to the fathers in the prophets in many portions and in many ways, in these last days has spoken to us in His Son, whom He appointed heir of all things..."* (Heb. 1:1-2) In His High Priestly prayer, Jesus said to His Father, *"...all things that are Mine are Yours, and Yours are Mine..."* (John 17:10) Since Jesus is the heir of all things and we as His bride inherit through Him, we are *"...fellow heirs with Christ...."* (Rom. 8:17)

The husband, who owned the land, provided a dwelling place for his wife. The eternal Son, our divine Bridegroom, is even now preparing a dwelling place for us in His Father's house. (John 14:2-3) One day He will say to His bride, *"Come, you who are blessed of My Father, inherit the kingdom prepared for you from the foundation of the world."* (Matt. 25:34)

Protection

❋❋❋

Not only did the husband of Bible times give material provision to his wife, but he also gave her protection. Women did not fight in the armies, nor could they protect themselves from attack. We wives represent the church, and our husbands symbolize Christ. Therefore, women are the weaker gender because the church is weaker than the Son of God. (See 1 Pet. 3:7.)

Suppose you and your husband are alone in the house and are awakened in the dark of night because of a sound in the living room. It sounds as if someone is moving around in there! What is the normal reaction to that scenario? I suspect that in such an instance you do *not* tell your husband, "You stay here, and I'll go see if there is a burglar." No, the *husband* goes out to investigate. Why is that? Because he is stronger, and because he is the protector.

As we said in an earlier chapter, the name of our heavenly Bridegroom—Jesus—means *Yahweh saves* or *Yahweh delivers*. He is our protector and the deliverer from our enemies.

*"I call upon the Lord, who is worthy to be praised,
and I am saved from my enemies."* (Psa. 18:3)

By the authority of our Husband's name—Jesus—the forces of darkness are defeated in our lives. (Remember what we said previously about a wife's taking her husband's name?)

Do you recall the slave girl who was in bondage to an evil spirit in Philippi? She was a fortuneteller, and she followed Paul and his companions around the city shouting about them. *"She kept this up for many days. Finally Paul became so troubled that he turned around and said to the spirit, 'In the name of Jesus Christ I command you to come out of her!' At that moment the spirit left her."* (Acts 16:18 NIV) This young woman was set free from her enemy (the evil spirit) by the name of Jesus Christ.

Like David, we can trust the Lord to protect us in the dark and dangerous places:

"Even though I walk through the valley of the shadow of death, I fear no evil, for You are with me..." (Psa. 23:4)

"In peace I will both lie down and sleep, For You alone, O LORD, make me to dwell in safety." (Psa. 4:8)

The name of our Bridegroom protects us, because His name represents all that He is.

The Lord puts restrictions upon us for our protection, however. When Israel fell into wickedness, God's protection was withheld from them.

"Then they will cry out to the LORD, But He will not answer them. Instead, He will hide His face from them at that time Because they have practiced evil deeds." (Mic. 3:4)

"Oh that My people would listen to Me, That Israel would walk in My ways! I would quickly subdue their enemies And turn My hand against their adversaries." (Psa. 81:13-14)

What are some of the restrictions that He places upon us, and how do they protect us? A prime example is found in the following passage about the works of the flesh.

"Now the deeds of the flesh are evident, which are: immorality, impurity, sensuality, idolatry, sorcery, enmities, strife, jealousy, outbursts of anger, disputes, dissensions, factions, envying, drunkenness, carousing, and things like these, of which I forewarn you, just as I have forewarned you, that those who practice such things will not inherit the kingdom of God." (Gal. 5:19-21)

We are restricted from practicing fits of rage, immorality, idolatry, envy, drunkenness, and the other behaviors in this list. Why? Is God holding out on us? Does He capriciously think up rules for us to keep? Nothing can be further from the truth. The fact of the matter is that God forbids those practices because they are harmful to us and/or to others. Paul tells us that those who make a practice of such things will not inherit the kingdom of God. Ladies, those are serious words!

In fact, *every* time God commands us to do or to avoid something, He does so for our good. Everything that God forbids or requires is aimed at our benefit. Moses told the children of Israel that they should observe the Lord's commands and decrees that he gave them *for their own good.* (Deut. 10:13) The same is true for the commandments that He gives to us.

If you don't believe that failure to heed God's Word brings disaster, talk to the drug addict who has contracted AIDS. Consider the alcoholic who has ruined her life or her health. Think about the unfaithful wives who have lost their husbands due to their immorality. What about the woman who does not control her tongue? She damages her relationships, and James furthermore tells us that the religion of the person who has an unbridled tongue is worthless. (Jas. 1:26)

It behooves us, therefore, to be intimately familiar with restrictions on our behavior as revealed in the Scriptures and to be obedient to His instructions. Ignoring them puts us outside the umbrella of protection.

In the same way, God has called our natural husbands to protect us; and we are wise to allow them to do so.

Let me tell you an incident that illustrates that point. It happened a number of years ago during an extremely busy time in my life. My father-in-law had suffered a stroke several years earlier, and he was disabled. Then my mother-in-law fell and broke her hip, leaving her disabled as well. In order to help them, I was driving into Little Rock from our suburb across the river several mornings a week.

We had only two garage door remotes for three drivers. My husband drove to work every morning, and our son drove to high school every day. Since I was a stay-at-home wife and mother except for the days when I was helping my in-laws, it was logical that my husband and son had the remotes.

My husband made one request of me that I considered completely unreasonable. He asked me to always back the car out of the garage, park the car, go back and close the garage door from the inside and then go through the house to lock up before I left. He specifically asked that I *never* push the button to close the garage door and then run under the door before it closed.

"How ridiculous!" I thought. "Running under the door saves me a couple of minutes each time, and I've never had any problems making it out before it closes. He's too cautious."

I wasn't willing to listen to the voice of my husband, but there came a day that I regretted it. That day, my shoes had soles that were a little too slick as I ran across the concrete. Down I went! It was a really hard fall on the cement floor. I tore a huge hole that destroyed my favorite slacks; and of course, I *lost* quite a bit of time when I had to go back inside and change my clothes. Worst of all, I also hurt my leg and knee. Within a short time, my shin was black from just under the knee to my ankle. Talk about sore! The injury to my knee was such that it caused me pain whenever I knelt on that leg during the next two years.

I had foolishly decided that I knew better than my husband did and that I wasn't going to yield to his word. Therefore, he was unable to protect me. I learned a painful lesson that day.

How about you? Does that story remind you of any events in your life?

Perhaps your husband has said, "I don't think you should drive when the roads are so icy." Did you tell yourself, "I can drive as well as anyone can," and go anyway? Or did you submit to his request?

Maybe he said, "I don't think you should go to that part of town alone." Did you ridicule him for excessive caution or angrily tell him that he is overbearing? Or did you instead appreciate having a husband who wanted to protect you?

Perhaps he said, "I think you need to get more rest." Did you complain that you were too busy to get more rest and ignore his protection?

Just as the Lord's commands will not keep us safe if we disobey Him, your husband cannot protect you if you rebel against his direction.

Embracing Passion

❋❋❋

Have you ever wondered why God created sex? Does the Bible indicate what He had in mind when He made man and woman with sexual natures? I think it does, and I believe it will help us to fulfill His plans for physical intimacy in marriage if we know what His purposes are.

Our sexual natures were not an accident. The Lord of glory, the giver of all good gifts, created us this way to bless us. Learning God's purposes for physical intimacy will encourage us to fulfill them, and being aware of Satan's schemes for this area of our lives will help us to resist the enemy's evil plans.

Procreation

The most obvious purpose for sexual relations is procreation. God chose to populate the earth through sexual intercourse and the resulting pregnancies.

"God created man in His own image, in the image of God He created him; male and female He created them. God blessed them; and God said to them, 'Be fruitful and multiply, and fill the earth, and subdue it; and rule over the fish of the sea and over the birds of the sky and over every living thing that moves on the earth.'...Now the man had relations with his wife Eve, and she conceived and gave birth to Cain, and she said, 'I have gotten a manchild with the help of the LORD.'" (Gen. 1:27-28, 4:1)

This was one of God's intentions for coitus: reproduction and the extension of the human race.

What does Satan do? As always, he opposes God's plan. Satan promotes immoral sexual unions and then abortion, which kills the resulting offspring.

Symbolizes Relationship with Jesus

Reproduction is not the only reason that God created us with sexual natures, however. Another reason for sexual intimacy is that—just like other aspects of our marriages—it symbolizes the union of Christ and the church.

"For this reason a man will leave his father and mother and be united to his wife, and the two will become one flesh. This is a profound mystery—but I am talking about Christ and the church." (Eph. 5:31-32 NIV)

I have said in earlier chapters that husbands are givers and wives are receivers. It's worth noting that a woman is the receiver even in the sexual relationship with her husband. Reproduction never occurs because the wife deposits eggs in her husband. Rather, children are born because the husband releases sperm into his wife. All sperm comes from the husband, not the wife. Woman does not contribute seed. Only one Man was called the seed of woman: Jesus, who had no earthly father, was the seed of woman promised in Gen. 3:15.

When a baby girl is born, she already has the entire supply of ova (eggs) that she will ever have. They are part of her body. We could say that she received them, in a sense, from her father. Most of these ova will decline and die over the years, but a few hundred of them will mature and be released between puberty and menopause for possible fertilization.

Baby boys are not born with a lifetime supply of sperm, however. A man continually produces new sperm, illustrating that the Lord Jesus is the *Source* of life. He *produces* new life.

The woman, on the other hand, first received life from her father (her own life and body, which included the eggs that she will contribute to the reproductive process), illustrating that the church receives life (new birth) from God. She cannot produce life herself.

The wife then receives life (sperm) from her husband. As a result of her intimacy with her husband, babies are born. God could have chosen to create every inhabitant on earth in the same way that He created Adam, but He didn't. Physical reproduction was designed to demonstrate the way that spiritual reproduction takes place.

The bride of Christ receives her life from the Lord. God created her and gave her new birth. The divine Bridegroom then gives her the ability to lead others to be born again. Is it not true that the more intimate we are with Christ and the more we continually receive of His life, the more likely we are to share our faith with others? And is it not true that we will be more likely to influence others if we daily spend time growing more intimate with Him?

It's possible that one of my close friends would perhaps be unaware that a certain person is a casual acquaintance of mine. The name of that acquaintance might never come up in a conversation with my friend. It's highly unlikely, however, that I would fail to mention my husband. Anyone who has been around me for even a short time knows that I am married to Charles. That's because I have an intimate relationship with him. My life is so intertwined with his that I cannot talk about my own life without mentioning my husband.

It's the same with our heavenly Bridegroom. If we have an intimate relationship with Him, we will talk about Him. There would be no way to discuss our own lives without speaking His name.

Indeed, we are expected to bear fruit when we are joined to Christ. *"Therefore, my brethren, you also were made to die to the Law through the body of Christ, so that you might be joined to another, to Him who was raised from the dead, in order that we might bear fruit for God."* (Rom. 7:4)

This would include the fruit of the Spirit. *"But the fruit of the Spirit is love, joy, peace, patience, kindness, goodness, faithfulness, gentleness, self-control; against such things there is no law."* (Gal. 5:22-23)

Bearing fruit isn't limited to the fruit of the Spirit, however, for it would also include spiritual reproduction. Jesus said that we become His witnesses when we are filled with the Spirit. *"But you will receive power when the Holy Spirit comes on you; and you will be my witnesses in Jerusalem, and in all Judea and Samaria, and to the ends of the earth."* (Acts 1:8 NIV)

Have you noticed that there is a vast difference in the strength of your husband's passion for physical intimacy and yours? Why did God give men sex drives that are so much more intense than those He gave to the women? I think that one reason the Lord gave the man a greater interest in sexual intimacy was to illustrate Christ's intense desire for *spiritual* intimacy with *His* bride, the church. A wife's relatively smaller libido illustrates the church's weaker desire for intimate communion with our heavenly Bridegroom. We are always on Jesus' heart. He desires us, pursues us, woos us, and longs for us to spend time with Him in prayer and personal worship. Far too often, we tell Him, "I'm too busy now."

In most marriages, the husband likewise desires physical intimacy with his wife with far more intensity and on many more occasions than she desires sexual relations with him. Just as Christians often put off the Lord's desire for spiritual intimacy because of busy-ness or lukewarmness, wives frequently utter the infamous "Not tonight; I have a headache."

When a husband pursues sexual intimacy, *nothing* would distract him. I think that the roof could fall in, and he would still be intent on intimacy. His wife, however, is easily distracted from her interest in sexual relations. A ringing phone, and her attention is fully diverted. Yes, even in the area of physical intimacy, our marriages portray the relationship of Christ and the church.

Spiritual Intimacy and Lavish Worship

Many scholars believe that while the Song of Songs of Solomon is the story of Solomon and his wife, it is simultaneously an allegory of the Lord's fervent love for us. As such, it teaches us concerning spiritual marriage to the Lord as well as natural marriage to a man. We can learn from both the failures and the right behavior of the bride in this passionate Biblical love story.

"How beautiful you are, my darling,
How beautiful you are!

Your eyes are like doves...
O my dove, in the clefts of the rock,
In the secret place of the steep pathway,
Let me see your form,
Let me hear your voice;
For your voice is sweet,
And your form is lovely." (S. of S. 1:15, 2:14 NASU)

"How beautiful you are, my darling!
Oh, how beautiful!
Your eyes are doves...
My dove in the clefts of the rock,
in the hiding places on the mountainside,
show me your face,
let me hear your voice;
for your voice is sweet,
and your face is lovely." (S. of S. 1:15, 2:14 NIV

I copied the above passage from both the NASU and the NIV so that you can easily compare the translations.

In S. of S. 1:15, the bridegroom likens the bride's eyes to doves. Let's consider a couple of Scriptures to find what our eyes represent.

"The lamp of the body is the eye; if therefore your eye is clear, your whole body will be full of light. But if your eye is bad, your whole body will be full of darkness. If therefore, the light that is in you is darkness, how great is the darkness!" (Matt. 6:22-23) Therefore, the eye is a lamp.

"The spirit of man is the lamp of the Lord..." (Prov. 20:27)

Since my physical eyes are my lamp, both eyes and lamp symbolize my human spirit. The prophet described the spirits of the cherubim as rims full of eyes, and John pictured the sevenfold Spirit of God as eyes. (Ezek. 1:18-21, Rev. 5:6) When the Holy Spirit descended upon Jesus, He took the form of a dove. (Mark 1:10) Thus, we see that lamps, doves, and eyes are all symbolic of spirits.

The bridegroom calls his bride to uncover herself. (S. of S. 2:14) The NASU speaks of revealing her *form*; the NIV renders that word as *face*. The Hebrew is less specific, referring to her *appearance,* and it comes from a root that means *to see.*

There is no hiding place where the Lord cannot see us, but we can hide our eyes, blocking our perception of Him. If we do so, we avoid spiritual eye contact, spirit-to-Spirit intimacy. A toddler thinks he is hidden if he hides his eyes, although we can still see the child because he has covered only his eyes. Likewise, we hide our "eyes" (our spirits) from the Lord, but He always sees us. He sees everything. *"And there is no creature hidden from His sight, but all things are open and laid bare to the eyes of Him with whom we have to do."* (Heb. 4:13)

Satan's goal is to lead us to "hide our eyes"—to withdraw from spiritual intimacy so that we can't perceive God—and then he tells us that God isn't near! The devil is a liar.

As a husband loves to behold his wife's uncovered form and as a man who loves his bride finds pleasure in gazing into her eyes, so also our glorious Bridegroom longs for us (His bride) to joyfully uncover our hearts and our eyes before Him. He yearns for us to enjoy intimate communion with Him, harboring no guile and withholding nothing in our lives from Him.

Men desire intimacy when they *see* their wives. A woman is led to intimacy when she thinks about her beloved and receives his touch. Our heavenly Bridegroom sees us all the time and always desires us. We must keep Him in our minds and receive His spiritual touch to increase *our* desire for spiritual intimacy. What sexual intercourse is to a marriage, intimate, personal worship is to our relationship with the Lord.

As we have said before, sexual desire is stronger in men than it is in women. Repeatedly in this spiritual love story recorded in the Song of Solomon, the bridegroom expresses his vision of the bride as beautiful and *desirable.*

"...The king has brought me into his chambers." (S. of S. 1:4)

This refers to the king's inner apartment. In all likelihood, it means the bedroom, the place of intimacy. Like a husband who desires sexual relations with his wife, the bridegroom/king constantly woos his bride to spiritual intimacy and expresses his longing for her. She makes his heart throb.

"You have made my heart beat faster, my sister, my bride;
You have made my heart beat faster with a single glance of your eyes..." (S. of S. 4:9)

With only a glance from His bride—with only a brief connection of her spirit with the Holy Spirit—the divine Bridegroom's heart begins to pound. Imagine what joy is sparked in His heart if we actually begin to gaze into His eyes, totally focusing our attention on Him. Jesus is wooing us. He is calling to us, "Come into the chamber of intimacy. Open your heart and uncover your eyes. Enter into communion and worship."

We, the church, are Christ's queen in gold. The Bridegroom asks us to regard everything else in our lives as secondary and focus our attention upon the King, listening for His voice.

"...At Your right hand stands the queen in gold from Ophir.
Listen, O daughter, give attention and incline your ear:
Forget your people and your father's house;
Then the King will desire your beauty.
Because He is your Lord, bow down to Him." (Psa. 45:9-11)

He already loves and desires us, but He can be rebuffed. Do you remember what the bride did in Solomon's Song? The bridegroom came to the door of his bride's chamber and asked her to open to him.

She told the story:

"I was asleep, but my heart was awake."

That her heart was awake typifies a regenerate person. She was asleep; that is, she was not alert or responsive. She was "deadened" to him.

"A voice! My beloved was knocking:
'Open to me, my sister, my darling,
My dove, my perfect one!
For my head is drenched with dew,
My locks with the damp of the night.'
'I have taken off my dress,
How can I put it on again?
I have washed my feet,
How can I dirty them again?" (S. of S. 5:2-3)

In other words, she indicated that this wasn't a good time for her to be intimate with him. What silly excuses! Her husband expressed his desire for intimacy, and she said that she didn't want to be intimate with him because she had already taken off her dress! Today's wife might say, "Not now. I'm all snug in the covers and it's cool in the bedroom," or, "Not tonight; I'm tired."

The bride went on to say,

"My lover thrust his hand through the latch-opening..." (S. of S. 5:4 NIV)

Her husband's longing for her was *so great!* Nevertheless, he withdrew his hand and removed His presence. Don't you find that when you repeatedly put off time with the Lord, you begin to feel distant from Him?

It's that way in marriages, too. When a husband is persistently rebuffed, he will sometimes withdraw. A woman who deprives her husband of physical intimacy places temptation in his path. Even if he does not actually stray into adultery or leave his wife, a wall grows between them.

Now, our divine Bridegroom is entirely faithful to us; but we must be on guard that we do not push Him away. Once you find yourself distant from Him, it's difficult to get back into His presence because your own heart will be hardened (deadened) toward Him.

"I arose to open to my beloved;
And my hands dripped with myrrh,
And my fingers with liquid myrrh,
On the handles of the bolt.
I opened to my beloved,
But my beloved had turned away and had gone!..." (S. of S. 5:5-6)

Although she made excuses and failed to respond to him, the bride in the Song of Songs later repented and went out to him. We too must repent when we have become "too busy" for intimate communion with the Lord.

At first, she couldn't find him. Then she began to praise him to the people she met along the way:

"My beloved is dazzling and ruddy,
Outstanding among ten thousand.

His head is like gold, pure gold;
His locks are like clusters of dates
And black as a raven.
His eyes are like doves
Beside streams of water,
Bathed in milk,
And reposed in their setting.
His cheeks are like a bed of balsam,
Banks of sweet-scented herbs;
His lips are lilies
Dripping with liquid myrrh.
His hands are rods of gold
Set with beryl;
His abdomen is carved ivory
Inlaid with sapphires.
His legs are pillars of alabaster
Set on pedestals of pure gold;
His appearance is like Lebanon,
Choice as the cedars.
His mouth is full of sweetness.
And he is wholly desirable.
This is my beloved and this is my friend,
O daughters of Jerusalem." (S. of S. 5:10-16)

It isn't surprising that when she began to praise him like that, she found herself once more in her husband's presence.

Praising the Lord will restore us to His presence also. The King James Version of Psa. 22:3 says that the Lord *inhabits* the praises of His people. Praising the Lord will invite His presence.

Your natural husband would love for you to praise *him* also. You perhaps would not wax eloquent by comparing his abdomen to carved ivory and his legs to alabaster pillars, but he would like to hear what you find desirable about his physical appearance.

The bridegroom and the bride in Solomon's Song were reunited, and he again declared his desire for intimacy.

"*How beautiful are your feet in sandals,*
O prince's daughter!
The curves of your hips are like jewels,

Here Comes the Bride

The work of the hands of an artist.
Your navel is like a round goblet
Which never lacks mixed wine;
Your belly is like a heap of wheat
Fenced about with lilies.
Your two breasts are like two fawns,
Twins of a gazelle.
Your neck is like a tower of ivory,
Your eyes like the pools in Heshbon
By the gate of Bath-rabbim;
Your nose is like the tower of Lebanon,
Which faces toward Damascus.
Your head crowns you like Carmel,
And the flowing locks of your head are like purple threads;
The king is captivated by your tresses.
How beautiful and how delightful you are,
My love, with all your charms!
Your stature is like a palm tree,
And your breasts are like its clusters.
I said, 'I will climb the palm tree,
I will take hold of its fruit stalks.'
Oh, may your breasts be like clusters of the vine,
And the fragrance of your breath like apples,
And your mouth like the best wine!" (S. of S. 7:1-9)
This time she joyfully yielded to Him:
"I am my beloved's,
And his desire is for me.
Come, my beloved, let us go out into the country,
Let us spend the night in the villages.
Let us rise early and go to the vineyards;
Let us see whether the vine has budded
And its blossoms have opened,
And whether the pomegranates have bloomed.
There I will give you my love...
Let his left hand be under my head
And his right hand embrace me." (S. of S. 7:10-12, 8:3)

There was a time when he brought her to his chamber, but there was also a time when he brought her to the banquet hall.

*"He has brought me to his banquet hall,
And his banner over me is love."* (S. of S. 2:4)

There his banner of love is over her for all to see. Private worship is necessary if our relationship with the Lord is to be as it should be. Nevertheless, intimate communion alone in His presence does not eliminate public worship; rather it prepares us for and enhances corporate worship. Corporate worship, moreover, trains us for further private communion with Him.

The bridegroom proclaims his love for her in the public place, and the bride can pour out perfume on the bridegroom when he is in the banquet hall.

*"While the king was at his table,
my perfume spread its fragrance."* (S. of S. 1:12 NIV)

Do you remember when Jesus was a dinner guest at Bethany? Mary the sister of Lazarus came in and poured perfume on Him. (You can read this story in Matt. 26:6-13, Mark 14:3-9, Luke 7:37-39, John 11:2, and John 12:1-8.) This woman had lived a sinful life, so vile that the host at this dinner was shocked that Jesus would even allow her to touch Him.

Yes, she was a sinner, but she was penitent. She began to weep over her sins. Her tears bathed His dusty feet, and she dried them with her hair. (Simon the Pharisee had neglected his duty as host to provide for the washing of Jesus' feet.)

The bridegroom says in the Song of Solomon that his bride's tresses captivate him. (S. of S. 7:5) A woman's hair is her glory and her covering, and her locks symbolize her submission to her husband. (See 1 Cor. 11.) The bride's hair captivates the bridegroom because it is a symbol of her submission to him. Mary—immoral, sinful Mary—used her hair to dry the feet washed by her tears of repentance. She submitted to the Holy One.

Then Mary broke an alabaster vial of costly, fragrant oil and anointed His head and feet. This spikenard oil was worth 300 denarii, a great deal of money. A denarius was a day's wage for a laborer. (Compare Matt. 20:2.) There were weekly Sabbaths in the year, plus several annual holidays when no work was to be done. Thus, Mary's expression of worship was the equivalent of about a year's wage for a laborer. Mark 6:37 indicates that with only 200 denarii, they could have purchased enough food to feed the 5,000 men plus women and children. Mary's gift was great.

Mary did not hold back. She poured it all out on the King of kings. She *broke* the vial. There was no pulling out a stopper, pouring a little on Jesus, and re-closing the container. No, Mary worshipped lavishly. She worshipped with abandon, nothing withheld.

David did that too. With great joy, he was bringing back the Ark of the Covenant to the city. (See 2 Sam. 6:12-23 and 1 Chron. 15:25-29.) David removed his royal robes and wore simple garments of fine linen.

When the bearers of the Ark had gone only six paces, David stopped to offer an ox and a fatling to the Lord. Seven bulls and seven rams were also sacrificed because the Lord helped the Levites who bore the Ark.

You can understand why they wanted to offer these sacrifices. On a previous attempt to bring the Ark, they had improperly loaded the Ark onto an oxcart. This disobeyed the Lord's instruction that the Levites should carry it with poles. Uzzah had reached out to steady the Ark when it nearly fell, although the Law forbade him to touch it. As a result, Uzzah had died before the Lord. (2 Sam. 6:2-11)

As David and the people were bringing the Ark the correct way and enjoying God's blessing, they worshipped and praised Him. This was no quiet, dignified procession. David and those with him were *shouting* to the Lord. There were blasts of trumpets and horns. The sounds of singing, cymbals, harps, and lyres filled the air. Moreover, David danced before the Lord with all his might.

Do you think everyone was happy about this outpouring of joy and praise before the Lord? The Bible says that when Michal, David's wife, looked out of her window and saw her husband's exuberant worship, she was greatly displeased. In fact, the Scripture says that she despised him. She held him in contempt. She was embarrassed by his undignified behavior. After all, Michal was not only the wife of King David; she was also the daughter of King Saul. She accused David of making a fool of himself before the peasants. His worship

Here Comes the Bride

wasn't regal enough for a king, in Michal's opinion. She rebuked her husband for his passionate expression of praise to God.

David was more concerned about pleasing God than about pleasing his wife. He replied to her rebuke, *"It was before the LORD, who chose me above your father and above all his house, to appoint me ruler over the people of the LORD, over Israel; therefore I will celebrate before the LORD. I will be more lightly esteemed than this and will be humble in my own eyes, but with the maids of whom you have spoken, with them I will be distinguished."* (2 Sam. 6:21-22) Rather than becoming more prideful because of his kingship, David said that he would choose to humble himself even more.

The text goes on to say that Michal, the daughter of Saul, was barren to the day of her death.

Just as Michal was displeased with David's exuberance, there were those who criticized Mary's lavish worship when she poured out the pure nard ointment on Jesus. They thought she was going overboard. While she did not please everyone, she did please the King. The diners criticized Mary, but Jesus told them to leave her alone. Furthermore, He announced that Mary's act of worship would be recounted wherever the gospel is preached.

When *we* pour out praise and worship to His name, this likewise pleases Him.

We must never have Michal's attitude. We must not act like those who criticized Mary when she lavishly poured out an offering of perfume on Jesus. We must not despise rich, abundant worship. The Lord *deserves* lavish worship! Like Michal, we risk barrenness and fruitlessness if we hold in contempt those who are willing to humble themselves and pour out all on the King.

"...(Y)our name is like perfume poured out.." (S. of S. 1:3 NIV)

His name is Jesus (*Yahweh* saves)...Immanuel (God with us)...Prince of Peace...King of kings...Lord of lords. His name is wonderful. His name is majestic. It is lovely, and it is worthy of praise. Let us delight Him by speaking of all His name implies as we praise Him.

"How beautiful is your love, my sister, my bride!
How much better is your love than wine,
And the fragrance of your oils

Than all kinds of spices! (S. of S. 4:10)

When Mary poured out the perfume, Jesus was pleased with her offering; and the fragrance *"filled the house."* (John 12:3) Mary's spikenard oil filled the house with a sweet scent. The fragrance of our worship likewise spreads to those who hear.

"Thanks be to God who always leads us in his triumph in Christ and manifests through us the sweet aroma of the knowledge of Him in every place. For we are a fragrance of Christ to God among those who are being saved and among those who are perishing—to the one an aroma of death to death, to the other an aroma of life to life..." (2 Cor. 2:14-16)

When Paul and Silas praised God in the dungeon, the other prisoners were listening. (Acts 16:25) Furthermore, the answer to their worship was an earthquake that loosed their bonds and led to the salvation of the jailer and his family.

Expression of Love

Another reason for the difference in the needs of husbands and those of their wives—not only in sexual matters, but in others as well—is that the differences invite loving, sacrificial behavior toward each other. It takes no love to do what I want to do anyway, but to meet my husband's need when it isn't so important to me is an expression of unselfish love. God wants us to love each other, and choosing to bless my spouse is showing love. In fact, that's what we often call it, isn't it? Lovemaking? It's a manifestation of love. We are to be looking for what blesses our husbands, and not just thinking about whether it strikes our fancy at the moment.

Agape love always wants to look out for the good of the beloved. Do you remember the description of *agape* in 1 Corinthians 13? Love behaves kindly, and it doesn't seek its own way. Paul also exhorts us to *"Do nothing from selfishness or empty conceit, but with humility of mind regard one another as more important than yourselves; do not merely look out for your own personal interests, but also for the interests of others."* (Phil. 2:3-4) God has created this avenue for you to bless your husband with your body.

You do not, in fact, have authority over your own body. As a wife, you do not have the right to bestow or withhold sexual favors according to your whim. Your body is under *your husband's* authority. The Bible says, *"The husband must fulfill his duty to his wife, and likewise also the wife to her husband.* **The wife does not have authority over her own body, but the husband does;** *and likewise also the husband does not have authority over his own body, but the wife does.* **Stop depriving one another**, *except by agreement for a time, so that you may devote yourselves to prayer, and come together again so that Satan will not tempt you because of your lack of self-control."* (1 Cor. 7:3-5, emphasis mine)

Since we are here considering the responsibilities of the wife, let's read that again leaving out the instructions to husbands: *"The wife does not have authority over her own body, but the husband does…Stop depriving* [your husband], *except by agreement for a time so that you may devote yourselves to prayer, and come together again so that Satan will not tempt you because of your lack of self-control."*

According to this passage, abstinence from sex within a marriage is permissible under certain circumstances:

- First, it is a mutual decision. That means that your husband concurs with the decision to enter this sexual fast.
- Next, the fast is for a specific period of time. In other words, the two of you set a time limit on the withdrawal from sexual activity.
- Finally, the sexual fast is for the same purpose that you fast from food: to devote yourselves to prayer. This is a far cry from refusing intimacy with your husband because you are "not in the mood."

In fact, Scripture indicates that your husband not only has *authority* over your body, but that your body is indeed *his body*—just as the church is Christ's body as well as His bride. *"In this same way, husbands ought to love their wives as their own bodies. He who loves his wife loves himself. After all, no one ever hated his own body, but he feeds and cares for it, just as Christ does the church—for we are members of his body."* (Eph. 5:28-30 NIV)

Here Comes the Bride

One reason that we have difficulty with obeying these Scriptures is that women's sexuality is strongly tied to emotion. Probably the most important sex organ for a woman is between her ears. She associates lovemaking with how affectionate she feels at the moment. If she is upset with her husband, it diminishes her desire for intimacy.

Her husband's desire for sex, however, is mostly physical. It's a physical need. While his wife sees sexual intimacy as a result of the love and emotional attachment in their relationship, the husband whose sexual appetite is being starved may find it a struggle to develop emotional intimacy and affection.

I once saw an e-mail joke that listed the steps that are necessary to make a wife happy and those required to give happiness to a husband. There were eighteen steps to making the wife happy, including loving her, complimenting her, hugging her, taking care of her, and spending money on her. The steps to pleasing a husband, however, were only two: showing up naked and bringing food.

There is a lot of truth in that joke. Women and men have needs that greatly differ, and fulfilling a husband's appetites for sex and food will go a long way in keeping him content.

Have you ever been busily loading the dishwasher when your husband began to interrupt your work by sensual touch? It was likely because he was thinking about sex, and he was touching you to attempt to interest you as well.

Men are aroused by what they see. If you are swaying back and forth to load the dishwasher or wash the windows, you don't in any way think of your movements as being sensual. If you notice your husband's motions as he washes the car, you see no sexual connotation at all. That's because you don't think like a man does, and you are not aroused in the same way a man is. As your husband watches your body swaying, however, he begins to imagine your doing that while you are nude. This is the contrast between your perception of the moment and his fantasy about it.

God's plan is that the husband and the wife lovingly bless each other. He created sex to give us a manifestation of the love between husband and wife that is to be shared nowhere else.

What is Satan's plan? His plan is that we regard our bodies selfishly, that we consent to lovemaking when it pleases us—but not unless it does. The enemy of our souls urges the spouses to use sex only for selfish gratification rather than as an expression of love that desires to bless the other. He tells the wife that she has no responsibility to give herself to her husband unless she is "in the mood," and he leads her to use sex as a weapon or reward to manipulate her husband.

Ladies, the opposite of love is not hatred. The opposite of love is selfishness! When we regard physical intimacy as something that we bestow when we desire it and withhold when we do not, we are showing selfishness instead of love.

Doesn't *agape* mean that we think of the other person's good above our own? It doesn't take as much love for a woman to give herself to her husband when she is flushed with passion as it does to yield to his desire when she herself has no particular interest.

A kind and loving husband often considers the condition of his wife and restrains himself when he knows that she is sick or weary. I suggest, however, that it is a wise wife who does not refuse him when he asks. In the case that she is extremely tired, she could offer him a choice between a McDonald's hamburger (a "quickie") right now, or a seven-course banquet (a really special expression of sexual love) the following morning when she is rested. Given these options, a man who is strongly aroused will choose the "hamburger," and the one who is less desperate will often elect to wait for the excitement to come. In either event, he will not feel rejected.

A wife will sometimes complain that if she yielded to her husband's every request for intimacy, she would spend all of her time in bed. She might be surprised, however. Most men who are regularly denied will ask for lovemaking with far greater frequency than they would otherwise. Because of the refusals, they will ask at every opportunity, even when their own interest is slight, for fear of missing an occasion when their wives would perhaps have said yes.

By the way, your husband's self-esteem and self-worth are tied up in his sexuality. A woman's self-esteem is connected to her sexuality too, for that matter. How would you feel if you thought your husband no longer found you desirable?

You must be extremely careful. Regardless of how confident your husband seems, he is fragile in this area. If you reject or ridicule your husband in that which relates to his sexuality, he will interpret it as rejection and ridicule toward his manhood—and in fact, toward his very self. Be very certain that you do not tease him in any way that could possibly be interpreted as rejection, ridicule, or criticism of his manliness.

Pleasure

Another reason that God created sex is to give us pleasure. Lovemaking is meant to bring us intense delight. The idea that sex is dirty or shameful (that we should not enjoy it) did not come from God. He created this aspect of our lives to illustrate the joy found in our intimacy with Him. When we are spiritually intimate with the Lord, it brings joy to Him.

"*...And as the bridegroom rejoices over the bride,*
So your God will rejoice over you." (Isa. 62:5)

Likewise, this spiritual intimacy also brings joy to *us*.

"*...In Your presence is fullness of joy;*
In Your right hand there are pleasures forever." (Psa. 16:11)

"*...And in the shadow of Your wings I sing for joy.*" (Psa. 63:7)

He finds joy in our intimacy with Him, and He gives joy to us. He wants us to find delight in our physical intimacy (which illustrates the spiritual intimacy with Him) as well.

"*Let your fountain be blessed,*
And rejoice in the wife of your youth.
As a loving hind and a graceful doe,
Let her breasts satisfy you at all times;
Be exhilarated always with her love." (Prov. 5:18-19)

God is the giver of good and perfect gifts, and His gifts bring enjoyment. James 1:17 says that every perfect gift comes down from the Lord. Paul tells us in 1 Tim. 6:17 that God richly supplies us with all things to enjoy. Pleasure in that which God gives us is right and good.

What then is Satan's strategy? His plot is to take the joy from the gift. He tempts people to commit rape or to molest children. The forces of darkness tempt women to give themselves to one man after another seeking love but never finding it. Satan and his servants lead people to engage in sexual activity outside of marriage, where the security of loving commitment is missing. He lures men to use women without loving them. He encourages the wives to withhold their bodies from their husbands, using the beautiful gift as a means to manipulate.

God's plan is infinitely better, don't you think?

Stress Relief

How do we deal with worries and stresses in life? How does the divine Bridegroom relieve our anxieties?

"Be anxious for nothing, but in everything by prayer and supplication with thanksgiving let your requests be made known to God. And the peace of God, which surpasses all comprehension, will guard your hearts and your minds in Christ Jesus." (Phil. 4:6-7)

"You will keep him in perfect peace,
Whose mind is stayed on You,
Because he trusts in You." (Isa 26:3 NKJV)

As we draw near to the Lord, He gives us peace.

Likewise, sexual activity within a marriage brings relief for the stresses of life and comforts us when we are down.

Do you remember the example of this in the Scriptures when Isaac's father, Abraham, sent a trusted servant to find a wife for Isaac in the land of Abraham's birth? God blessed the servant's search, and he brought back Rebekah.

Because he was mourning the death of his mother, Isaac was sorrowful when the servant returned with the bride-to-be. The Bible says, *"Then Isaac brought her [Rebekah] into his mother Sarah's tent, and he took Rebekah, and she became his wife, and he loved her; thus Isaac was comforted after his mother's death."* (Gen. 24:67)

Part of this relief may be because of the close intimacy with someone we love and who loves us. Even the physical touch of a hug is comforting, and total intimacy greatly multiplies the comfort of an embrace.

There is more to it than that, however. The physical exertion and the orgasm release endorphins into our bodies that bring us ecstasy and then contentment.

When I was a young wife, I attended a women's retreat where I met a woman (perhaps 45 years old) who told in one of the discussion groups about the failure of her husband's business. She described the anxiety that he had undergone during that difficult season. This woman told us that during that time, she had considered her primary role to be a sex partner to give relief to her husband's stresses. Those of us in our twenties marveled that this "older woman" would think about that and feel free to speak of it. (Forty-five sounded a great deal older to me when I was in my twenties than it does now!)

Perhaps because I had thought it was unusual for a woman "of that age" to have that attitude toward sex, I always remembered her words. When my husband and I were in *our* forties, I had the opportunity to put her counsel to work when *my* husband was without a job. I found that her sage advice was very helpful.

Do you find yourself thinking, "I can't get into the mood for lovemaking when I'm stressed out! How can he think of sex when money's tight and the car just broke down?"

Actually, stressful times are *great* occasions for passion since—as I said earlier—orgasms release endorphins into your body. The word *endorphin* means "endogenous morphine" (M-W Web Site); and indeed endorphins are a drugless way to kill pain, to relieve stress, and to produce euphoria. Even if you are unable to have an orgasm, your husband's stress will be relieved. That will elevate *his* mood, and in turn, will make your day better too. Furthermore, the exercise will benefit your emotions and the closeness with your husband will comfort you.

Now you may be saying, "I don't ever have an orgasm, so I don't get many endorphins." You and your husband need to remember that men and women don't function the same way. When a man sees his partially clothed wife or sees her bend over or any one of a thousand other movements that excite him, he is *ready*! We women are not wired that way. We need romantic overtures, sensual physical touch, and slower foreplay.

It seems to me that sex is the part of marriage that is most difficult for spouses to discuss. I hope that those of you who do not customarily experience orgasm will find a time when both you and your mate are calm, and explain to your husband that you need more time in foreplay. Prepare for this discussion by thinking about your favorite sexual memories. Then when you discuss it with your husband, you can tell him what turns you on.

During an actual sexual episode, you could whisper a reminder to go slower or to use a gentler touch. Perhaps you would remind him of ways that you like for him to touch you. Then you can praise him when he does something that excites you. If you can approach it from the angle of "I love it when you do this" (instead of complaining about what you don't like or expressing disinterest in sex altogether), you may find yourself in ecstasy.

God's plan is to bring joy and tranquility to His people through the outlet of sexual love. What does the prince of darkness desire? Satan's plan is to convince wives to refuse to engage in it because they are too stressed! That, it seems to me, is like a woman thinking that she's too sick to take medicine or too hungry to eat.

Health

Closely related to the stress-relieving benefits of sexual love is the physical exercise that it gives to your body. Everywhere we turn, we are told that we need more exercise. As the time of physical intimacy progresses, your muscles contract. Your body moves, and you raise your heart rate. You are burning calories. Let me tell you: This is way more fun than a treadmill, any day!

Promotes Emotional Intimacy

The next benefit of sexuality in marriage is that a husband and wife enhance the emotional intimacy in their relationship when they participate in physical union. Just as their bodies are joined and there is nothing between them, the union of every aspect of their beings becomes more intimate.

The Bible often uses the word *know* to describe sexual relations. When Gen. 4:1 tells us that Adam had sexual intercourse with Eve, it uses a Hebrew word that is rendered as *know* in a great many passages. This is a primary root word, and it literally means *to know* (properly, *to ascertain by seeing*). This is an interesting play on words, since men are sexually ignited by what they see.

When Mary told the angel that she was a virgin, she said that she did not know a man. (Luke 1:34, Greek) Likewise, when Matthew recorded that Joseph did not have marital relations with Mary until after the birth of Jesus, he said that Joseph did not know her until then. (Matt. 1:25, Greek) In these and other passages about sexual intimacy, the New Testament uses a Greek word that means *to know absolutely*. Joseph's knowledge of Mary could not be complete until they consummated the marriage through sexual intimacy after the birth of Jesus.

The Lord, our heavenly Bridegroom, knows us fully; there is nothing about us—in body, in soul, and in spirit—which He doesn't see. *"And there is no creature hidden from His sight, but all things are open and laid bare to the eyes of Him with whom we have to do."* (Heb. 4:13)

One day we will also know the Lord fully: *"For now we see in a mirror dimly, but then face to face; now I know in part, but then I will know fully just* **as I also have been fully known.***"* (1 Cor. 13:12, emphasis mine) Until we see Him face to face, spiritual intimacy—deep, personal worship—creates a greater closeness to the Lord and helps us to know Him better.

Thus, our enemy also tempts us to neglect spiritually intimate occasions with our Lord and entices us to fall for spiritual seductions that lead us to unfaithfulness to the heavenly Bridegroom.

Sexual union encourages us to truly "see" our spouses and to "know them absolutely." It goes without saying that our husbands can see more when we wear less! It's also easier to be emotionally transparent when you aren't wearing any clothes.

You may find that even if your husband isn't an ace communicator, you have his full attention in the early stages of a sexual encounter and that he will more easily participate in conversation then. (Obviously, you have his attention in the latter stages too, but that might not be a good time for discussion!)

Now, I am not advocating that you complain that he didn't carry out the trash—or even ask if he did—at such a time. This is not the time for criticism or an argument. It may, however, be a time when you can have heart-felt discussions about some things that are deep in your heart.

God's intention for the sexual relationship is to nourish intimacy in every part of the marriage. It's only for those two—the husband and the wife—and excludes all others. This should encourage you to freely give your body to your husband, because you undoubtedly desire emotional intimacy with him.

That's God's plan, but there's another plot out there. What does Satan promote? His scheme is to convince people to engage in sexual intercourse outside the marriage relationship with no overall intimacy, often with partners they hardly know. The opponent of God leads people to public sex rather than limiting it to the intimate relationship of husband and wife. Sexual activity is splashed on TV and movie screens for all to see. The tempter entices women to walk around in scanty or seductive clothing, allowing men who are not their husbands to "see" them.

Or perhaps Satan will persuade the wife that her body is not alluring to her husband. She will decide, since she has too much fat on this part of her body or not enough fat on another part, that she is too embarrassed to display it for her husband. Ladies, you might be surprised to learn how sexy your husband thinks you look, particularly if you make every effort to make your sex life exciting for him.

I would like to insert here that he might think you look sexy in things that you think are unbecoming. For example, sometimes the lingerie that he chooses would not be your personal selection because you think it accentuates the bulge in your tummy or is otherwise unflattering to your figure. Remember that no one else is going to see you. If your husband likes the way you look in it, that's all that matters.

Nevertheless, one of your husband's basic needs is for you to be physically attractive to him. Because men are attracted by what they see, it is important that you look pretty in his eyes when you go to bed. Very few men appreciate seeing their wives sleep in an old, worn-out T-shirt. Surely you can find something that is comfortable for you and pretty for him. For those times when you know he desires physical intimacy, have some seductive apparel to model for him. We will talk more in a future chapter about dressing to look beautiful for our husbands.

One thing that creates excitement for husbands is variety. While many women don't need this as much, most men crave change. Every man is different, of course, and what is exciting to one man may seem silly to another. You might be surprised, however, at what he finds thrilling in the bedroom—even if he's very conservative elsewhere.

Try planning a really sultry and seductive occasion for him. Vary the sexy nighties that you model for him. Move to a different room. Or simply ask him what special thing you can do to please him in that night's sexual episode. He may suggest something for you to wear to bed, certain ways that he wants you touch his body, or ways that he wants to touch you. Maybe he would like for you to wrap yourself in scarves, do a striptease for him, or make love in front of a mirror.

I'm not asking you to do anything that you consider perverted or wrong, but it doesn't have to turn *you* on to be exciting to *him*. Men and women are different. If it brings joy to him and there's nothing wrong with it, why not? Besides, you may be surprised. The new expression of passion may become a source of excitement to you as well.

Is this not true in our worship to the Lord? I was a little uncomfortable the first time I raised my hands to praise the Lord and the first time I worshipped by dancing before Him, but these things have now become wonderful expressions of praise and worship that bless me as well as the Lord.

The Holy Estate of Matrimony

In my wedding vows, I promised to live together with my husband in the holy estate of matrimony. Have you ever thought about that phrase?

Every once in a while, one hears of a man and woman who are legally married but who live separately. The husband lives in this city, and his wife resides in that city. Sometimes such an arrangement is temporarily necessary—because the man has a new job and the wife is finishing out the school year or selling the house, for example—but they soon return to living together. In a few cases, however, a man and his wife actually live apart long-term, but remain legally married.

Other couples live in the same house with each other, but they do not "live together." They live separate lives and are hardly involved in each other's lives at all. If I am to fulfill my marriage vows, I must "live together" with my husband. Our lives must be intertwined.

We vowed to live together, and we promised that our life together would be in holy matrimony. It's interesting how the word *matrimony* came to mean *marriage*. The word *matrimony* came to us from the Latin word *mater*, which means *mother*. Since this word is related to the word *matrix*—which means *womb, source*, or *origin*—it appears that matrimony is related to the sexual aspect of marriage. The word *matrimonial* pertains to connubial, nuptial, or hymeneal duties or rights, so our matrimony refers to the entrance into marriage and the consummation of the marriage through sexual intercourse. (Webster)

I want you to notice, however, that I promised that my marriage (my matrimony) would be holy. Marriage was God's idea, after all. If matrimony refers to the sexual relationship, then *holy* matrimony brings to mind this Scripture: *"Marriage is to be held in honor among all, and the marriage bed is to be undefiled; for fornicators and adulterers God will judge."* (Heb. 13:4) Holy matrimony means that marriage is sacred. We are to be holy—set apart—to God and to each other. My relationship to my husband is sacred, and our union is to be one that is devoted to God.

Marital intimacy should be reserved for the husband alone. Some women, when their husbands are away, have intimate relationships with other men as well.

"I have spread my couch with coverings,
With colored linens of Egypt.
I have sprinkled my bed
With myrrh, aloes and cinnamon.
Come, let us drink our fill of love until morning;
Let us delight ourselves with caresses.
For my husband is not at home,
He has gone on a long journey." (Prov. 7:16-19)

Such a woman, willing to receive seed from a man who doesn't have the right to that intimacy, is a harlot—an adulteress.

The woman described in Proverbs 7 had spread her couch with linens, but they were not the fine, clean and white linens of righteousness. (Compare Rev. 19:8.) Rather she had spread them with *dyed* linens of *Egypt*. They were dyed (that means that they were stained) and they were from Egypt (a type or symbol for the world).

Listen to what James says about an inappropriate relationship with the world: *"You **adulteresses**, do you not know that friendship with the world is **hostility toward God**? Therefore, whoever wishes to be a friend of the world makes himself an enemy of God. Or do you think that the Scripture speaks to no purpose: 'He **jealously** desires the spirit which He has made to dwell in us'?"* (Jas. 4:4-5, emphasis mine) Sexual union joins two bodies; spiritual union with Christ means that His bride is one spirit with Him. (1 Cor. 6:16-17) If we are caught up in the seductions of the world, we are spiritual adulteresses.

The Lord said, *"...I, the LORD your God, am a jealous God..."* (Ex. 20:5) He is jealous in an appropriate sense, not in an unreasonable way. As our God and as our spiritual Bridegroom, He has the right to expect faithfulness from His bride.

Just as the Lord does not want to share His bride with the seductions of the world, your husband has the right to expect purity of both body and mind in your relationship with him. When a woman allows herself to be drawn into a close relationship with another man, when she begins to discuss intimate parts of her life with another man, when she talks about her marriage problems with another man without her husband's presence—then she is at risk to follow the path of physical impurity as well.

We have discussed in depth how we ought to show passion toward our husbands and toward the divine Bridegroom. In the next chapter, we will discuss ways to assure that we are passionate.

Defeating the Passion-killers

❋❋❋

I would like to discuss several passion-killers that damage both our passion for the Lord and our passion for our husbands.

Fear and Unbelief

One passion-killer is fear, which is linked to unbelief. Have you ever been afraid to trust the Lord in something? Afraid that if you yielded to what He called you to do, you would be unhappy?

That fear is from the enemy of your soul, and it indicates that you do not believe that Christ loves you and has your best interest at heart. Thus, unbelief hampers our passion for the Lord.

If we don't believe that He loves us supremely, we are afraid to trust Him. Hebrews 11:6 says, *"And without faith it is impossible to please Him, for he who comes to God must believe that He is and that He is a rewarder of those who seek Him."* We must believe not only that He exists, but also that His actions toward our faith are rewards—that they are beneficial to us as we yield to Him.

What is the antidote to passion-killing fear and unbelief? Repeatedly we find words addressed to the people of God like those in Deut. 31:6: *"Be strong and courageous, do not be afraid or tremble at them, for the LORD your God is the one who goes with you. He will not fail you or forsake you."* These words are commands to be obeyed. We must *choose* to have courage. Courage is not the absence of fear, but the choice to do the right thing in spite of fear.

Just as fear damages our intimacy with the Lord, it can inhibit passion for our husbands as well. Do you fear pregnancy? Do you fear that your husband is using you? Do you find it hard to believe that your husband really loves you? Do you fear losing control? Do you fear that you will be aroused, but left frustrated and unfulfilled because you didn't experience orgasm?

I exhort you to have courage as you yield yourself to your husband. I challenge you to courageously yield to his desires and choose to believe in his love for you. (In reality, sexual intimacy is probably the ultimate act of submission to him.) If you have been sexually frustrated, communicate your needs to him. He may not yet understand what lights your fire.

Selfishness

Another passion-killer is selfishness. When we are consumed by selfishness, we will be unwilling to yield to the Lord. Living according to our selfish desires (the desires of the flesh) sets us on an opposite path from what the Lord would have us do. *"For the flesh sets its desire against the Spirit, and the Spirit against the flesh; for these are in opposition to one another, so that you may not do the things that you please."* (Gal. 5:17) If we are walking according to our fleshly desires, we will not be passionate about our relationship with the Lord.

Too often natural wives rebuff their husbands' longing for intimacy with excuses like those given by Solomon's bride. In self-centeredness, these women think that they shouldn't have to meet their husbands' needs unless they themselves are interested in intimacy. They think, "I have my rights." They ask, "What's in it for me? Why should I do this for him unless it pleases me?"

Where is love in that? Such an attitude ignores the admonition of Scripture: *"Do nothing from selfishness or empty conceit, but with humility of mind regard one another as more important than yourselves; do not merely look out for your own personal interests, but also for the interests of others."* (Phil. 2:3-4)

Does yielding to your husband's desires only when you feel passionate yourself picture the response that the church should give to the Lord's call to spiritual intimacy? Unfortunately, it does depict the actual response of many Christian people. It does not, however, demonstrate what we *should* do when He calls.

It is far too common for a wife to use sex as a bartering tool to manipulate her husband and to get her way about other things. Such wives openly say or in some other way convey the thought, "If you want sex, then do this thing that I want." Some women, filled with resentment or unforgiveness, withhold sexual intimacy as punishment. These are dangerous courses of action.

Sex should never be used as a weapon against your husband, offered as a bribe to manipulate him to do what you want, or really even reserved as a reward for when he pleases you. Sexual intimacy is an opportunity to demonstrate love to your husband and to experience closeness with him.

A woman who cheapens it to the level of payment for getting him to do the dishes or take her out to dinner is making an extremely foolish mistake. She is relegating the physical intimacy in her marriage to the level of prostitution—giving sex for the payment of getting what she wants.

Frequently when marriages go on the rocks, the rocks are at least partly in the bed. That's because sexual problems will create problems in other areas of the marriage and because problems in other areas will damage the sexual relationship. A passionless marriage may survive, but it will not thrive. It won't flourish.

Jesus' desire for us is far stronger than ours is for Him; and as a rule, husbands have stronger sex drives than their wives have. A wise and loving woman, however, will give herself willingly to her husband—and to the Lord—even when she isn't particularly in the mood.

Sex is a very real need in your husband. When I was a young woman, I heard a television interviewer ask a physician if a man's sexual desire could be compared to his appetite for food. The doctor indicated that it did not compare to his hunger instinct, but to his *survival* instinct—his instinct for self-preservation. This sexual yearning in your husband is extremely strong, and it is an opportunity for you to express your love for him. Remember, ladies: Selfishness is the opposite of love.

Fatigue

It isn't uncommon for women (especially young mothers or employed wives) to feel so tired by bedtime that sexual activity doesn't sound like fun. If that describes you, perhaps you can arrange your schedule to include times of rest so that you will have energy for lovemaking. This could include being careful not to fill your day with so much work that you are always exhausted or taking a nap when the children sleep in the afternoon. (This is a benefit of being a stay-at-home wife and mother!) Or you might go to bed a little earlier than your husband does, either to sleep a little while or just to rest and think about the coming sexual joy. If your schedules permit, you might also try making love in the daytime, when you are more rested.

Fatigue does kill your appetite for physical intimacy, and it is a picture of something in the spiritual marriage. Have you sometimes found yourself neglecting your quiet times with the heavenly Bridegroom because of busy-ness? The Lord has work for us to do, but we must exercise care that we do not allow work to rob us of time in His presence. Busy-ness is one of the primary causes of our "hiding our eyes" from our heavenly Bridegroom. (S. of S. 1:15 and 2:14) Do you find that you become too spiritually weary to desire His fellowship and that your passion for Him wanes? I urge you to make spending time in the Lord's presence a daily priority in your life.

Perhaps you need to remember the Sabbath rest that is promised to God's people. *"There remains, then, a Sabbath-rest for the people of God; for anyone who enters God's rest also rests from his own work, just as God did from his."* (Heb. 4:9-10 NIV) Our Sabbath rest is to be more than a day of physical rest each week. It is to be a daily life of desisting from our own ways and our own works, choosing instead to live in dependence upon the power of God. (Compare Isa. 58:13-14.) If we truly find rest, we will no longer do our own works or do our own thing.

Even *good* works done in our own fleshly effort, after all, are unacceptable.

"All of us have become like one who is unclean,
and all our righteous acts are like filthy rags..." (Isa. 64:6 NIV)

The Hebrew word rendered as *filthy* in this verse is the word that was used to describe soiled menstrual cloths, which to an observant Jew would have been even more unclean than they are to us. Whatever we do in the flesh—be it "good" or evil—is unclean in the sight of God. Works done in the flesh will burn up in the Day of the Lord. They are wood, hay, and stubble. (See 1 Cor. 3:10-15.) Christ calls us to abandon our own works and enter His Sabbath rest.

Many experts tell us that for an activity to be relaxing, it must be different from the work we usually do. For example, if a man's employment requires him to do manual labor, he needs physical inactivity to rest. Perhaps he will read a good book or work a crossword puzzle to rest. A person whose work is mental, however, often finds relaxation in a physical activity such as tennis or golf.

My brother is an engineer. Throughout his career, he primarily did his work at a desk, planning and designing water systems on a map. Once a project started, he sometimes traveled to the site to observe how things were progressing; but he did no physical labor. He spent most of his work time in his office writing, organizing, communicating, and coordinating. He had done no physical labor, but when he went home in the evening, he was tired. Why? Because he had been doing his work.

Over the years, however, he frequently spent evenings and weekends using the woodworking tools in his basement. A talented craftsman, he designed and created various items of wood—everything from exquisite pen and pencil sets to beautiful lawn furniture to intricate trivets—and each piece was a work of art. When he finished a woodworking project, he was physically tired but mentally refreshed.

Now at times in his life, my father worked as a carpenter. When *he* came home from a day spent laboring on the construction of a house, he had no desire to make things of wood in order to relax. When *he* made things of wood, he was doing his work.

Rest requires ceasing from our own labors. What are the works from which we are to rest? They are anything that we do apart from the Lord. Our own strengths can truly become our weakness. Laboring at what God doesn't call and empower us to do will bring about weariness.

Furthermore, continual labor without refreshing ourselves in His presence wearies us as well. Jesus said, *"Come to me, all you who are weary and burdened, and I will give you rest. Take my yoke upon you and learn from me, for I am gentle and humble in heart, and you will find rest for your souls. For my yoke is easy and my burden is light."* (Matt. 11:28-30 NIV)

Accepting the Wrong Viewpoint

Sometimes our passion wanes because we have accepted the wrong viewpoint. What did Jesus say about this?

"He replied, 'Isaiah was right when he prophesied about you hypocrites; as it is written:

"'These people honor me with their lips,
but their hearts are far from me.
They worship me in vain;
their teachings are but rules taught by men.'

"You have let go of the commands of God and are holding on to the traditions of men." (Mark 7:6-9 NIV)

Sometimes people lose passion for the Lord because they have begun to focus on the *traditions* of religion and have lost sight of *Him*.

Others find their passion waning because they have become worldly-minded. They are influenced by the attitudes of the world. The Bible says, *"You adulteresses, do you not know that friendship with the world is hostility toward God? Therefore whoever wishes to be a friend of the world makes himself an enemy of God."* (Jas. 4:4)

Likewise, a woman's passion for her husband is damaged when she begins to be influenced by the world's ungodly view of marriage. The world proclaims that we should look out for number one and that our husbands have no rights to physical intimacy unless we are equally impassioned at the moment.

The solution in the natural marriage is the same as in the spiritual one: She needs to consciously change her perspective. Jesus calls us to be servants, to think of the other person before ourselves. (Mark 9:35, Phil. 2:4-7) Just as the traditions of men and worldly attitudes can kill your passion toward the Lord, looking at marriage the way the world does can damage the physical relationship in a marriage.

Disinterest

While it is true that men as a rule have greater sex drives than their wives have, women do have libido. One way to cultivate this is to spend time thinking about physical intimacy with your husband. If you have ever experienced an orgasm, think about how it felt; you will want to experience it again! If you have never experienced this, you may want to visit your Christian bookstore to find a good book on sexuality to help you and your husband in this area.

Women tend to find more pleasure in sex if they experience it more often. From that angle, we could say that neglecting this area of your marriage tends to *weaken* your interest.

Do you want your husband to think you are the most wonderful wife in the world? Very few husbands fail to respond positively and gratefully to wives who make sex exciting for them.

Watch your husband, and you will be able to tell what creates ecstasy for him; then give him more of that. Those times when you are not really all that excited yourself are golden opportunities to learn new ways to please him sexually, because you can concentrate more on watching him than when you are feeling so much passion yourself.

God has created human beings with a desire to commune with Him. This is why people who haven't known the true God tend to create and worship false gods. Just as a wife needs to cultivate her natural libido, we also need to choose to do what increases our longing for spiritual intimacy with the Lord. Our desire for that will weaken if we neglect our personal time alone with Him. Worshipping and praising the Lord need not wait until we are "in the mood." Many,

many times, our desire for spiritual intimacy grows as a *result* of praise and worship.

Praise is a sacrifice, and we are priests. (Heb. 13:15, 1 Pet. 2:9) In the Old Testament, we read that the Levitical sacrifices were food both to God and to the priests who offered them. (See Lev. 2:3, 3:11, 3:16, 6:16, 6:25-29, 21:6-8, and 21:17.) Giving ourselves with abandon (in praise and worship of the Lord, just as in physical intimacy with our husbands) can give us exquisite joy as well as the delight that it gives to our Bridegroom.

I urge you to give yourself fully to the heavenly Bridegroom and to experience the joys available to you. Joy is the result of being filled with the Spirit of Christ. (See Gal. 5:22.) Loving and worshipping the Lord with all your being, holding back nothing, will bless you. I challenge you to worship the Lord with abandon and minister joy to *Him*.

May you repent of your busy-ness and return to intimacy with the divine Bridegroom/King. May you be like Mary, pouring out lavish worship and praise as fragrant ointment to the Son of God without fearing the criticism of other people.

I pray also that your every sexual encounter with your husband will remind you of how deeply the Lord desires to commune with you in spiritual intimacy.

Furthermore, I encourage you to give yourself to your husband with abandon. God created marriage, and He created the sexual relationship to flourish within marriage. He pronounced everything that he had created as "very good," and every gift that God gives is good and perfect. I hope that you will begin to see this part of your marriage as an opportunity both to receive and to give joy. I pray that you will learn to eagerly receive the gifts that the Lord offers to you through physical union with your husband. I urge you to allow your husband to be exhilarated and satisfied by your body and by your love.

Through physical lovemaking, may you grow in the *emotional* intimacy in your marriage. May you and your husband learn more and more how to please each other and to bring ecstasy to each other. In so doing, you will extend a joyful blessing to your husband and will cement your relationship with him.

Looking Beautiful

❀❀❀

Have you ever seen an ugly bride? I never have. Even plain women are beautiful when they walk down that center aisle, because they are radiant with the joy of being joined to a husband. The young man who awaits her at the altar does not see an unattractive bride. He sees the most beautiful woman in the world at that moment, because he loves her.

Do you remember the words of the bridegroom in Solomon's Song of Songs? This is what he said to his bride:

"You are altogether beautiful, my darling,
And there is no blemish in you...
You have made my heart beat faster, my sister, my bride;
You have made my heart beat faster with a single glance of your eyes,
With a single strand of your necklace.
How beautiful is your love, my sister, my bride!
How much better is your love than wine,
And the fragrance of your oils
Than all kinds of spices!" (S. of S. 4:7, 9-10)

If (as many believe) the Song of Solomon is an allegory of Christ and the church as well as Solomon's own story, then these are words that the Son of God would say to His bride. He sees us as a beautiful bride.

That was the goal of His sacrifice: *"Christ also loved the church and gave Himself up for her, so that...He might present to Himself the church in all her glory, having no spot or wrinkle or any such thing; but that she would be holy and blameless."* (Eph. 5:25-27)

Bright, clean linen (linen that has not been stained with dye or something else) is creamy white. The bride of Christ wears white to the wedding. Look at John's words in the book of Revelation: *"Let us rejoice and be glad and give the glory to Him, for the marriage of the Lamb has come and His bride has made herself ready. And it was given to her to clothe herself in fine linen, bright and clean, for the fine linen is the righteous acts of the saints."* (Rev. 19:7-8)

Likewise, most women wear a white gown when they are united with their natural husbands in marriage. The bridal gown symbolizes the white wedding garment of the bride of Christ, as well as the purity of life that the bride promises on the day that she is joined to a natural husband.

Remember that the husband is the giver. Even our righteousness is a gift from the heavenly Giver to us, His beloved bride. *"And it was **given** to her to clothe herself in fine linen."* (Emphasis mine)

Linen is expensive to produce, because it is a time-intensive project to grow flax and manufacture the fabric. Spiritual linen is expensive too; our Bridegroom paid a dear price (His own blood) for the righteousness that He makes available to us.

Every bride's beauty pleases her husband, and the beauty of the bride of Christ pleases the Son of God. Although of herself she is swarthy, He sees her as without blemish. (See S. of S. 1:5-6 and 4:7.)

We have no righteousness of our own. Jesus said in John 15:5 that apart from Him we can do nothing. Now we are obviously capable of doing many things apart from Him, but they are worthless. Jesus meant that in our own fleshly effort we could do nothing of godly, spiritual value.

The true beauty of the bride is not found in her own flesh, nor is it in bright jewelry, a fancy coiffure, or an expensive wardrobe. Paul wrote, *"Likewise, I want women to adorn themselves with proper clothing, modestly and discreetly, not with braided hair and gold or pearls or costly garments, but rather by means of good works, as is proper for women making a claim to godliness."* (1 Tim. 2:9-10)

It is the inner adornment of a gentle and quiet spirit that Christ finds attractive. Peter tells wives, *"Your adornment must not be merely external—braiding the hair, and wearing gold jewelry, or putting on dresses; but let it be the hidden person of the heart, with the imperishable quality of a gentle and quiet spirit, which is precious in the sight of God. For in this way in former times the holy women also, who hoped in God, used to adorn themselves, being submissive to their own husbands."* (1 Pet. 3:3-5)

The Greek word that is rendered *precious* in 1 Pet. 3:4 means *extremely expensive*. The same Greek word was used in Mark 14:3 to describe the spikenard perfume with which Mary the sister of Lazarus anointed Jesus, and in 1 Tim. 2:9 to describe costly clothing. Peter associates this gentle and quiet spirit (highly valued by the Lord) with our chaste and respectful behavior toward our husbands. (See 1 Pet. 3:2.)

We also find that the Proverbs 31 excellent wife wears the fine linen symbolic of righteous acts.

"...Her clothing is fine linen and purple." (Prov. 31:22)

If we tried to produce our *own* righteousness, the result would not be fine, white linen, but rather filthy rags.

"All of us have become like one who is unclean,
and all our righteous acts are like filthy rags..." (Isa. 64:6 NIV)

Notice that it doesn't say that only our *sins* are like filthy rags; it rather refers to even our fleshly attempts at righteous acts as filthy rags. Fleshly efforts at producing righteousness will fail. *"For I know that nothing good dwells in me, that is, in my flesh; for the willing is present in me, but the doing of the good is not."* (Rom. 7:18) Only what the Lord works in us will produce fine, white linen.

Indeed, anyone who has ever worn linen knows that linen without spot or wrinkle *must* be supernatural linen. Natural linen almost forms wrinkles as one walks from the closet to the front door! Furthermore, spots are obvious on white linen. Although linen resists stains, the smallest stain that does occur will be noticeable on the solid white garment. If no spots of filth can be seen on our robe of righteousness, it is certainly the work of the Lord.

Depending on the quality of the flax plant, the skill of the spinner, and the intended use of the cloth, linen thread can be spun for coarse fabric or it can be spun into extremely fine thread. The Egyptians made sails out of coarse linen, for example, but used fine linen for the most expensive garments. The Lord Himself spun the linen for our robe of righteousness, for it's made of His own righteousness. Therefore, it's the very finest linen.

Nonetheless, it is still true that even though the bride of Christ cannot provide her own righteousness, she has *made herself* ready to receive it.

"Let us rejoice and be glad and give the glory to Him, for the marriage of the Lamb has come and His bride **has made herself ready**. *It was given to her to clothe herself in fine linen, bright and clean; for the fine linen is the righteous acts of the saints."* (Rev. 19:7-8, emphasis mine)

The Greek word that is translated as *made ready* literally means *to prepare* and comes from a root that means *ready*. She makes herself ready—prepares herself—through repentance and her choices to receive what He offers. The righteousness of Christ is a gift, but we choose whether or not we will wear it. Peter reminds us, *"But according to His promise we are looking for new heavens and a new earth, in which righteousness dwells. Therefore, beloved, since you look for these things,* **be diligent** *to be found by Him in peace, spotless and blameless..."* (2 Pet. 3:13-14, emphasis mine)

In fact, the NASU translation of Rev. 19:8 is accurate. The Greek word that is rendered as *righteous acts* refers to *deeds* of righteousness, not solely to imputed righteousness. It's not only that we have received His grace, but also that we are choosing to live holy lives.

Furthermore, James tells us that we must keep ourselves unstained by the world's influence. The word that James employed for *unstained* is the same one used by Peter for *spotless*. (Jas. 1:27, 2 Pet. 3:14) This Greek word and the Greek word that Paul used in Eph. 5:27 to tell us that the bride of Christ will be presented without spot both share the same root.

Wearing the spiritual white linen wedding garment of righteousness is not optional. Do you remember the parable that Jesus told about the wedding feast?

"But when the king came in to look over the dinner guests, he saw a man there who was not dressed in wedding clothes, and he

said to him, 'Friend, how did you come in here without wedding clothes?'...Then the King said to the servants, 'Bind him hand and foot, and throw him into the outer darkness; in that place there will be weeping and gnashing of teeth.'" (Matt. 22:11-13)

We dare not fail to wear the garment of righteousness that He provides for us!

The Fashion Show

Imagine for a moment that you are attending a fashion show, where a model walks down the runway wearing a pair of wool slacks and a sweater. Flashbulbs pop from all sides as the model walks, turns this way and that, and strikes poses for the cameras. Soon she tops the outfit with the bulky matching jacket that rests across her arm. More cameras flash. Then it is time for her to model a clingy dress, so she attempts to pull it over the pants, sweater, and jacket. It simply will not fit!

What's wrong with that scenario? She needed to go take off the first outfit before she attempted to dress herself in the second one.

There are several passages in the New Testament that talk about our taking off and putting on various things. I would like for us to consider those, and to see that—just as the model's second outfit wouldn't fit properly when she attempted to pull it over the first— we need to take off some characteristics to make it easier to put on others. It isn't enough to put on the new; we must also remove the old.

17 So this I say, and affirm together with the Lord, that you walk no longer just as the Gentiles also walk, in the futility of their mind,

18 being darkened in their understanding, excluded from the life of God because of the ignorance that is in them, because of the hardness of their heart;

19 and they, having become callous, have given themselves over to sensuality for the practice of every kind of impurity with greediness.

20 But you did not learn Christ in this way,

21 if indeed you have heard Him and have been taught in Him, just as truth is in Jesus,
*22 that, in reference to your former manner of life, you **lay aside** the old self, which is being corrupted in accordance with the lusts of deceit,*
23 and that you be renewed in the spirit of your mind,
*24 and **put on** the new self, which in the likeness of God has been created in righteousness and holiness of the truth.*
*25 Therefore, **laying aside** falsehood, SPEAK TRUTH EACH ONE OF YOU WITH HIS NEIGHBOR, for we are members of one another.*
26 BE ANGRY, AND YET DO NOT SIN; do not let the sun go down on your anger,
27 and do not give the devil an opportunity.
28 He who steals must steal no longer; but rather he must labor, performing with his own hands what is good, so that he will have something to share with one who has need.
29 Let no unwholesome word proceed from your mouth, but only such a word as is good for edification according to the need of the moment, so that it will give grace to those who hear.
30 Do not grieve the Holy Spirit of God, by whom you were sealed for the day of redemption.
*31 Let all bitterness and wrath and anger and clamor and slander be **put away** from you, along with all malice.*
32 Be kind to one another, tender-hearted, forgiving each other, just as God in Christ also has forgiven you. (Eph. 4:17-32, emphasis mine)

Look at how this passage describes the old self: callous, hard-hearted, impure, greedy, corrupt, deceitful, bitter, and malicious. The old self seethes in anger and steals from others. Those are the kinds of things that we must remove—take off, so to speak—so that our new nature fits.

The Greek word for laying aside in verses 22 and 25 means to place something away from oneself. It can be translated as *cast away* or as *lay aside*. The word that is rendered *put away* in verse 31 means *to take up* or *to take away*. When he tells us in verse 24 to put on the new self, he uses a Greek word that means *to sink into a garment* or *to invest with clothing*. So Paul is telling us here that we must take off some things in order to clothe ourselves with some others.

There is a similar passage in Colossians. Let's look at that.

*9 Do not lie to each other, since you have **taken off** your old self with its practices 10 and have **put on** the new self, which is being renewed in knowledge in the image of its Creator. 11 Here there is no Greek or Jew, circumcised or uncircumcised, barbarian, Scythian, slave or free, but Christ is all, and is in all. 12 Therefore, as God's chosen people, holy and dearly loved, **clothe yourselves** with compassion, kindness, humility, gentleness and patience. 13 Bear with each other and forgive whatever grievances you may have against one another. Forgive as the Lord forgave you. 14 And over all these virtues **put on** love, which binds them all together in perfect unity.* (Col. 3:9-14 NIV, emphasis mine)

In Col. 3:9, Paul uses a Greek word that the NIV renders as "*you have taken off.*" This word means *to wholly divest oneself*. It comes from a Greek word that means *off* or *away*, and from a second word that *means to cause to sink out of, especially out of clothing*. One meaning of the English word *divest* is *to strip, of clothing, arms, or equipage, etc.* (Webster) So again, Paul is telling us to remove (as clothing) some things and to clothe ourselves with others.

Now let's look at another passage that talks about removing and enrobing.

*12 The night is almost gone, and the day is near. Therefore let us **lay aside** the deeds of darkness and **put on** the armor of light.*

13 Let us behave properly as in the day, not in carousing and drunkenness, not in sexual promiscuity and sensuality, not in strife and jealousy.

*14 But **put on** the Lord Jesus Christ, and make no provision for the flesh in regard to its lusts.* (Rom. 13:12-14, emphasis mine)

Again we have the Greek words for *cast off* and *sink into as into a garment*. We are to cast aside the deeds of darkness and clothe ourselves with Christ.

Do you think that Paul wants us to get the idea that we are to rid our lives of some things and cover ourselves with others? He uses this analogy repeatedly.

So what do we need to sling away? In Ephesians 4:22, he tells us to cast away our old self, our old nature. In Colossians 3:9, he tells us to remove—as if removing a garment—our old self and its practices. In Romans 13:12 and 14, he indicates that we must hurl away the deeds of darkness, and that this involves making no provision for the flesh. In other words, the things that he tells us to throw away are aspects of our old nature, the flesh.

What is our flesh like? Paul lists several manifestations of our flesh in the passages we just read: unwholesome words, jealousy, clamor (the Greek means *crying out*, like *shrieking* or *screaming*), bitterness, strife, deceit, wrath-controlled or anger-controlled actions, malice, slander, greediness, theft, carousing, drunkenness, impurity, sensuality, and sexual promiscuity.

He recaps some of those and adds others in Gal. 5:19-21:

19 *Now the deeds of the flesh are evident, which are: immorality, impurity, sensuality,*
20 *idolatry, sorcery, enmities, strife, jealousy, outbursts of anger, disputes, dissensions, factions,*
21 *envying, drunkenness, carousing, and things like these, of which I forewarn you, just as I have forewarned you, that those who practice such things will not inherit the kingdom of God.*

Paul is telling us that these things have no place in our lives.

One thing that our divine Bridegroom would like for us to remove is hypocrisy. *"Therefore, rid yourselves of all malice and all deceit, hypocrisy, envy, and slander of every kind."* (1 Pet. 2:1 NIV) The Greek word that is translated *hypocrisy* in this verse involves playing a false part or pretending. It's being an actress who wears a mask that says she is one way, while in her heart (and perhaps in her actions as well when she is with different people) she is another. A hypocrite is one whose desire is to please people rather than God or to deceive people into believing she is more righteous than she is. This was the big problem with the Pharisees. (See Matt. 6:2, Matt. 22:15-18, and John 12:43.) Jesus' harshest words were to hypocrites. (See Matt. 23:13-36, for example.) We must make sure that we remove this terrible garment.

Now some of these may not give you any trouble. Those don't really tempt you, but others are such a part of your flesh that it "feels like" you can't help yourself. Another woman will find your temptations easier to withstand but will be sorely tempted by a different set of failures.

Perhaps you have no problem resisting drunkenness, but you habitually lie. Or possibly you never steal, but you dress sensually (1 Tim. 2:9), use unwholesome language (Eph. 4:29 and 5:4), or harbor bitterness in your heart (Heb. 12:15). Maybe you are never tempted with sexual immorality, but you regularly allow wrath to control your words and actions.

Do you ever say, "He made me so angry that I couldn't help myself"? My sisters, that's Satan's lie! You *can* resist the temptation. *"No temptation has seized you except what is common to man. And God is faithful; he will not let you be tempted beyond what you can bear. But when you are tempted, he will also provide a way out so that you can stand up under it."* (1 Cor. 10:13 NIV)

Sometimes we find ourselves beginning to believe that the acts of the flesh are attractive. We hear and see those things exalted on television and in movies. We listen to the world's opinion, and we begin to be deceived. That's why it's a good idea to take heed to the Psalmist's words in Psa. 101:3:

"I will set no worthless thing before my eyes..."

If we hear a lie often enough, it begins to sound like truth.

Unfortunately, there is a *bit* of truth in the lie. Hebrews 11:25 tells us that there *is* pleasure in sin. If there were no pleasure in it, we would not be much tempted. There is pleasure in sin, but it's a *passing* pleasure. The pleasure doesn't last. It's followed by shame and death.

The Bible tells us to take off those old garments of the flesh. Regardless of which ones are ingrained in your flesh, the commandment is that you should cast them away from you. Take them off, as if removing filthy garments, and throw them away from you. Jude tells us that such fleshly clothing will pollute us. (Jude 23) James warns us that such garments have become moth-eaten. (Jas. 5:2)

Linen resists moths and repels dirt. We are better off clothed in the spiritual white linen of righteousness than in the filthy rags of the flesh. Don't forget the words of Isaiah that we considered earlier in this chapter:

"All of us have become like one who is unclean, and all our righteous acts [that is, attempts to do "good" out of our own flesh] *are like filthy rags..."* (Isa. 64:6 NIV)

You don't want to cover yourself with something that is tattered, polluted, and contaminated!

Paul wrote, *"For we are His workmanship, created in Christ Jesus for good works, which God prepared beforehand so that we would walk in them."* (Eph. 2:10) The word that Paul used for *workmanship* means *a product*, i.e. *fabric* (literally or figuratively). When God created our new natures, He also wove garments of righteous acts for us to do.

He did not, however, make us to be robots. We are to clothe *ourselves* with these righteous garments. We have a choice! That's why Paul commands us to put on *"...the new self, which in the likeness of God has been created in righteousness and holiness of the truth"* (Eph. 4:24) and *"...which is being renewed in knowledge in the image of its Creator."* (Col. 3:10 NIV) Putting on the new nature is in fact putting on Christ, for He is our righteousness. (Rom. 13:14, 1 Cor. 1:30)

You may be thinking, "Well, I put on Christ when I was born again." Yes, you were plunged into Christ when you chose to receive Him; but Paul is talking to *Christians* when he instructs us to clothe ourselves with the Lord Jesus Christ. (See Rom. 1:7, 13:14.) He clarifies the instruction when he adds, *"...and make no provision for the flesh in regard to its lusts."* (Rom. 13:14)

Even Christians, who have been placed into Christ at conversion, must "put on Christ." That is, we are to divest ourselves of the acts of the flesh and clothe ourselves with the new nature that will reflect the character of Christ. The new nature is filled with righteousness, holiness, truth, and the knowledge of God. (Eph. 4:24, Col. 3:10)

Dressing in the new nature means that we wear kindness, compassion, forgiveness, gentleness, and patience. (Eph. 4:32, Col. 3:12) Peter instructs us to put on humility: *"...all of you, clothe yourselves with humility toward one another, for GOD IS OPPOSED TO THE PROUD, BUT GIVES GRACE TO THE HUMBLE."* (1 Pet. 5:5)

Finally, we cover all of these with love. *"And **over all** these virtues put on love, which binds them all together in perfect unity."* (Col. 3:14 NIV, emphasis mine) Love will fit over the other appropriate clothing. It is not compatible with the deeds of the flesh (we must remove these if we would wear love) but it works well with every truly righteous act. *"But the fruit of the Spirit is love, joy, peace, patience, kindness, goodness, faithfulness, gentleness, self-control; against such things there is no law."* (Gal. 5:22-23)

Furthermore, the white linen garment is comfortable and durable. Wearing linen keeps the wearer cool; it protects from heat of the day. When the heat of persecution or trouble comes, our linen is protection for us. Linen can take the heat. We can even use the hottest setting of our irons on linen without scorching it.

Suppose your husband went to Paris or New York and bought for you a designer wardrobe. He spared no expense and bought only the very best. Would you stick the new garments in the back of your closet and continue to wear the old, tattered things you already had? I think not. How do you think your husband would feel if you continued to wear the worn-out clothing and shunned his lovely gifts to you?

Jesus (your heavenly Bridegroom) paid an *enormous* price so you could wear the robe of righteousness. In fact, He paid the highest price ever paid for anything: His own blood. I encourage you to ask the Lord to "go through your spiritual wardrobe." As you re-read the passages in this chapter that deal with taking off and putting on characteristics, ask the Lord to show you what you need to discard. Invite Him to show you which garments you should be wearing but have neglected. Then respond to His voice and remove the offending clothing so that the white linen robe of righteous acts will fit well as you clothe yourself in it.

"Give unto the LORD the glory due to His name;
Worship the LORD in the beauty of holiness." (Psa. 29:2 NKJV)

The NASU renders that verse to say that we should worship Him in holy attire. The Hebrew word that is translated *beauty* in this verse is the word for *decoration* or *ornament*. When we bow down before our heavenly Bridegroom, the King of kings, we are adorned and made beautiful by holiness.

Think about the people in your life whom you consider to be beautiful inside. Do you see goodness and faithfulness in them? Are they "wearing" the "garments" that we have been commanded to cast away, or are they "dressed" in kindness, compassion, forgiveness, humility, gentleness, and patience? Which do you find more attractive in other people: arrogance, or humility? Which do you find more appealing: greed, or generosity? Every woman wants to be beautiful. Here is an opportunity to beautify ourselves.

We must be careful that our desire is to please the Lord, however, and not merely to please the people around us.

"...The LORD does not look at the things man looks at. Man looks at the outward appearance, but the LORD looks at the heart." (1 Sam. 16:7 NIV)

John tells us about some people who believed in Jesus, but who were more concerned about pleasing other people: *"Nevertheless many even of the rulers believed in Him, but because of the Pharisees they were not confessing Him, for fear that they would be put out of the synagogue; for they loved the approval of men rather than the approval of God."* (John 12:42-43)

When I was a teenager and even a young woman, I often wore certain clothing because I'd been told that it was fashionable. I didn't stop to think whether the style was becoming to me, because I wanted to wear what others had determined were the "right" kinds of clothing.

I have become less concerned about wearing the latest fad as I have grown older. Instead, I now look for garments that are becoming to me—that look better on me. In the same way, we begin to look for "clothing" that enhances our beauty in the eyes of the divine Bridegroom as we grow more spiritually mature.

"How can you believe, when you receive glory from one another and you do not seek the glory that is from the one and only God?" (John 5:44)

"...We must obey God rather than men." (Acts 5:29)

Dressing for the Natural Husband

Just as we must dress to please the heavenly Bridegroom, we must also strive to make ourselves look attractive for our natural husbands. Proverbs 31 says that the wife described there wore garments of scarlet and purple as well as white linen. (Verses 21-22) King Lemuel could afford expensive scarlet and purple fabrics for his bride, but not everyone could.

It isn't necessary to wear luxurious, costly attire, but you should do everything possible to dress attractively for your husband. Put on a little makeup and fix your hair. Wear something that he likes. Neatness, cleanliness, and becoming styles are far more important than the cost of the outfit. The way you look affects how he thinks about you all day. If you look frumpy most of the time, that's how he will picture you when he thinks about you.

A wise wife wants to dress to make herself more beautiful to her husband. I have always tried to make it a point to look my best when I have been out in public with Charles or when I visited his office. I didn't want him to be ashamed to be seen with me.

"An excellent wife is the crown of her husband,
But she who shames him is like rottenness in his bones."
(Prov. 12:4)

Didn't you do this during your courtship? When you and your husband were dating, did you wear your sloppiest clothes, neglect your hair, and skip the makeup? I think not. I believe that you wanted to look beautiful to him.

When Naomi sent Ruth to the threshing floor to meet with Boaz, she instructed her to make herself appealing to him. *"Wash yourself therefore, and anoint yourself and put on your best clothes, and go down to the threshing floor..."* (Ruth 3:3)

Or consider the story of Esther. The Persian king was seeking a new queen, so beautiful young virgins were brought from all over the kingdom for his consideration. Among the young women who were gathered to the palace was the Jewess Hadassah, who is also known as Esther.

One by one, the maidens were taken to the king for his decision about them. The Bible tells us that when a young woman was summoned to the king's presence, *"...anything that she desired was given her to take with her from the harem to the king's palace."* (Esther 2:13)

"When the turn came for Esther (the girl Mordecai had adopted, the daughter of his uncle Abihail) to go to the king, she asked for nothing other than what Hegai, the king's eunuch who was in charge of the harem, suggested. And Esther won the favor of everyone who saw her. She was taken to King Xerxes in the royal residence in the tenth month, the month of Tebeth, in the seventh year of his reign. Now the king was attracted to Esther more than to any of the other women, and she won his favor and approval more than any of the other virgins. So he set a royal crown on her head and made her queen instead of Vashti." (Esther 2:15-17 NIV)

Ruth and Esther listened to wise council so as to please Boaz and the Persian king. They could have chosen to listen to other young women. Ruth chose to listen to the wisdom of Naomi, and Boaz was pleased with her. Knowing how women are, I would not be surprised if the other virgins advised Esther as they all waited for their turns to go to the king. Esther wisely chose, however, to listen to the king's servant, who knew his master's tastes. She didn't just take what the other virgins took. It turned out that the other virgins didn't know what would please the king, for he didn't choose any of them. He chose Esther.

Have you noticed that some women often dress to please other women rather than their husbands? Has your husband ever expressed frustration because you would not wear a coat on a very blustery, cold winter day? Your reasoning might be that you couldn't wear your coat because it was not the right length or color for your outfit. As a woman, I could understand your thinking, but it probably would seem foolish to your husband…and to mine.

What if your husband were to request that you wear a certain piece of jewelry when you go out on a date night? Perhaps you don't want to do as he requests because you think the jewelry doesn't match your clothes. Again, as a woman, I understand your discomfort in wearing what you consider a mismatched combination. What we need to ask ourselves, however, is whether we want to look beautiful for our husbands, or whether we desire to wear what other women consider fashionable.

This tendency of wives who want to please others in their appearance rather pleasing their husbands reminds me of those things that Jesus said about folks who were more interested in pleasing other people than in pleasing Him. Choosing whether we will dress for other women or for our husbands illustrates how we must notice whether we are wearing unrighteous qualities that would please the world rather than putting on things that please our heavenly Bridegroom.

Natural Beauty Isn't Enough

Society exalts beauty as the source of self-worth in women. Even for the most beautiful woman, however, appearance means little to her husband if she is an unpleasant companion. Truth to tell, the beauty that even your husband sees in you will probably be enhanced as much by your wearing the white linen of righteousness as it will by your wearing flattering clothing.

"Like a gold ring in a pig's snout
is a beautiful woman who shows no discretion." (Prov. 11:22 NIV)

Furthermore, physical attractiveness invariably fades with passing years. Proverbs 31 ends with these words:

"Charm is deceptive, and beauty is fleeting;
but a woman who fears the LORD is to be praised.
Give her the reward she has earned,
and let her works bring her praise at the city gate." (Prov. 31: 30-31 NIV)

Ladies, may this be our goal. Let's make sure that our priorities are straight. May we always seek to please our heavenly Bridegroom and our husbands in what we wear.

Opening Your Heart

❃ ❃ ❃

Importance of communication

Almost every time I read or hear commentary from marriage counselors, their words include something like this: Communication is essential to a successful marriage.

When you tell your husband, "The weather is nice today," it's communication, isn't it? "The telephone call is for you." If you say that to your husband, you have communicated. But what happens if that is as deep as your conversations ever go? Those are words that you would feel comfortable saying to a total stranger.

What if you never talk to your husband about the things that are deep in your heart, things that are too personal and intimate to discuss with other people? What if you never tell him about your hopes, desires, needs, and dreams? What if you don't discuss your plans for the week? What if you never discuss what's bothering you? What if you don't tell him how much you treasure him? Experts repeatedly tell us that if husbands and wives don't open their hearts to each other, the marriage is damaged.

Have you ever had a close friend with whom you did everything? Maybe you lived next door to her. You were constantly together. You likely shared secrets. You worked on hobbies together and took your children to the park together. You loved her dearly.

Here Comes the Bride

Then one day, she moved away. She lived in the next town, and you rarely saw her anymore. At first, you continued to call each other for chats on the phone and frequently made dates to meet for lunch; but as other things entered your schedules, you had less and less contact. You don't dislike her now—in fact you still care a great deal for her—but you probably wouldn't tell your deepest heartbreaks to her after being out of touch for a while. If nothing else, there would be too many things you would have to say to bring her up to date before you could explain the latest problem.

What happened? Friendships cannot be built or maintained unless we spend time together, either in person or via telephone or other communication. They can't be sustained without conversation to knit your hearts together.

Husbands and wives in ideal marriages are "best friends." If you desire to maintain a loving friendship with your husband, you must make spending time in conversation and togetherness a priority.

At the very least, couples need to communicate about their daily lives. Far too many hurt feelings occur because one spouse doesn't know what the other is planning.

Suppose you had invited a couple for dinner a week ahead of time, and the wife called to reschedule the evening before the planned dinner. She was rather irritated that her husband had other plans that he wouldn't or couldn't cancel. Moreover, it turned out that she had agreed on a date with you without ever consulting her husband about his schedule! She had mentioned it to him only that evening, 24 hours before the time that you and she had chosen.

What if that wasn't the only mistake she made? What if, while you were discussing in your telephone conversation a future date for the postponed dinner, she agreed to a time immediately on the telephone? Perhaps you would ask if she didn't need to check with her husband about the rescheduled date, but she would reply, "Oh, no, I always make these plans. He will be able to come." I would say that such a woman has much to learn about communication in marriage, wouldn't you? Sadly, such situations are not rare.

If couples are to truly blend their lives, they must consult each other about plans for couple events. In fact, they should discuss their daily lives even when the event involves only one of them. A marriage is not merely two people who happen to share the same house and the same bed. Marriage means that their lives are blended together.

Developing Transparency

Transparency is an important ingredient in successful communication in marriage. "Pass the corn, please," is talking—but it's at a pretty low level of communication.

If you are a wise wife, you will allow your husband to see parts of your heart that no one else is allowed to see. Make yourself vulnerable to him! Openness in communication invites emotional communion between the two of you. Is that not your desire? Do you not long for affectionate closeness between his heart and yours? A husband and wife should be able to voice their deepest concerns and embarrassments without fear of betrayal. They should be comfortable to convey their hopes, dreams, and happy accomplishments without fear of sounding ridiculous or prideful. This is your husband! Open your heart to him. Give yourself fully to him emotionally, just as you yield completely to him sexually.

Most women like to talk, but we must be certain that we speak the *truth*, including those areas of our hearts where we are afraid or ashamed. Even if you have done something about which he will not approve, you must be truthful. I have met many people who see no problem with lying and practice it regularly. I have never known even one person, however, who approved of another person's lie to her. Jesus said, *"In everything, therefore, treat people the same way you want them to treat you..."* (Matt. 7:12)

Can He Trust You?

Can your husband trust you with his secrets? While Proverbs 31:11 seems to single out the importance of our being trustworthy in the area of finances, we must not limit our faithfulness to money. It's important that we be worthy of our husbands' trust in all things.

The excellent wife *never* betrays her husband's confidence. She repeats to *no one*, including her mother or her closest friend, the words that he has spoken for her ears alone. The ability to keep confidences is important in any relationship, but particularly in the marriage partnership. Husbands and wives need the assurance that they can speak their most private thoughts without fear of their being repeated to others.

Can your spouse trust you to avoid advertising his secret fears, his confessed sins, his failures, his shortcomings, and his embarrassments? The Bible teaches us to confess our sins to one another. (See Jas. 5:16.) It refers, however, to confessing our *own* sins, not those of our husbands. Let *your husband* confess *his* sins.

Women frequently complain because their husbands won't discuss their deep feelings with their wives. If you desire that kind of intimacy, you must be worthy of his trust.

The Lord says that there are conditions to *His* confiding in us:
"The LORD confides in those who fear him;
He makes his covenant known to them." (Psa. 25:14 NIV)
"In this case, moreover, it is required of stewards that one be found trustworthy." (1 Cor. 4:2)

Fearing the Lord refers to respecting and reverencing Him. If we respect and reverence Him, we will not be untrustworthy. Our husbands represent Christ, and we must respect them. Showing that respect to our spouses will mean that we must be trustworthy in that relationship as well.

Keeping Your Promises

Can your husband trust you to do what you say you will do, or does he always wonder if you will change your mind? You may say, "Well, when I told him I would do that, I didn't know that my friend was going to ask me to lunch," or, "That was before I saw how busy I would be today." Perhaps you think, "I'm just not in the mood to do that today," or, "I'm too tired."

The Psalmist asked the question, *"...Who may dwell on Your holy hill?"* Among the qualities that he listed in reply are, *"He who walks with integrity,"* and, *"He swears to his own hurt and does not change."* (Psa. 15:1-4)

Sometimes things do come up. My suggestion is that in such situations, you call your husband and ask if it would be okay with him if you do the promised thing later. Rather than just failing to do what you said that you would do, you instead ask for a postponement. Remember, however, that this is a request and not a statement of fact. You are asking to be released from your promise, not declaring that you have decided not to fulfill your word. Most husbands will be flexible when possible, so long as you are not doing this too often.

Wisely Building Him Up

When the queen mother advised her son of the qualities of the excellent wife, she included these words:
"She does him good and not evil
All the days of her life." (Prov. 31:12)
One way that the godly wife does her spouse good and not evil is by building him up rather than tearing him down. She *en*courages rather than *dis*courages him.
"The wise woman builds her house,
But the foolish tears it down with her own hands." (Prov. 14:1)
It is the wise woman who builds her house. She has learned that she must build up her husband as a part of building her home and marriage. In order to know how to encourage him, she needs wisdom.

Yes, we must exercise wisdom when we speak. Communicating wisely requires that we first obtain wisdom. That seems obvious enough, doesn't it?

According to James, however, there are two kinds of wisdom. There is a wisdom that is earthly, unspiritual, and demonic. It is envious and selfish. (See Jas. 3:14-15) Excellent wives will not speak or display that kind of wisdom. That is the wisdom found in the world.

Instead, we are to open our mouths with *godly* wisdom. *"But the wisdom from above is first pure, then peaceable, gentle, reasonable, full of mercy and good fruits, unwavering, without hypocrisy."* (Jas. 3:17) Are your words pure, peaceable, and gentle? Are they reasonable and merciful? Are your words sincere? Do they reflect the fruit of the Spirit described in Gal. 5:22-23?

Godly wisdom doesn't come naturally to us. Whatever is natural is fleshly and earthly. If a woman attempts to "build her house" in her own strength, employing natural wisdom, she will not do very well.

"Unless the LORD builds the house,
They labor in vain who build it..." (Psa. 127:1)

A wife must depend upon the Lord's work within her if she wants to be successful in "building her house." Solomon's mother told him, you recall, that the excellent wife fears the Lord. (Prov. 31:30) The Bible further says that reverence for God brings godly wisdom:

"The fear of the LORD is the beginning of wisdom..." (Psa. 111:10.)

In fact, the *only* way we can have godly wisdom is to receive it from God. *"But if any of you lacks wisdom, let him ask of God, who gives to all men generously and without reproach, and it will be given to him. But let him ask in faith..."* (Jas. 1:5-6)

There is humility — not pride — in godly wisdom, for it's not our own wisdom. *"Who is wise and understanding among you? Let him show it by his good life, by deeds done in the humility that comes from wisdom."* (Jas. 3:13 NIV)

Listening

Most of the time we think of only the speaking part when we consider communication, and that *is* an important aspect of it. It's an area in which most of us need to improve.

Another side of communication, however, is listening; and the admonition of Scripture is, *"...But everyone must be quick to hear, slow to speak..."* (Jas. 1:19) I think it was Mark Twain who said that if we were supposed to talk more than we listen, we'd have two mouths and one ear. The listening side of communication is more difficult for most people than the speaking part.

The first thing to remember when you are listening is that you must *listen*. That seems obvious enough, doesn't it? But when I say "listen," I don't mean that you should just sit there quietly while he speaks, but *really listen*. Focus on his words. Women regularly complain that their husbands don't talk to them. Many times, however, the wives don't listen when the men do have something to say. (The Lord speaks to us constantly, and too often we don't pay attention to His voice either!)

Perhaps when you are supposedly listening to your husband, you sometimes are in reality thinking about what you are going to say in reply. To the degree that you are formulating your response instead of paying attention to your mate's words, to that same degree you are not listening. This habit is a symptom of being more interested in winning than in finding truth, or being more concerned with putting forth your own ideas than with considering his.

In discussing problems with her husband, the successful wife will be careful to avoid focusing on getting her way and instead be vigilant about seeking truth and wisdom. We will talk more about that in the next chapter.

Have you done this to the Lord? Have you ever read the Bible to prove what you want to believe (or what you've been taught) rather than to find what truth really is? This attitude, whether shown to our husbands or to our heavenly Bridegroom, is a sign of selfishness, pride, and arrogance. It *should* be a call to repentance.

Remember this Proverb:
*"He who gives an answer before he hears,
it is folly and shame to him."* (Prov. 18:13)

Another listening failure is thinking about something entirely different while your mate is talking. Suppose, for example, that your husband is telling you about something that happened at work that day or talking about a football game. Instead of listening, are you deciding what to have for dinner, thinking about the book you have been reading, or considering your schedule for the following day?

Or perhaps you are busy with some activity and listening with "half an ear." I would suggest that you turn off the TV, put down your magazine, or get off the Internet to focus completely on what he is saying. Otherwise, you will convey the message that what he says is not important to you. You would not want that attitude from him when *you* have something to say, would you? I have to remind myself of this, because I tend to think I can multitask. I find, however, that I sometimes miss part of what he is saying. Besides, my divided attention on those occasions communicates to him that I am neither listening nor interested.

Our apparent inattention may discourage our husbands from talking on another day, and we certainly don't want that. Remember that your husband needs your respect. He needs to know that he is important to you. Make every effort to develop an interest in the things that interest your husband.

Another difficulty is that when I am concentrating on some task and my husband begins to speak to me, it sometimes takes me a second or two to make the transition from what I'm reading or doing to what he is saying. If you find yourself arriving at the conversation in the middle of your husband's sentence, you might want to admit that you didn't catch the first part. Otherwise, you may give an inappropriate reply!

Good communication is indeed necessary to a successful marriage, and communication includes both listening and speaking. Remember to temper your speaking with love, and to give him the benefit of the doubt when you listen. Good communication will strengthen the unity of your marriage; angry or harmful dialogue will bring discord and destruction.

Communicating with the Heavenly Bridegroom

Now, remember that marriage is a picture of the union of Christ and the church. Just as communication is vital to an intimate marriage relationship, prayer is essential for a close walk with the Lord.

Too often, however, we are negligent in the area of communication with the divine Bridegroom, as is frequently the case with our earthly husbands. The result is the same in the spiritual realm as it would be in an earthly union: Lack of communication causes our relationship with Christ to deteriorate. Our appetite for spiritual things begins to wane when we get too busy to communicate with the Lord. Thus, we soon find ourselves neglecting the Word and prayer, even when we are *not* busy.

The Psalmist said,

"Seven times a day I praise You..." (Psa. 119:164)
You may think, "I don't have time to pray seven times a day." Another Psalm says,
"Evening, morning, and noon
I cry out in distress,
and He hears my voice." (Psa. 55:17 NIV)

If you are in distress or in times of trouble, you might be more motivated to *find* time to cry out three times a day...or seven times... or even twenty times a day!

Sometimes our prayers are what a friend of mine calls *arrow prayers*. These are short conversational prayers, perhaps only a sentence or two at a time, that go up to the Lord all day long. The Bible instructs us to *"pray without ceasing."* (1 Thess. 5:17)

Obviously, we cannot devote our entire attention to speaking to the Lord 24 hours a day, seven days a week. We must sleep, work, eat, interact with our families, and so forth.

We can, however, remain in a running conversation with the Heavenly Bridegroom. As situations come up, we discuss them with the Lord much as we would discuss things that come to mind as we sit with our husbands. There will be times of silence and times of speaking, but we are connected and available to each other for conversation. Probably this is the kind of prayer to which Paul referred when he exhorted us to pray constantly.

Sometimes our prayers are what my friend calls *soaking prayers*. This is when we settle down for focused time with the Lord. Jesus discussed this kind of prayer when He said, *"But you, when you pray, go into your inner room, close your door and pray to your Father who is in secret, and your Father who sees what is done in secret will reward you."* (Matt. 6:6) It is like the times when Jesus prayed all night long to His Father. (Luke 6:12) It's like the prayer meeting that was held at Mary's house for the purpose of asking the Lord to bring about Peter's release from prison. (Acts 12:12) In this kind of prayer, we are totally focused on prayer alone.

These two kinds of prayer remind me of the altar of incense in the ancient Tabernacle as described in the book of Exodus.

"Aaron shall burn fragrant incense on it; he shall burn it every morning when he trims the lamps. When Aaron trims the lamps at

twilight, he shall burn incense. There shall be perpetual incense before the LORD throughout your generations." (Ex 30:7-8)

The incense (which symbolizes prayer) was replenished twice a day, but it burned continually. (Rev. 8:3-4, Psa. 141:1-2, and Ex. 30:8.) When the fresh incense was added in the morning and at twilight, it typified the "inner room" prayers in which we stop and devote our entire attention to prayer. Yet the incense smoldered all day, with its smoke ascending and the fragrance filling the Sanctuary. The continual burning of the incense reminds us of our flowing conversation with the Lord as we *"pray without ceasing"* throughout the day.

I believe that both of these types of prayer are crucial to developing greater closeness to the divine Bridegroom. We don't want to limit our conversations with the Lord to a couple of sessions a day when we take time to stop all else and talk to Him. You wouldn't corner your husband twice a day and reel off everything that you wanted to say that day and then ignore him the rest of the time. On the other hand, we do need times when we can communicate with our spouses without distractions; and it is critical to our spiritual walk with the Lord that we do find those times when we *can* devote our full attention to conversation with Him.

Do you remember when you were dating your husband? In all likelihood, you had no problem spending two hours on the telephone with him. Likewise, it wasn't difficult for the two of you to find things to say when you were out on a date. Why was that? It wasn't that you had two hours' worth of news or information to give him. Rather, it was that you loved talking to him and hearing his voice. Didn't the two of you repeatedly proclaim your love to each other during those conversations? I dare say that you didn't often consider yourself too busy to take his phone calls!

David wrote of the Lord,

"...In Your presence is fullness of joy..." (Psa. 16:11)

Those who are in love with Jesus will find joy in conversing with Him.

When our prayer lives begin to drift, we may find ourselves merely listing everything we want the Lord to do for us and making that the whole of our prayers. "Please do this, Lord." "I need that,

Lord." Neglected are the words of gratitude and thanksgiving. Forgotten are the words of praise and honor. Absent are the words of adoration and love.

Suppose you and your husband went out for a special evening. Maybe it was for your wedding anniversary or for Valentine's Day. Over a romantic candlelight dinner, you started listing everything you wanted him to do for you: Clean out the garage; fix the little crack in the sheet rock over the living room door; wash the car; rearrange the bedroom furniture.

Perhaps your husband would take your hand and begin to tenderly tell you how beautiful you are, how much he loves and cherishes you—but you return to your list: Put up a new ceiling fan; re-caulk the bathroom, build shelves in the laundry room; etc.

How do you think your husband would feel? Do you think that date night would strengthen your marriage relationship? Do you think that your hearts would be more intimate with each other after that evening? You had ignored his proclamations of love and affection. Do you think that your love for him would have grown in that climate?

Now we do need to communicate our needs to our husbands, and the Lord wants us to come to Him for our needs to be met as well. Although He fully knows before we ask, the Lord has chosen to fulfill our needs in response to our prayers. Christ teaches us to ask and keep on asking Him for what we need. (See Matt. 7:7, Jas. 4:2, and Luke 18:1.)

The problem comes when that is the sum total of what we say. He yearns for us to open our hearts to Him and to grow more and more spiritually intimate with Him. Jesus always loves us; when we open our hearts to Him, our love for Him and our intimacy with Him grow.

In the Song of Solomon, the bridegroom tells the bride that He longs to hear her speak:

"...*Let me hear your voice;*
For your voice is sweet..." (S. of S. 2:14)

He wants her to *talk* to Him. If these were words from a natural husband, many wives would consider them to be the fulfillment of a fondest dream come true!

The heavenly Bridegroom seeks more conversation and communion with us. He invites us: "Talk to Me. Pray. I love to hear you speak to Me." He yearns for us. He woos us. Let us not withhold our words from the Lover of our souls.

Isn't it wonderful to know that when we speak, the Lord is listening? That He is devoting His attention to us?

"I love the LORD, because He hears
My voice and my supplications.
Because He has inclined His ear to me,
Therefore I shall call upon Him as long as I live." (Psa. 116:1-2)

I love that. The Lord inclines His ear to me when I speak to Him.

A few years ago, the Lord said to my heart, "Your prayer life needs a little work."

Shortly after that, my husband and I received a newsletter from our friend Dr. Jim Mackey, in which he discussed Psa. 116:1-2, quoted above. Jim has given me permission to share an excerpt from what he had written that especially ministered to me:

"...(W)hat is **_GOD's_** posture when you pray? This little thing can maximize your prayer life! **_'Because He has inclined His ear unto me...'_** He is leaning forward...leaning toward *you!*

"What are you communicating when you lean toward someone speaking to you?
- I want to hear what you are saying
- What you are saying is important to me
- I don't want to miss a single word

"When the psalmist understood **GOD'S POSTURE** and what that posture was meant to convey to the pray-er, it made him understand how eager and ready God was to engage in his life!

"God didn't want to miss a single word of his prayer! God *wanted* to hear what he had to say!"

What a delight to know that the Lord is inclining His ear toward us to hear our prayers! What a joy that the Creator of the universe listens intently when we speak to Him!

There's another problem in many people's prayer lives, however. Just as we often think only of speaking in communication with our husbands, we tend to think of prayer as only the speaking part when we consider communication with the Lord. The other side of communication—with the Lord as with our husbands—is listening.

Now, it's abundantly clear that Jesus Christ is the *perfect* Bridegroom. I've heard many women complain because their husbands wouldn't talk to them, but the Lord isn't like that. He loves to speak to His bride. He has written us a letter—the Bible—that teaches us and reveals His heart to us. His Spirit continually speaks to our spirits to lead us, to encourage us, to reassure us, and to exhort us.

If that were the whole conversation, we would be describing a monologue. Real communication is a dialogue. Even two monologues don't equal a dialogue, however. Conversation means that *each* person has the opportunity to talk, *and* that each listens when the other speaks.

Unfortunately, our prayers frequently gravitate toward being monologues from *our* end. We rattle off everything that we want to tell the Lord without waiting to hear His response. We ask for help and answers, but we don't wait to hear what He says in reply. We fail to incline *our* ears to *His* voice. Instead, we quickly jump up as soon as we finish talking and go on with the busy-ness of everyday life. Then we wonder why our prayers are fruitless!

Perhaps you will say, "My time is all taken up with serving the Lord. That's why I don't have enough time to sit and listen to Him. Sometimes He doesn't speak quickly enough."

Do you remember the story of Mary and Martha? (See Luke 10:38-42.) Not only did Martha's work distract her, but she was unhappy that her sister was not distracted as well!

Martha was serving, and service is a good thing. It was not wrong for Martha to want to prepare food for everyone. They needed to eat, and cooking a meal was an appropriate way for her to serve. (In fact, it's also a problem when people think they are too spiritual to do mundane ministry like that.)

Only when Martha allowed the preparation of the meal to distract her from being in the Lord's presence did she go wrong. I suspect that she was not putting out plates of sandwiches. I don't think this was unleavened bread and dried fish. I picture her putting on the finest feast she knew how to cook: roast fatted calf with all the trimmings, perhaps, and her famous almond-honey cakes for dessert. There is a time to lavish on friends, but Martha allowed this activity to prevent her from being in the Lord's presence and hearing His voice.

Her sister, on the other hand, chose to sit at the Master's feet and cling to His every word. Jesus praised Mary for this.

If we want to grow closer to the Lord—if we want our hearts to become more intimate with His—then we cannot view prayer as optional or as a chore to be hurriedly done. It must not be relegated to times when we can think of nothing else to do. This is a love relationship with our heavenly Bridegroom, and love grows through opening our hearts to one another—speaking to Him from the depths of our hearts and listening carefully to His responses.

Are you actively cultivating that communication (both speaking and listening) with your husband? Moreover, are you faithful to pray and listen to the Lord, your heavenly Bridegroom? I urge you to speak to Jesus *about* your natural marriage and to listen to His voice to tell you what *you* (not your husband) should change. Are you communicating your love both to your earthly mate and to the Lord that he represents? Both the divine Bridegroom and your earthly husband long for you to express your love, honor, and devotion. Let's commit to making this a priority in our lives.

The Battle

❋❋❋

Do you and your husband ever disagree? Do you argue? If you are honest, you answered in the affirmative to the first question. Whether you would say that you argue partly depends upon your definition of the word *argue*. Most couples argue. Some would say that they *discuss problems* instead of that they argue. Whatever you want to call it, conflict resolution is an important aspect of your marriage, for no two people will always agree with each other.

Now in our relationship with the heavenly Bridegroom, conflict resolution is a pretty easy matter, so it won't take me long to discuss that. He has *infinite* wisdom, and He is *always* right. Any time that we disagree with Him, we are dead wrong.

Sometimes we bristle because the Lord hasn't done for us what we wanted. Sometimes we think that our situation is "different" and that we shouldn't be required to obey His word. Our flesh wants God to give us our way about everything.

Nevertheless, He is the perfect Bridegroom and His bride is imperfect. He is invariably right. Resolving the conflict requires us to acknowledge that we are wrong and He is right, and to align ourselves with His way of thinking. This is called repentance.

Conflict resolution in a human marriage, however, is another matter. In this relationship, we must deal with problems between two imperfect spouses. When one partner in a marriage sweeps under the carpet an issue that really bothers her, the issue doesn't disappear. Eventually, it will erupt like a volcano—probably with more negative emotion than would have been the case if she had dealt with it earlier.

Married partners certainly need to discuss what is bothering them. Wives shouldn't expect their husbands to be mind readers. It's important to convey one's own thoughts honestly, effectively, and kindly. If a wife bottles up her dissatisfaction about an issue, resentment and bitterness are likely to eventually develop. This is certainly something to avoid. *"See to it that no one comes short of the grace of God; that no root of bitterness springing up causes trouble, and by it many be defiled."* (Heb. 12:15)

Frequently a woman will allow problems to seethe under the surface because she wants to avoid conflict or because she thinks she is "unspiritual" if she says anything about what bothers her.

I don't like conflict. My *natural* preference—and more so as I get older—is to avoid conflict by clamming up. Conflict is unpleasant. I have learned by experience, however, that I should resist that tendency to hide from problems, because evading the issue allows it to fester and grow foul. Eventually, it will probably boil over in angry, hurtful words or develop coldness in our relationship; and then it *would* be sinful.

These bitter, resentful feelings will harden our hearts. They will damage not only the human marriage union, but will also mar the relationship with the heavenly Bridegroom. If we fail to communicate with our husbands about these issues, we risk becoming resentful. Then we are at odds with the spiritual Bridegroom as well, because that attitude displeases Him.

The key to success in this kind of communication is *"speaking the truth in love."* (Eph. 4:15) Yes, address the problem, but address it lovingly. Speak the truth, but speak it in love.

What kinds of problems are we addressing here?

Sometimes marital difficulties are the result of family background or personality differences. Perhaps the wife needs frequent expressions of non-sexual affection from her husband. Her husband, who is less demonstrative, doesn't give many hugs and kisses apart from sexual occasions. Maybe her family had a real Christmas tree, while his clan always put up an artificial one. Perhaps her family had frequent parties, but his family rarely entertained.

If she has been inviting 40 people in for parties or if he brought home a small "permanent" tree for their first Christmas and they have put it up every year, then they probably need to discuss how to solve these differences in a way that doesn't leave one of them feeling overwhelmed or cheated.

Perhaps he has a habit that drives her up the wall, and she regards it as a lack of consideration for her. Or maybe she *thinks* she understands what is going on, but she doesn't.

Years ago, I became more and more annoyed because Charles sometimes threw his handkerchief to the floor of our shared walk-in closet when he hung up his suit pants. Later, when I retrieved it and put it into the hamper, I invariably thought, "Why can't he put that into the hamper when he puts his shirt in there instead of throwing it on the floor?" I never mentioned it to him, however. (I just perfected my "martyr skills.")

After this had gone on for quite a while, I was in the bedroom one day when he replaced his suit in the closet after work. When he draped the pants over the hanger, the handkerchief slipped from the pocket and landed silently on the carpet. Charles was totally unaware that this had occurred.

When I laughed and told him what I had been thinking, he was amazed that I would believe he would just throw them down. He had never noticed when the handkerchiefs had fallen, and I had picked them up before he could notice them later.

It turned out that the pocket on the pants of just one suit allowed the handkerchief to fall after he folded the pants over the hanger. After that day, he was careful to observe whether he was littering the closet floor with handkerchiefs. If I had mentioned the handkerchiefs to him when they first began to appear in the floor, I could have spared myself many moments of frustration.

There are countless other ways that these kinds of misunderstanding occur, and good communication can be the solution. It has been my observation that timely and loving communication can resolve problems like the aforementioned issues before they begin to imperil the relationship.

The words *timely* and *loving* are important here. *Timely* means that you discuss it when you first realize that you aren't going to be able to live with it without developing frustration. Moreover, it also means that you find a time when the two of you are alone and relatively relaxed and upbeat. It may mean, as well, that the two of you take a break to cool off before you discuss an especially volatile issue.

Ask yourself if the issue is really important to you. If it is, talk to him. Discussing an issue early on, before resentments grow in your heart, will help you to employ tenderness when you talk to your husband about things that bother you. Talking about the problems when the two of you are in a good frame of mind will make it easier for you both to exercise self-control.

Loving means that you use kind words and a gentle tone of voice. It means that you are willing to listen to reason, instead of aiming only to get *your* point across. Trying to find a solution that will please you both will lead to a more successful marriage. One spouse should seek the happiness of the other. *"Each of you should look not only to your own interests, but also to the interests of others."* (Phil. 2:4 NIV)

Too often a hurt or angry wife will think that her husband should automatically know what she needs or should know that what he's doing bothers her. It's unreasonable to think this way, ladies.

Marriage is a type (a shadow or symbol) of the relationship with Christ, but it is *only* a shadow. The Lord *does* know what we need before we ask, but even He desires that we ask Him for what we need so that *we* will recognize our dependence upon Him.

Your husband, on the other hand, will many times be unaware that you need or desire something unless you tell him. You are setting yourself up for disappointment if you expect your husband to read your mind. Only God has that ability. While your spouse knows you better than anyone else does and he may be able to decipher more without words than anyone else could, he will not *always* know what you're thinking.

I suspect that *you* sometimes misunderstand or fail to notice *his* desires and needs. Do you not sometimes misinterpret the clues? In fact, aren't there times when you *think* you are doing something that will really please him, and then later you find out that you have done the opposite of what he wanted? I know that I have.

As a wife, you can *try* to hear what he means, not just the words that he has spoken. Watch his countenance. Listen to the tone of his voice. Consider the things you know to be his insecurities. We can't be mind-readers, but it is important to *try* to focus not merely on the words being said, but also on what may possibly be the motivation for the words.

The one caution here is that in some situations you would be wise to verify your perceptions rather than presuming that you know what he meant and didn't say. You know your husband better than anyone else does, but you cannot read his mind any more than he can read yours.

When you are unsure of his unspoken thoughts, it never hurts to ask him to clarify it for you. He probably won't mind. Although women frequently want to give hints, men are often much more willing to be forthright. It's always possible that you are misreading him. I've done that many times.

Have you ever thought something like this? "He knows we're having company tonight and I'm overwhelmed with work today. Why doesn't he help me?"

Some women would interpret the failure to help to mean that their husbands don't care about them. In all likelihood, however, it means only that a husband in that situation didn't think about it because his wife always takes care of the chores in question.

Most men are by nature less nurturing than most women are; therefore, things of this sort are less likely to occur to them. If you need a hand with the children's baths, ask him. If you are sick or extremely tired or busy, call him and ask him if he will stop by a fast food place for you. In all likelihood, he will do it—presuming you don't call him when you are "not feeling well" too often!

When you feel as though he is not being thoughtful of you, give him the benefit of the doubt. Patiently explain what you need. I have found that hints are many times unnoticed. I'm preaching to myself here, because my *fleshly* tendency would be to give hints—and then be hurt if he didn't do what I wanted!

Do you think that his action isn't sincere if you have to ask him? Perhaps you find yourself thinking something like this: "He's just doing it because of what I said. If he really cared about me, he would think of it himself."

When he hears your request and willingly chooses to bless you, he is responding to your need. It takes far more love for him to do something that he has no particular inclination to do (at the petition of the one he loves) than to do something that's *his* idea of helping or something that he *enjoys* doing for you. It's like the times when you freely meet your husband's sexual needs. It takes much more love to do this when you have no particular interest yourself than when you are panting with passion.

The Bible mentions *"speaking the truth in love."* (Eph. 4:15) Later in that chapter, Paul adds these words: *"Therefore, laying aside falsehood, SPEAK TRUTH EACH ONE OF YOU WITH HIS NEIGHBOR, for we are members of one another."* (Eph. 4:25) While we are to avoid harsh words, we must communicate our feelings honestly to avoid misunderstandings that lead to resentment.

When you fail to tell your spouse what you are thinking in order to avoid conflict or when you tell "white lies" to keep the peace, you are setting yourself up for disaster. Even a lie spoken with good intentions will likely be harmful rather than helpful. If you tell your husband what you think he wants to hear in order to keep from hurting his feelings or making him angry—but it is a lie—then you are not being honest.

Jesus said, *"I am...the truth."* (John 14:6) He also told us that Satan is *"a liar and the father of lies."* (John 8:44) There is really no such thing as a "white lie." A lie is from the devil, and the truth is from Christ. God has said that He *hates* a lying tongue. (Prov. 6:16-17)

Has this ever happened at your house? Your husband noticed that your countenance wasn't good and asked you what was wrong. Because you were angry with your husband but you preferred not to discuss what was wrong, you sharply replied, *"Nothing!"* as you loudly slammed the cabinet door. I have occasionally done that myself, but was it not a lie? And aren't we shutting down the communication in our marriages when we do it?

Besides, the angry tone of voice and the force with which you close the cupboard door exposes the falsehood of your reply that nothing is amiss. Your husband is not fooled. He knows something is wrong, but he can't do anything to fix it until he knows why you are upset.

That doesn't mean that you should harshly dump negative, hurtful words on your husband. Every word that we speak is to be for the purpose of edification. *"Do not let any unwholesome talk come out of your mouths, but only what is helpful for building others up according to their needs, that it may benefit those who listen."* (Eph. 4:29 NIV) You cannot build him up if your words are destructive. Kindness and gentleness soften truth without compromising it.

The right path, the path that Jesus would have us walk, always has a ditch on each side. In the area of communication, the ditch on one side is clamming up and shutting down communication. The ditch on the other side of the path is speaking hurtful words in the guise of communicating. The right path is *"speaking the truth in love."*

If you are by nature one who shies away from conflict, you probably will have to work on speaking up before anger clouds your judgment and you explode or grow bitter. If your natural tendency is to be too outspoken and demanding, you will likely need to work on your listening skills and on softening your words with kindness and consideration.

Another word of warning: When we do decide to repent and change our past behavior, there is a tempting tendency to cross the path and run down to the other ditch. That is, if you realize that your communication has been too harsh, you may be tempted to shut down altogether to avoid saying too much. If you realize that you have allowed bitterness to grow in your heart because of undiscussed problems, however, you may be tempted to attack in the name of communication. Be quick to turn back toward the path when you see that you are "over-correcting," but don't return to your original ditch.

Here's one reason that expecting your husband to know what you want (without your telling him) will not work: You and your husband do not think alike. This is due partly to the differences between men and women. They do *not* think alike. No two people

Here Comes the Bride

explain feelings in exactly the same way, but this is especially true in communication between men and women.

To avoid misunderstandings, it's sometimes helpful to repeat the thought to him using your own words. "I think you are saying ___. Is that what you mean?" "Do you mean ___?" "Are you saying ___?" If you have misunderstood, he can rephrase what he has said. Sometimes he may be shocked to think that you could interpret his words in the way you did. Rephrasing to clarify meaning will make it more likely that the two of you are on the same wavelength. This is especially helpful if the issue at hand is important or if it is something about which you strongly disagree.

Suppose *he* seems to misunderstand what *you* have said. It would probably be a good idea to recognize the possibility that you have not communicated your thoughts well. If he seems not to understand your train of thought, try saying it in different words.

I once heard a woman say that little girls talk, but little boys make noise. I found that this was often true when my children were small. Our daughter was a real chatterbox from a very early age. When she played with her dolls, I could hear the conversation that she pretended was occurring. It was easy to follow her story line.

Our son at that age—although he also talked early—could perfectly imitate the sounds made by a helicopter or a motorcycle, and frequently did. Listening to him as he pretended a story involving his G.I. Joe figures or toy cars meant that I heard as many sound effects as words. Unless I was nearby and could see the action, I had no idea what he was pretending.

The gender differences in conversation continue into adulthood, but they spread to involve how the man or the woman views communication. A man will usually see dialogue as a means to give his wife some information or to solve a problem. Conversely, a wife will likely see the same discussion as a means to express her feelings to her spouse and to share her life with him.

These contrasting views exist because God made men and women to be different from each other. The men need facts and information to be leaders, problem solvers, protectors, and providers. The women need the emotional communication to be nurturers and to feel loved.

The wise couple will not see these differences as a hindrance, but will embrace them as that which makes the two spouses to be one whole. A husband and wife should not only *compliment* one another but also *complement* each other; that is, they should complete each other.

Years ago, I heard a man say that if he asked his neighbor where he bought his lawnmower, the neighbor would tell him where he purchased it. If he asked his wife where she bought the steak, on the other hand, she would ask, "Is it tough? Is something wrong with the meat?" That's because his words are information-oriented, while hers are often emotion-oriented. We wives should try to remember that our husbands' questions and comments might not be complaints.

Presumption and defensiveness can also present real problems in communication. When I was a new bride, I was an inexperienced cook who burned the dinner more often than I do today. Now, I don't remember a single occasion that Charles actually complained about my cooking in all the years that we have been married. Nevertheless, I would get upset with myself if I scorched the potatoes in the early days of our marriage.

I would begin thinking to myself, "Charles won't like this food." Then I would start a conversation with him in my mind, defending myself for my cooking mistake. I would think what I would say to him when he complained about the food, then what he would reply to that, then how I could respond to his reply. By the time he came home from work, I had already had an argument with him in my mind—and I was angry. Poor Charles had no idea why he came home to an irate wife! It would have been helpful if I'd waited for an actual complaint before I began to argue.

Often when a woman tells her husband about some huge problem (like a serious illness or a major unkindness that has been done to her by a friend) he will be overwhelmed because it is something that he cannot fix. He is the protector, and he feels compelled to handle any problem.

In all likelihood, however, she really doesn't *expect* him to fix that. She probably isn't asking for advice. She wants him to listen, to care about her pain, and to hold her in his arms. She wants him to make her feel loved and cherished and comforted. Because he speaks Man and she speaks Woman, this can be a bit of a problem in communication. In a case like this, reassure your husband of what you really need.

On the other hand, we wives may need to put a limit on *how often* we tell our husbands what we want, at least when it involves telling them the same thing over and over. A woman may think, "He always forgets what I ask him to do, so I have to keep reminding him time and again." A husband, on the other hand, may think, "She nags me." A woman tends to presume that if her husband hasn't done what she asked, that he needs prodding. I remind you (and myself!) to avoid nagging.

*"A constant dripping on a day of steady rain
And a contentious woman are alike."* (Prov. 27:15)

That verse always reminds me of a dripping faucet when I'm trying to go to sleep, or maybe of Chinese water torture. Because a man by his very nature fears being dominated by a woman, he will usually resent (and probably resist) nagging. Even if he abdicates and gives in to the haranguing, he will believe that she doesn't respect him.

Since discussing issues and resolving problems in our marriages are so important, we need to acquaint ourselves with how to do it in a godly manner. Just as nations follow rules of engagement when their armies go to war, we need rules of engagement for handling the battles in our marriages.

The Enemy

One of the rules of engagement that the U.S. Army follows in times of conflict is this: Always defend yourself and friendly forces from attack. In other words, a soldier must protect himself and his fellow soldiers from the damage the enemy wishes to inflict.

Before an army can be expected to fight a war, it must first be able to *recognize* its enemy. This is what makes fighting guerilla warfare so difficult. Terrorists' methods make it nearly impossible to know whether a person is a threat to you or not. So also in your marriage battles, you need to identify the enemy—and it is not your husband!

"For our struggle is not against flesh and blood, but against the rulers, against the powers, against the world forces of this darkness, against the spiritual forces of wickedness in the heavenly places." (Eph. 6:12)

The adversary that you face in marital conflicts is the same enemy who opposes you in every arena of your life—Satan—and he is aided by the hordes of spirits who follow him. The devil's goal is to devastate you and to destroy your marriage. He would like for you to attach the "enemy" label to your husband as one means of accomplishing his evil objective, but you must remind yourself that the devil is the real foe in your marital skirmishes.

In order to protect your marriage, you and your husband need to be on the same team. If you turn on each other, your marriage will suffer. Jesus said, *"Every kingdom divided against itself will be ruined, and every city or household divided against itself will not stand."* (Matt. 12:25 NIV)

The United States Army grants to its soldiers the right of self-defense and the right to respond to hostile intent toward themselves, their comrades, or the civilian population. Our true enemy has made clear his intention toward each of us and toward our marriages. We *must* return fire.

Avoid Friendly Fire and Collateral Damage

Next, soldiers are to avoid friendly fire and collateral damage. This rule of engagement means that the soldier must be alert to avoiding injury to his comrade-in-arms with friendly fire (accidentally wounding him).

When we are in the midst of a conflict resolution in our homes, it's vital that we remind ourselves of the identity of our enemy so that we can stand together with our husbands and protect each other from the devil's schemes. Our true adversary is treacherous, and he will attempt to use us to do his bidding and accomplish his ends: wounding our mates and (ultimately) destroying our marriages.

How can we resolve the conflict while avoiding injury to our husbands? Remember that it isn't necessary to be unkind in order to express our concerns. The Bible tells us that *everything* that we do should be done in love, and that love is kind. (1 Cor. 16:14, 13:4) While it's important to bring problems to the light and discuss them in order to resolve them, it is equally essential to guard our words to protect the one we love.

Words that are motivated by anger (instead of a desire to bring righteousness to the household and to find wisdom for the problem at hand) will do harm rather than good, *"...for the anger of man does not achieve the righteousness of God."* (Jas. 1:20)

Our tongues can be weapons aimed at our husbands, but we must guard against that.

"There is one who speaks rashly like the thrusts of a sword,
But the tongue of the wise brings healing." (Prov. 12:18)
"With his mouth the godless man destroys his neighbor..." (Prov. 11:9)

We don't want to be like the godless person. We don't want to aim our weapons at our husbands. We want to bring healing to our marriages.

If you hurl angry accusations at your husband, he will likely respond in one of two ways:

- Perhaps he will become defensive and entrenched in his position.
- Perhaps he will agree with you and get down on himself because of guilt.

Neither of these is desirable. The first encourages him to cling stubbornly to his previous stance even if he's wrong, and the problem will not be solved. The second is destructive to your husband, throwing him into depression or despair. He might give in to your position because of guilt, but the problem will not permanently be resolved.

To avoid these undesirable results, make sure that your weapons are aimed at the *problem*, not at your husband. Work *together* with your mate to eliminate the difficulty. Remember: You are on the same side of this war! The Bible says that Satan is the accuser of the brethren. (Rev. 12:10) We don't want to join the enemy in his evil activity.

What is your goal for the argument? What do you hope to accomplish? Do you really want the best answer to the problem you are discussing? Do you really want what is best for your family? Or do you just want your way? Remember that we must discuss our problems in love. The Bible says that love doesn't seek its own way. (1 Cor. 13:5) I fear that sometimes we find ourselves arguing for our own opinion or preference, whether or not it is the best answer.

The Bible says,
"A fool does not delight in understanding,
But only in revealing his own mind." (Prov. 18:2)
Since the Lord is checking our motives, we would do well to examine them ourselves.
"All the ways of a man are clean in his own sight,
But the LORD weighs the motives." (Prov. 16:2)
If you are really right about the issue at hand, you can be more persuasive with kind words than with harsh ones.
"Through patience a ruler can be persuaded,
and a gentle tongue can break a bone." (Prov. 25:15 NIV)
"The wise in heart will be called understanding,
And sweetness of speech increases persuasiveness...
The heart of the wise instructs his mouth
And adds persuasiveness to his lips." (Prov. 16:21, 23)
Although I cannot guarantee that your sweet words will persuade your husband to see things your way, I *can* tell you that you will be *more likely* to be persuasive that way.

Furthermore, humility demands that you consider the possibility that your husband is right and you are wrong. The wise woman allows her heart, influenced by the Spirit of God, to instruct her mouth instead of allowing her flesh to reign there.

I have known some women who made requests of their husbands in very sweet voices, but the requests were in reality veiled demands. If you are going to go ballistic in the event that he doesn't go along with your idea, your sweetness is really hypocrisy. You aren't requesting in that case; rather, you are demanding.

Inappropriate Weapons

Another Army rule of engagement is this: "Use the minimum level of force."

When the United States went into Afghanistan and Iraq several years ago, we had some plans about what kinds of weapons we would and would not use, and on whom. It was predetermined that we would not use weapons of mass destruction (nuclear, biological, or chemical weapons) because these would assault the general population instead of attacking only the enemy armies.

Not only must we guard against friendly fire (injuring our husbands) but we must be careful to avoid collateral damage as well. In Iraq, our enemy was not the Iraqi people in general, but Saddam and those loyal to him and fighting for him. We tried to deal gently with the general population and to win their hearts. We didn't want to injure innocent bystanders.

Your children are in the battle zone, and they will be victims of any careless words that you hurl toward your husband. I urge you not to argue about emotional issues in their presence, for the little ones will be wounded with deep insecurity that will follow them even into adulthood.

For that matter, I would advise you to avoid arguing in front of *any* audience, so that you do not disgrace your husband in the minds of your listeners.

It's really important that when you decide that you must air a complaint to your husband, you take care to do it privately. The Bible instructs us as to how we should let people know when they have hurt or offended us. *"If your brother sins, go and show him his fault **in private**..."* (Matt. 18:15, emphasis mine)

When Charles and I were newlyweds, I was usually afraid to tell him what I didn't like about something he did. This hesitance was because of my own insecurities about conflict, not because of anything that Charles had done to intimidate me. Nevertheless, these unpleasant thoughts about something that Charles did or said (or at least my perceptions of those incidents) didn't just go away. When other people were with us, I found the courage to rehearse what I considered his shortcomings because I knew that strong conflict was less likely when others were present.

Finally one day when we were alone, my husband asked me to please stop talking about problems in the hearing of other people. I now know what I did not know then, that men desperately need the honor of their wives, *particularly* in the presence of others. Publicly advertising his shortcomings will humiliate your husband. You want to honor him, not shame him.

"An excellent wife is the crown of her husband,
But she who shames him is like rottenness in his bones."
(Prov. 12:4)

Obviously, if the two of you go to someone for counsel about a problem, you will both need to talk about what is wrong; otherwise the third party could not help you. What I want to convey here is that it is harmful to your marriage if you complain about his faults in social settings with friends or relatives.

The goal of the Army is to use the minimum level of force that is required to eliminate the threat. In the same way, we must decide that certain weapons are not acceptable when we are attempting to resolve conflict in our marriages. It's vital that we choose weapons that thwart the purposes of hell's forces and spare our families. We should also avoid using weapons that don't work properly—that don't help us to come to the godly result in our disagreements. We must be certain that any weapon we use attacks the problem and not our husbands. We don't want to launch any "misguided missiles" that will strike our mates or our families.

When a respectful wife disagrees with her husband, she attacks the *problem* instead of attacking *him*. Her words must always aim at resolving the problem rather than wounding her husband or getting even. Her approach is, "Have you considered this?" or "Let me explain my thinking." She might say, "Your words were unkind." If she is to be an excellent wife, however, she will never scream, "I don't know why I married you. You're worthless. I hate you."

If she thinks he is too tight with the money, she may appeal to him. Perhaps she would ask, "Can you help me make a new budget? I can't seem to stretch the household money enough to last through the pay period." This demonstrates a problem that the two of them will attack together. It would be decidedly unhealthy to the relationship if she were to say, "You're a cheap, tight-fisted tyrant," or "I don't know why I couldn't have married a man who could make me a decent living." "I don't think that's a wise course of action" attacks the problem. "You're a jerk!" attacks the person.

The closer the relationship, the greater the capacity to injure. For example, if a stranger says something horribly unkind to you on the street, you may become irritated; but it won't really hurt you. If your closest woman friend says that same thing, it wounds you deeply. If your spouse says it, you are devastated and heartbroken.

As a wife, you know where your husband is the most vulnerable; and he values your respect more than anyone else's opinion. Therefore, you can hurt him more than anyone else could. Be on guard to use only the right weapons and to aim them properly.

What are the weapons to avoid in our conflicts?

History: One banned weapon is "history." Don't bring up past mistakes when you are discussing the current problem. If the past error was resolved, it must be dropped completely. If it has not been resolved, you should save it for another occasion. When you are discussing the toothpaste he leaves in the sink, don't bring up your desire for him to spend more time with you and the children. In a discussion about money problems, don't bring up the clothes that don't make it to the hamper. You can solve only one problem at a time.

Volume and Angry Words: Another weapon we should avoid is "volume." Don't yell. A man of my acquaintance once said that his wife thought that if he disagreed with her, it must mean that he surely didn't hear what she said—so she said it louder. Ladies, it's thoroughly possible for your husband to hear and understand every word that you have spoken and still disagree with you.

Perhaps you are thinking, "Well, he started the angry, harsh words—not me. I just responded in kind." Remember the words of the wise man:

"A gentle answer turns away wrath,
But a harsh word stirs up anger." (Prov. 15:1)

The best way to cool a hot situation is to respond to his angry words with quiet, gentle ones.

Another common remark is, "Well, I couldn't help speaking harshly. He made me mad." Ladies, the Word of God reminds you that *you* are responsible for controlling your words and actions.

"A fool always loses his temper,
But a wise man holds it back." (Prov. 29:11)

Perhaps right now you are thinking, "It's only natural that I would scream insulting words at him when I am angry." Ladies, if we are Christians, *natural* is what we do *not* want to be. *Natural* is what we do in the flesh. Listen to what the Bible says about living according to what is natural: *"The acts of the sinful nature are obvious: sexual immorality, impurity and debauchery; idolatry and witchcraft; hatred, discord, jealousy, **fits of rage**, selfish ambition, dissensions, factions and envy; drunkenness, orgies, and the like. I warn you, as I did before, that those who live like this will not inherit the kingdom of God."* (Gal 5:19-21 NIV, emphasis mine)

There are default settings on my computer. I have it set to use Times New Roman 12-point type. Unless I specifically choose another setting on a particular document, it will use that font. Times New Roman 12-point is "natural" to my computer. In the same way, the flesh (or human nature) is the default setting on people. If we do not choose to yield to the will of God, we will "do what comes naturally." That is, if we do not choose to walk in the Spirit of God, we *will* fulfill the desires of the flesh. *"But I say, walk by the Spirit, and you will not carry out the desire of the flesh."* (Gal. 5:16)

Everyone gets angry occasionally; but even in our anger, we must avoid sin. *"In your anger do not sin..."* (Eph. 4:26 NIV) *"...Everyone should be quick to listen, slow to speak, and slow to become angry."* (Jas. 1:19 NIV) Obeying that command to listen promptly, to speak unhurriedly, and to guard against swift anger will help us to avoid words that injure.

Some of the most sober words in the Bible are these: *"If anyone thinks himself to be religious, and yet does not bridle his tongue but deceives his own heart, this man's religion is worthless."* (Jas. 1:26) Women—who often are quick to talk—must take these words to heart.

In order to be sure that your words are kind when you address a big problem with your husband, I would suggest that when possible you communicate with the Lord about the issue first. Ask the Lord what *you* are doing wrong here. In most instances, both spouses need to improve in a given issue since we are all imperfect. Even if you were entirely without fault in the problem to be discussed, however, it would still be a good idea to seek the Lord's guidance on how to approach the discussion and to receive His help to avoid sinful attitudes in the argument.

You may think, "I thought you said it was important not to sweep problems under the carpet, and now you are saying I can't argue with angry words." Yes, speak the truth. Tell him how you feel and why, but do it gently and kindly.

*"Brethren, even if anyone is caught in any trespass, you who are spiritual, restore such a one **in a spirit of gentleness**; each one looking to yourself, so that you too will not be tempted."* (Gal. 6:1, emphasis mine)

Every time we speak unkindly, we display a lack of love. The Scripture says, *"...love is kind..."* (1 Cor. 13:4) Anger is never a justification for unkind speech. Too many people think that they must be the slaves of their emotions. They think that if they are upset, their wrath justifies hurtful words. "I couldn't help it," they say, "because I was angry."

The apostle Paul wrote, *"BE ANGRY, AND YET DO NOT SIN; do not let the sun go down on your anger, and do not give the devil an opportunity."* (Eph. 4:26-27) The NIV says, *"In your anger do not sin: Do not let the sun go down while you are still angry, and do not give the devil a foothold."* The Greek word that is rendered *opportunity* in the NASU and is translated as *foothold* in the NIV literally means *a spot, a place,* or *a location.* It is also a word used to refer to a scabbard, a sheath for the blade of a sword. It's the same Greek word that was used for the place to put a sword in Matt. 26:52.

If you allow your anger to lead you into sinful words or behavior, you are giving the devil a scabbard. When you permit your anger to linger, you will give Satan a place to conceal his sword. It allows him to keep his weapon in readiness to attack both you and your husband.

Now you might think on one occasion, "It's almost sundown, so I must forgive quickly," and another time think, "It's only 8 o'clock in the morning. I can keep my wrath all day." That's not the point, ladies. The apostle is warning us about the importance of forgiving *quickly*. More on this in a later chapter.

Ridicule: Closely related to angry words are words of ridicule. I strongly urge you to ban this weapon, for its only result will be to wreak destruction in your husband. It will actually aid and abet your enemy, the devil, in destroying your husband's self-confidence and his assurance that you love and respect him. Name-calling often falls into this category. Ban ridicule from your war zone.

Violence: Never use the weapon of violence on your husband. I really shouldn't have to say that to Christian women, but I have actually known Christian women who used this weapon against their husbands. Banning this weapon means that you *never* slap your husband, pour something on him, or throw something at him. You *never* scratch him with your fingernails or gouge him with some object. The weapon of violence in a marriage will always attack your husband instead of the problem, and it has no place in the conflicts in Christian marriages. Even if you know that you are not going to actually physically hurt him, striking him will humiliate him and tempt him to sin.

Threatening Divorce: This is the equivalent of a nuclear bomb. Satan loves divorce, and he loves to hear this threat. The Bible says in Mal. 2:16 that God *hates* divorce, so naturally His adversary would promote it.

Divorce and remarriage are acceptable in very limited circumstances, according to the Word of God. *"And I say to you, whoever divorces his wife, except for immorality, and marries another woman commits adultery."* (Matt. 19:9) Don't make this as an idle threat simply because you are angry and want to hurt your husband. Don't say it to scare him into doing what you want. This weapon doesn't belong in your arsenal. We will discuss this more thoroughly in another chapter.

Appropriate weapons

Then what weapons shall we use? We must select weapons that will defeat our true enemy. Our desire must be for godliness in our marriages, so our weapons must be those that drive out *un*godliness.

Taking thoughts captive: One of the most important weapons that we have is the weapon of taking captive our thoughts. *"For though we walk in the flesh, we do not war according to the flesh, for the weapons of our warfare are not of the flesh, but divinely powerful for the destruction of fortresses. We are destroying speculations and every lofty thing raised up against the knowledge of God, and we are taking every thought captive to the obedience of Christ…"* (2 Cor. 10:3-5)

Our natural tendency is to allow our thoughts to drift wherever they may go, believing that we cannot do otherwise. The Bible teaches, however, that we can and must control our thoughts in order to defeat the enemy's schemes. When we do not choose to capture our thoughts and bring them to obedience, the flesh *will* control them. Allowing our thoughts to skim along uncontrolled means that they will roll toward the low place.

Paul teaches us that we are to avoid dwelling on certain thoughts and to choose to meditate on others. *"Finally, brethren, whatever is true, whatever is honorable, whatever is right, whatever is pure, whatever is lovely, whatever is of good repute, if there is any excellence and if anything worthy of praise, dwell on these things."* (Phil. 4:8)

When you dwell on thoughts critical of your husband, you develop a critical *attitude* toward him. This will decrease your love and esteem for him.

Matthew 12:36-37 tells us a serious reason why it's important to choose our words wisely. We will be judged by our words.

Have you ever said something that you regretted and then asked yourself, "Why did I *say* that?" In many instances, we say something we wish we hadn't because we have been thinking those words over and over. If you take captive your thoughts, it will be easier to restrain your words. To avoid wrong speech, therefore, remember that thought-control helps with word-control.

Sword of the Spirit: The next weapon is the sword of the Spirit, which is the Word of God. The armor of God includes this offensive weapon to defeat our devilish foe. *"Therefore, take up the full armor of God, so that you will be able to resist in the evil day, and having* *done everything, to stand firm...And take...the sword of the Spirit, which is the word of God."* (Eph. 6:13, 17)

Even Jesus used this weapon in His battle with temptation. (Matt. 4:1-11) Using this sword against the devil and his hordes will defeat their purposes and drive them away for a season. Speaking the words of Scripture to yourself (and to your husband in a non-accusatory manner) will help the two of you to set your priorities in the marriage and to come to a righteous decision in the problem at hand.

Now there's a prerequisite to using the sword of the Spirit: You must first know what it says. How can you wield these holy words against the enemy if you don't know what the applicable words are?

Thus you must set aside time for regular Bible study. You will not be equipped with this sword merely by attending church and women's meetings, and you must arm yourself before the crisis comes. If you start leafing through the Bible in time of trouble, you are unlikely to find the needed passage. Even when we have read the Bible many times, we tend to forget if we haven't made Scripture study a continual practice.

Self-control: Earlier we considered the problem of allowing anger to control our words in a time of disagreement. Instead of that inappropriate weapon, we must choose to wield the weapon of self-control.

"Like a city whose walls are broken down
is a man who lacks self-control." (Prov. 25:28 NIV)

When we lack self-control, we lose the wall of protection against our enemy's attack.

I have oftentimes heard people say that they just can't control their tempers. They explain that being hot-tempered is just part of their personalities, that it is because of the way they were brought up, or that it is due to their red hair. Regardless of what weaknesses or tendencies we may have inherited because of our genes or upbringing, Christians do not have to give their tempers full reign.

"The fruit of the Spirit is...self-control..." (Gal. 5:22-23) The Holy Spirit will produce this quality in Christian people, *if* they will yield to Him and will choose to obey Him.

The excellent wife has her tongue under control:
*"She opens her mouth in wisdom,
And the teaching of kindness is on her tongue."* (Prov. 31:26)
*"A constant dripping on a day of steady rain
And a contentious woman are alike;
He who would restrain her restrains the wind,
And grasps oil with his right hand."* (Prov. 27:15-16)

A nagging and quarrelsome wife is out of control. Let us seek to be women in whom the spiritual fruit of self-control is evident. Communication is good, but we must be diligent to speak wisely and kindly. This is true even when we are upset, *"for the anger of man does not achieve the righteousness of God."* (Jas. 1:20)

Listening: One of the most difficult weapons for many women to use is the weapon of attentive listening. Too often we have the tendency to plan our next remark while our husbands are still talking.

The Bible says, *"He who gives an answer before he hears, it is folly and shame to him."* (Prov. 18:13) Therefore, a wife must avoid interrupting her husband's words to give her reply. I think, however, that it also means that she is not *forming* a response before she has really listened to and weighed his ideas. After all, how can she truly listen if her thoughts are occupied with what *she* will say? As a talker myself, I know how difficult it is to avoid this pitfall; and in fact, it is one of my most frequent failings—particularly during an emotional discussion of some disagreement.

Army units communicate via two-way radios. A microphone, in appearance and shape somewhat resembling a cordless phone, is attached to the radio with a cord. When a soldier talks, he must hold down a rectangular button on the side of the mic. He can transmit as long as this button is activated, but he cannot hear anything the person on the other end might be saying. After he finishes transmitting, the other person can activate *his* microphone; then the first soldier can listen. Only one of the soldiers can talk at a time if they want to communicate effectively. That's really true in any communication.

Tolerance: Different is not the same thing as wrong. You don't have to have the same opinion about everything. It's not always necessary to agree. If he likes hot salsa and you like mild, buy two jars.

If he likes the electric blanket set on low and you like it on high, get a dual-control blanket. If he likes to watch football and you hate it, read a book while he watches the game.

Counselors: Sometimes soldiers find themselves outnumbered, and they need to call for backup. When you find yourself overwhelmed by the enemy, don't continue to try to fight alone.

"For by wise guidance you will wage war,
And in abundance of counselors there is victory." (Prov. 24:6)
"Make plans by seeking advice;
if you wage war, obtain guidance." (Prov. 20:18 NIV)

It has been my observation that people who delay too long in getting help with their marital difficulties often reach the point that they no longer want help; they just want out. It's better to seek counsel before your hearts harden to each other.

Now, I don't recommend talking to every friend you have about the disagreements with your husband (in fact, I recommend that you do not) but sometimes you do need counsel. The natural thing to do when you are unhappy with your spouse is to tell your story to someone who will agree with you. Unfortunately, doing what comes naturally means acting in the flesh. If we want *godly* counsel, we must go to someone who knows God, who is familiar with His word, and who has a successful marriage.

Jesus said that the pupil, when fully trained, will be like his teacher. (Luke 6:40) Be sure that the people you choose to advise you are people who will give spiritual counsel. For example, don't go to your neighbor who has been divorced four times, to your sister who has a terrible relationship with her husband, or to the atheist who works with you. They will likely give you bad advice.

I would also warn you about the danger of talking to *any* man about your marital problems unless his wife or your husband is also present—preferably both. Men are drawn into affairs because of sexual attraction and the need for respect or honor, but women are looking for relationship and the feeling of being loved and cared for. When you cry on the shoulder of another man, he will have heard only your side of the story. He will likely sympathize with your position, making you feel loved and protected. Your seeking his counsel will make him feel that you respect him. This will put you both in danger of falling into sexual sin. Sometimes the Bible warns us to stand firm against sin, but of immorality it says that we should flee—run from it! (1 Cor. 6:18)

The best solution is for you and your husband to go to a couple that you trust and discuss your problems in a four-way conversation. If he is not willing to go for counsel, I encourage you to talk to a godly, trustworthy Christian woman with a successful marriage. At any rate, you should choose a counselor who is going the direction that you want to go. Look to someone with a holy life and a successful marriage to be your counselor.

Prayer: Our soldiers have night vision goggles to see at night. When we find ourselves back in darkness during an argument, we need the light shined on the situation. We need to seek direction from the Lord, for He can see in the darkness.

"If I say, 'Surely the darkness will overwhelm me,
And the light around me will be night,'
Even the darkness is not dark to You,
And the night is as bright as the day.
Darkness and light are alike to You." (Psa. 139:11-12)

Thus, we must pray and seek the Lord's guidance in the darkness. When Paul writes about our equipment for battle in Ephesians 6, he includes the instruction to pray. (Eph. 6:18)

When your marriage is in a dark place, be sure that your prayers include a request for the Lord to illuminate and reveal to you any area in which *you* are walking in darkness.

Avoid Engaging Medical Units

Another rule of engagement of the American Army is that it does not engage medical units or hospitals in the war zone. In other words, our military forces do not make a battle out of something that is meant to bring healing.

How can we apply that rule of engagement to conflict resolution in a marriage? I believe that many times women do violate this principle. Some women refuse to have sexual relations until their husbands do what the wives want. If you hold back sexual intimacy from your husband because he has displeased you in some way, you are attacking something that can bring healing in your marriage.

Besides, using sex as a weapon indicates that you are withholding forgiveness as well. Again, this makes a battle of something that is meant for healing.

Another way that women use something meant for healing as another opportunity to attack is the improper apology. Have you ever "apologized" by sarcastically saying, "Well, I'm SOR-ry!" or "Well, ex-CUSE *ME*!" Some wives "apologize" by saying, "I shouldn't have done that, but you made me *so mad!*" My sisters, none of those is an apology. That kind of "apology" is really another assault.

A true apology would be, "I'm sorry that I said, '___.' Will you forgive me?" Or, "I was wrong to do ___. Will you forgive me?"

An apology means that you take responsibility for what you have done wrong, acknowledge your fault, and ask for forgiveness. It should not be used as a means of attack or as manipulation to get your husband to apologize. The Bible says, *"Therefore, confess your sins to one another, and pray for one another so that you may be healed. The effective prayer of a righteous man can accomplish much."* (James 5:16)

Prisoners of War

Soldiers in the U.S. Army are instructed to respect and protect enemy prisoners of war. Rarely (if ever) have Americans faced an enemy who treats well our soldiers that they capture. We, however, are a people who value human life. The regulations of our military forces require that our soldiers feed our prisoners well and give them medical attention.

How does this apply to conflict resolution in the marriage? Some women are married to men who are in bondage to Satan or who do not serve the Lord. These ladies must remember to treat kindly these prisoners of the evil one. The goal should be liberation of the captives!

Jesus said that He was anointed to set free those in bondage. Listen to His words:

"The Spirit of the Lord is on me,

*because he has anointed me
to preach good news to the poor.
He has sent me to proclaim freedom for the prisoners..."* (Luke 4:18 NIV)

Let's join Him in this ministry to set the captives free.

Tending the Wounded

American soldiers are instructed to collect and treat the wounded on the battlefield. They are required to never leave their wounded fellow warriors on the battlefield to die. Instead, they must carry them to a hospital for treatment. In fact, we give medical care even to those who are the soldiers of our *enemy* as well as those who are our comrades.

Sometimes in the heat of a battle in your home, wounds will be suffered. Please resist the temptation to storm out of the house, leaving your husband injured. Be sure that you comfort and encourage him if he is hurt, even if you believe that he was serving our adversary during the argument.

"In the same way, you wives, be submissive to your own husbands so that even if any of them are disobedient to the word, they may be won without a word by the behavior of their wives, as they observe your chaste and respectful behavior. Your adornment must not be merely external—braiding the hair, and wearing gold jewelry, or putting on dresses; but let it be the hidden person of the heart, with the imperishable quality of a gentle and quiet spirit, which is precious in the sight of God." (1 Pet. 3:1-4)

We all fall into the enemy's trap sometimes. Reassure your husband of your love and soothe his wounds. Develop a gentle and quiet spirit, to which God attributes great value. Make sure that your behavior is chaste (clean, pure, and holy) and that you show respect to your husband. (Eph. 5:33)

Disagreements come up in every marriage. You must make wise choices, ladies.

You must choose, first of all, to fight. If you allow discontentment to fester, it will damage your marriage.

Secondly, you must decide to fight *against* the right enemy (Satan) and to fight *alongside* your fellow soldier (your husband). The two of you are in the same army (your marriage). The Lord provides what you need to defeat the enemy who comes against your union, but the choice whether or not to make use of God's provision is yours.

"Finally, be strong in the Lord and in the strength of His might. Put on the full armor of God, so that you will be able to stand firm against the schemes of the devil. For our struggle is not against flesh and blood, but against the rulers, against the powers, against the world forces of this darkness, against the spiritual forces of wickedness in the heavenly places. Therefore, take up the full armor of God, so that you will be able to resist in the evil day, and having done everything, to stand firm." (Eph. 6:10-13)

A Forgiving Heart

✽✽✽

Let's face it: Spouses are going to disagree, and we discussed in the previous chapter the ways to deal with those differences. Holding grievances would be a terrible way to deal with problems in a marriage. Communication is vital.

Although we should always aim to avoid it, sometimes during those discussions words will be spoken that cause hurt feelings. At other times, a husband will do some thoughtless thing or make an unwise decision that hurts his wife. How should we as wives deal with such situations?

In the previous chapter, we considered appropriate and inappropriate weapons to wield in our marital battles. Perhaps your husband has used an improper weapon in your arguments. Maybe he has yelled at you or ridiculed you. Or perhaps he has sinned against you in some way that has caused the argument in the first place. Does this entitle you to use improper weapons against him? No. The Word of God does not permit us to take revenge.

"Do not say, 'I'll do to him as he has done to me;
I'll pay that man back for what he did.'" (Prov. 24:29 NIV)

Forgiveness is an appropriate response when your husband sins against you. Forgiveness is sometimes difficult, but it's a very important weapon. It disarms your true enemy in his plan to bring division in your home through the sin committed against you.

Besides, Jesus said, *"For if you forgive others for their transgressions, your heavenly Father will also forgive you. But if you do not forgive others, then your Father will not forgive your transgressions."* (Matt. 6:14-15) These are very serious words.

Our heavenly Bridegroom is in every way perfect, so He never needs our forgiveness. He is always right. Our husbands, however, are imperfect and do need our forgiveness.

Moreover, we had to *receive* pardon for our many sins before we could become a part of the bride of Christ. Having entered that relationship with our gracious Groom, we daily need His kind and merciful cleansing as we sin again and again. The hardness of our hearts grieves Jesus. (See Mark 3:5.) Like His people in the Old Testament, we hurt Him with our sins.

"How often they rebelled against Him in the wilderness
*And **grieved Him** in the desert!*
Again and again they tempted God,
*And **pained the Holy One** of Israel."* (Psa. 78:40-41, emphasis mine)

Furthermore, we need repeated mercy from our individual earthly husbands for our failures toward them. I once heard a preacher say that a great marriage is a union of two good forgivers. The reason that is true is that all husbands and wives do things that need forgiving. Every wife sins against her husband, and the husbands all sin against their wives.

Forgiveness is one of the primary themes of the Bible, yet many people struggle with what forgiveness really is.

What Forgiveness Is Not

First, before we talk about what forgiveness *is*, let us establish what forgiveness is *not*.

Forgiveness does *not* mean that what he did was okay. If he did nothing wrong, there is nothing to forgive.

When I receive forgiveness from the heavenly Bridegroom, it isn't because He thinks my sin was no big deal. What does He think of our transgressions?

*"There are six things which the LORD **hates**,*
*Yes, seven which are **an abomination** to Him:*
Haughty eyes, a lying tongue,

And hands that shed innocent blood,
A heart that devises wicked plans,
Feet that run rapidly to evil,
A false witness who utters lies,
And one who spreads strife among brothers." (Prov. 6:16-19, emphasis mine)

"Do you not know that the wicked will not inherit the kingdom of God? Do not be deceived: Neither the sexually immoral nor idolaters nor adulterers nor male prostitutes nor homosexual offenders nor thieves nor the greedy nor drunkards nor slanderers nor swindlers will inherit the kingdom of God." (1 Cor. 6:9-10 NIV)

"Now the deeds of the flesh are evident, which are: immorality, impurity, sensuality, idolatry, sorcery, enmities, strife, jealousy, outbursts of anger, disputes, dissensions, factions, envying, drunkenness, carousing, and things like these, of which I forewarn you, just as I have forewarned you, that those who practice such things will not inherit the kingdom of God." (Gal. 5:19-21)

"For the wages of sin is death, but the free gift of God is eternal life in Christ Jesus our Lord." (Rom. 6:23)

The Lord *hates* sin. Our sins cause Him anguish, grief, and pain. In fact, our sins are so heinous that they are all capital offenses; but He loves us so much that He prepared a plan to take our punishment Himself and to provide forgiveness to us.

Likewise, we must provide forgiveness when our husbands hurt us.

Next, forgiveness does *not* mean that the memory of the hurt is gone. "Forgive and forget," we hear so often. "If you haven't forgotten, then you haven't forgiven." Is that true?

Suppose a woman becomes involved with another man. Does her husband have to forget that she was unfaithful in order to forgive her? Or maybe the husband has struck his wife and broken her nose. Does forgiving him mean that she doesn't remember what he has done? Of course not! These are huge offenses. It's lunacy to think these things could be forgotten.

Moreover, forgiveness is *not* a warm, fuzzy feeling. Feelings are unreliable, but forgiveness is a choice you must make. If you wait for the feelings, you may never forgive. The choice to forgive is the locomotive; the feelings are the caboose. You will probably start feeling better after you forgive, but feelings are not a prerequisite to offering forgiveness.

Finally, forgiveness does *not* always mean that everything is as it was before. Sometimes there are consequences even after forgiveness. The person who has abused drugs or alcohol may sustain liver damage. God forgives him when he repents, but his body may still suffer.

Trust is destroyed by certain sins against a spouse (especially if the sin is a serious betrayal or if it is the repetitious commission of an especially hurtful sin) and restoring trust requires that the injured spouse see right behavior over time. Forgiveness is a gift; trust, however, may need to be re-earned.

What Forgiveness Is

The Lord, our heavenly Bridegroom, has set for us the example of forgiveness. He has shown us how to do it. God said,

"I, even I, am the one who wipes out your transgressions for My own sake,

And I will not remember your sins." (Isa. 43:25)

"Their sins and lawless acts

I will remember no more." (Heb. 10:17 NIV)

Some would ask, "Does that not mean that when the Lord forgives, He also forgets?" I think not. If God forgets, then there is something that He doesn't know. The Bible teaches that He knows everything:

"And there is no creature hidden from His sight, but all things are open and laid bare to the eyes of Him with whom we have to do." (Heb. 4:13)

"...For God is greater than our hearts, and he knows everything." (1 John 3:20 NIV)

When the Bible tells us that God no longer remembers the sin of the penitent one, it means that He no longer remembers the sin *against the sinner.* When He forgives me, the sin is no longer charged to my account.

"Blessed is the man

whose sin the LORD does not count against him..." (Psa. 32:2 NIV)

Thus, if you are to follow His example when you forgive your spouse, you will no longer remember the sin *against your husband*. In today's vernacular, we might say, "I don't hold it against him."

Indeed, love demands that you refrain from holding ill will about your husband's wrongdoing. *"Love...keeps no record of wrongs."* (1 Cor. 13:4-5 NIV) Another rendering of that passage says that love does not hold grudges. (TLB)

You see, forgiveness is a sign of love. It demonstrates that you love the one who has sinned against you. *"...(Y)ou should rather forgive and comfort him, otherwise such a one might be overwhelmed by excessive sorrow. Wherefore I urge you to reaffirm your love for him."* (2 Cor. 2:7-8) While forgiveness doesn't mean that the hurt is gone, it does mean that the resentment is gone.

Necessity of Forgiveness

You might ask, "How can I do that? How can I forgive him when he hurt me so badly?" Or maybe you would even say, "I *can't* forgive!" I have even heard women make such remarks over very trivial offenses by their husbands.

Have you suffered greater injustice than what Jesus endured on the cross? Certainly not! Yet He prayed this way about those who sinned against Him: *"Father, forgive them; for they do not know what they are doing..."* (Luke 23:34)

You may be thinking, "Yeah, but that was Jesus. He's the divine Son of God. I'm only human, and I can't do that."

On the contrary, the Bible instructs us to follow His example. *"Be kind to one another, tender-hearted, forgiving each other, **just as God in Christ also has forgiven you**."* (Eph. 4:32, emphasis mine) We are to forgive in the same way that the Lord has forgiven us.

When Jesus taught us to pray, He said that we should pray this way: *"Forgive us our sins, for we also forgive everyone who sins against us..."* (Luke 11:4 NIV) Then He added, *"For if you forgive men when they sin against you, your heavenly Father will also forgive you. But **if you do not forgive men their sins, your Father will*** *not forgive your sins."* (Matt. 6:14-15 NIV, emphasis mine) Ladies, those are strong words. You are in extreme peril if you refuse to forgive.

Do you think that's too hard? Do you think that Jesus could do it because He was the Son of God but it's too hard for us?

Stephen followed Jesus' example. When he was being martyred, he said, *"Lord, do not hold this sin against them!"* (Acts 7:60) Stephen forgave.

Would Jesus command us to do something that we could not choose to do? I'm not saying that it's easy (it definitely is not) but we can do it. If we were unable to offer forgiveness, would He say that we couldn't receive His pardon until we forgave others? He is not an unjust judge. He requires only what He empowers us to do.

When you find yourself saying, "I can't forgive," you are repeating what the enemy is telling you. Unforgiveness gives the advantage to Satan. *"But one whom you forgive anything, I forgive also; for indeed what I have forgiven, if I have forgiven anything, I did it for your sakes in the presence of Christ, **so that no advantage would be taken of us by Satan**, for we are not ignorant of his schemes."* (2 Cor. 2:10-11, emphasis mine)

You *can* forgive! When the forces of darkness bring the temptation to unforgiveness, you can remind the adversary of what the Bible says: *"No temptation has seized you except what is common to man. And God is faithful; he will not let you be tempted beyond what you can bear. But when you are tempted, he will also provide a way out so that you can stand up under it."* (1 Cor. 10:13 NIV)

Or perhaps you are thinking, "Well, I have forgiven him a dozen times for that same offense. He continually says that he won't do it again, but it remains his regular habit." Perhaps he has repeatedly used sarcastic, hurtful words to you or he has chronically shown a lack of punctuality. Maybe he has continued to create work for you by scattering newspapers all over the place or forgetting the dirty dishes he left drying out in the den.

Does that sound like what you have done to your divine Bridegroom? Have you found that you have committed the same sin over and over again? Are you grateful that the Lord continued to offer forgiveness to you as you repented?

For that matter, aren't there also certain failings toward your *husband* that *you* have repeated many times? We need to be honest with ourselves about these things, because humility requires us to avoid justifying our own failures.

Peter asked Jesus one day about how many times he must forgive someone. *"Then Peter came and said to Him, 'Lord, how often shall my brother sin against me and I forgive him? Up to seven times?'"* Listen carefully to Jesus' answer: *"I do not say to you, up to seven times, but up to seventy times seven."* (Matt. 18:21-22)

Now, Peter probably thought that he was being exceptionally generous and gracious when he offered to forgive seven times. Jesus didn't think that was adequate, however. He indicated that Peter should forgive *490 times!* I suspect that if we try to do that, we will likely lose count, and that is probably the idea.

Breaking out of Prison

Unforgiveness creates bitterness; and when someone is bitter, she becomes her own jailer. She imprisons *herself* with bitterness. Unforgiveness often causes more pain to the person who doesn't forgive than to the person who is unforgiven.

In Matt. 18:23-26, Jesus told the story about a king who decided to settle accounts with slaves who owed him money. One of these men owed the king ten thousand talents, an incredibly vast fortune. The margin of my Bible says that *one* talent was worth more than fifteen years' wages for a laborer. (NASU) It follows, then, that ten thousand talents would be the equivalent of more than *fifteen years'* wages for *ten thousand laborers!*

The man obviously didn't have the means to repay the debt; he was a servant, after all. Some scholars indicate that the slave in this case was likely a satrap or steward who had access to the king's assets. (Wycliffe)

The king ordered that the slave and his family be sold so that repayment could be made, although even that would not have come near to repaying the debt. The slave fell down before the king and begged for patience, telling the king that he would repay all that he owed. The monarch, knowing that it was not possible for the man to repay, was compassionate and merciful toward the man. He forgave the whole debt.

Jesus went on to say that the forgiven slave then left the king's presence and came across one of his fellow slaves. This second slave owed 100 denarii to the first slave, equivalent to *100 days'* wages for *a single laborer*. (Compare Matt. 20:2.) This debt amounting to a worker's earnings for only a few months perhaps could have been repaid eventually, although it may have taken a while. Nonetheless, the forgiven slave seized the man who owed him money and began to choke him. He demanded that his fellow slave pay back the debt.

Listen to Jesus tell the remainder of the story:

"So his fellow slave fell to the ground and began to plead with him, saying, 'Have patience with me and I will repay you.'

"But he was unwilling and went and threw him in prison until he should pay back what was owed. So when his fellow slaves saw what had happened, they were deeply grieved and came and reported to their lord all that had happened.

"Then summoning him, his lord said to him, 'You wicked slave, I forgave you all that debt because you pleaded with me. Should you not also have had mercy on your fellow slave, in the same way that I had mercy on you?'

"And his lord, moved with anger, handed him over to the torturers until he should repay all that was owed him. My heavenly Father will also do the same to you, if each of you does not forgive his brother from your heart." (Matt. 18:29-35)

The forgiven slave owed an enormous debt. There was no way that he, a slave himself, could ever hope to pay back that huge sum. We are like that forgiven slave. There is no way that we could ever repay the debt for our great sin against God. The slave who owed his fellow slave 100 denarii was like the person who sins against us. I believe that Jesus used these monetary amounts (10,000 talents and 100 denarii) to demonstrate that the debt of which we have been forgiven is far beyond comprehension. Anything that someone does to us is a pittance by comparison.

Here Comes the Bride

I want you to notice that according to this parable, we make ourselves vulnerable to the torturers if we refuse to forgive. The prison of unforgiveness is a place of torture.

Several years ago, I was having trouble forgiving an adult friend who had done something hurtful to my teenage son. The Lord sometimes speaks to me in dreams, and I had such a dream during that time. I would like to share with you some excerpts from my journal following that dream:

"Last night I dreamt that I needed to go a considerable distance down a long street. Although I had a car, I decided to walk...I hurried along the deserted street toward my destination, occasionally glancing into the adjoining lawns...I soon noticed that the sun was beginning to set. I chastised myself for choosing not to drive the car, for about half of my journey still lay before me. As the light slipped away, I uneasily noticed some ruffians standing near one of the houses and watching me pass them. Fear began to grip and overcome me as the darkness increased and I perceived that they intended to harm me."

When I awoke, the Lord began to interpret the dream to me. Listen to words from the remaining entry in my journal:

"The trip down the long street was something I really did need to do. This represented [dealing with the offense]. However, as the Lord had provided me with an automobile and I chose not to take it, so also He has provided a way to deal with hurts and disappointments in a relationship...Instead of following the Father's instructions, however, I responded in my flesh with anger and unforgiveness...I continued this way as the light began to fade and I began to walk in darkness. The thugs that I saw watching me and making ready to destroy me are spoken of in Scripture. *'Do not let the sun go down on your anger, and do not give the devil an opportunity.'* (Eph. 4:26-27)"

I went on in my journal to recount the parable of the unmerciful slave in which the person who refuses to forgive is vulnerable to the torturers, and to say that I believed that these represented demonic attack against the unforgiving one.

Remember that the Greek word rendered *opportunity* in Eph. 4:27 is a word that is sometimes used for a scabbard, a sheath for the blade of a sword. Ladies, it is in your own best interest to forgive, for you lock up your heart in sorrow when you decline to do so. Retaining your anger and refusing to forgive creates a stronghold for the enemy in your life and a place for him to keep his weapon in readiness to use against you and against your marriage.

Setting the Captive Free

Not only do you find yourself set free when you forgive, but you also release your husband from a prison when you forgive him. By forgiving your husband, you free him from the debt caused by his sin against you.

Unforgiveness is a method of getting revenge—of repaying him or punishing him for what he has done. When we do this, we usurp God's place.

"Never pay back evil for evil to anyone. Respect what is right in the sight of all men. If possible, so far as it depends on you, be at peace with all men. Never take your own revenge, beloved, but leave room for the wrath of God, for it is written, 'VENGEANCE IS MINE, I WILL REPAY,' says the Lord." (Rom. 12:17-19)

We must not seek revenge. Rather, Jesus has told us that we should treat our husbands in the same way we want to be treated. (Matt. 7:12) Do you want forgiveness when you mess up? Then forgive your husband when *he* errs. Do you want mercy when you sin? Then offer mercy, *"For judgment will be merciless to one who has shown no mercy; mercy triumphs over judgment."* (Jas. 2:13)

Jesus said, *"Blessed are the merciful, for they shall receive mercy."* (Matt. 5:7) I believe that is true on two levels. If we want God's mercy, we need to offer mercy to others. Additionally, I have found that other *people* are usually more merciful to a person who is merciful.

In the Old Testament, Joseph's brothers committed a terrible sin against him. They threw him into a pit in the desert, sold him as a slave to some traders, and then deceived his father into believing that a wild animal had killed him.

The caravan of traders took him to Egypt and sold him as a slave to an Egyptian official named Potiphar. In time, Potiphar's wife took a fancy to Joseph. When he refused her advances, she told her husband that Joseph had come to seduce her and had fled when she screamed. This falsehood resulted in Joseph's imprisonment in the dungeon. (Gen. 37:18-36, Gen. 39:1-20)

Would you say that Joseph's brothers had wronged him? Would you say that his brothers deserved no mercy? If so, you would be right. To show mercy, according to my dictionary, means that you show compassion to an offender, to one who has done wrong. (M-W) Mercy is a gift of the one who extends it, not wages for what is earned.

Eventually, Joseph was not only released from prison, but he also became second in command after Pharaoh himself. In a time of famine, Joseph's brothers had to come to Joseph to buy food for their families.

Joseph, a godly man, chose to extend mercy to his brothers. *"...Joseph said to them, 'Do not be afraid, for am I in God's place? As for you, you meant evil against me, but God meant it for good in order to bring about this present result, to preserve many people alive. So therefore, do not be afraid; I will provide for you and your little ones.' So he comforted them and spoke kindly to them."* (Gen. 50:19-21)

Can you find it in your heart to offer merciful forgiveness to your husband, to comfort him, and to speak kindly to him when he has sinned against you? You would be wise to do so. Forgiveness restores peace and joy not only to the forgiven, but also to the forgiver.

Reconciliation

While reconciliation requires both repentance and forgiveness, you can offer forgiveness whether or not your husband receives it through his repentance. Isn't that the way God's forgiveness works? He has offered forgiveness to all people, but His offer doesn't bring about reconciliation between God and the people who refuse to repent and receive His forgiveness. If a wife is to be godly, therefore, she must offer forgiveness whether or not her husband recognizes, repents of, and confesses his sins.

Perhaps you think it's too difficult to forgive when you have not seen evidence of repentance. I confess that I also find it far easier to forgive people when they repent. Nonetheless, we must not decide how we will behave based on whether it is easier to do it that way. We can never choose what the other person will do, but we can and must choose godliness in the way that we respond to those who sin against us. The Bible exhorts us this way:

"So, as those who have been chosen of God, holy and beloved, put on a heart of compassion, kindness, humility, gentleness and patience; bearing with one another, and forgiving each other, whoever has a complaint against anyone; just as the Lord forgave you, so also should you." (Col. 3:12-13)

Receiving Forgiveness

But remember this: Your husband isn't the only one who errs. You also sin against him, and repentance is vital to the health of your marriage. If you realize that you have done wrong to him, be quick to apologize and ask for his forgiveness.

Since some people find it difficult to do this, they simply begin to be extra sweet and nice as an attempt to make up for wrongdoing. This does not truly remedy the situation.

Other wives will apologize, but they have ulterior motives. That is, they apologize for their own shortcomings with the goal of manipulating their husbands into apologizing. Sometimes such a woman will even say, "Well, I'll apologize if you apologize." Or she will say, "I'm sorry I did that, but you made me *so mad!*" Neither one of those is a true apology. Those are attacks.

If something he did angers you and you sin in your anger, first apologize for your own sin. Do not attempt to manipulate an apology from him. Such an apology from him is useless anyway. His apologies must come from a recognition that he has sinned against you. Confront him with what he has done and explain how it has hurt you. That is not to be a part of your own apology, however, and your request for forgiveness should not hinge on whether or not he apologizes.

As I said in the previous chapter, the best apology that you can offer will specifically acknowledge your own sin and also ask your spouse to express forgiveness. A person who does not think what he/she has done is wrong will often repeat the action when similar circumstances arise. Because of this, your spouse's trust will be diminished by your sin. To restore the trust, you need to acknowledge that you know your words or behavior was wrong, ask for forgiveness, *and* begin to demonstrate right behavior.

"I was wrong" are three of the most difficult words in the English language, but they are invaluable. Merely saying, "I'm sorry" may leave your spouse wondering, "Sorry for what? Sorry that you got caught? Sorry that I am hurt or angry about it? Or are you actually sorry that you did or said it?" Furthermore, knowing that you will need to confess your sin if you do it again may help you to avoid repeating the violation.

If you and your mate have not been in the practice of doing this, your husband may say something like, "Oh, that's okay," or, "Don't worry about it." I encourage you, however, to pursue his verbalized forgiveness. Try saying, "No, I must know. Will you forgive me?" Confessed sin and vocalized forgiveness put closure on a problem in a way that "I apologize," and, "Oh, that's okay," usually cannot accomplish.

We will be well served to take to heart the words of James: *"Therefore, confess your sins to one another, and pray for one another so that you may be healed..."* (Jas. 5:16)

Let us open our locked hearts and extend the liberty that giving and receiving forgiveness brings.

Fulfilling Responsibilities

❋❋❋

It seems to me that today's society places too little emphasis on fulfilling our responsibilities. People everywhere want to talk about rights, but responsibilities are greatly neglected. If we are to be excellent wives and if we are to live as our heavenly Bridegroom desires, then we will make every effort to fulfill our responsibilities.

Some people would have a wife to believe that serving her husband indicates that she is abused. Others would contend that it is legalism to consider obedience and working for the Lord as important. I am convinced that both assertions are dead wrong.

Serving the Heavenly Bridegroom

Jesus indicated that His bride has work to do, saying, *"If you love Me, you will keep My commandments."* (John 14:15) The parable of the talents and the three servants further teaches us that we are to work. (See Matt. 25:14-30.) In fact, James tells us that if our faith does not produce works, it is dead faith.

"What use is it, my brethren, if someone says he has faith but he has no works? Can that faith save him? If a brother or sister is without clothing and in need of daily food, and one of you says to them, 'Go in peace, be warmed and be filled,' and yet you do not give them what is necessary for their body, what use is that? Even so faith, if it has no works, is dead, being by itself. But someone may well say, 'You have faith and I have works; show me your faith

without the works, and I will show you my faith by my works.' You believe that God is one. You do well; the demons also believe, and shudder. But are you willing to recognize, you foolish fellow, that faith without works is useless?...For just as the body without the spirit is dead, so also faith without works is dead." (Jas. 2:14-20, 26)

The church is the household of God as well as the bride of Christ. (Eph. 2:19) The bride is to minister to His family and to others who don't yet belong to His family. *"Therefore, as we have opportunity, let us do good to all people, especially to those who belong to the family of believers."* (Gal. 6:10 NIV)

Never think that serving others is beneath you, ladies. It is work of the highest order. Remember the words of Jesus: *"The greatest among you will be your servant. For whoever exalts himself will be humbled, and whoever humbles himself will be exalted."* (Matt. 23:11-12 NIV) He illustrated this when He washed His disciples' feet, doing work that was ordinarily relegated to slaves. Then He said, *"If I then, the Lord and the Teacher, washed your feet, you also ought to wash one another's feet. For I gave you an example that you also should do as I did to you."* (John 13:14-15)

There are countless ways that we may serve the family of the Lord or those who need Christ. A young mother might need a baby-sitter while she shops for groceries. Perhaps you could help an elderly neighbor with yard work or drive her to an appointment with her doctor. A sick or bereaved friend would benefit from a hot meal delivered to her door. Someone might need help with housework after surgery. Perhaps you could take a plate of cookies and a hearty welcome to a new neighbor. The downhearted need encouragement. Students may need tutoring in a subject that comes easily to you. Perhaps you can teach a young bride to cook. Maybe you can pass along the coupons that you don't need from your Sunday newspaper. Maybe you are to lead the church women's ministry. You could cut out visuals and handwork for the teacher of a children's Sunday school class. The possibilities are limitless.

You aren't on your own here. The heavenly Bridegroom has plans for how you personally should fulfill your responsibilities to His family. *"For we are God's workmanship, created in Christ Jesus* *to do good works, **which God prepared in advance for us to do.**"* (Eph. 2:10 NIV, emphasis mine) He has given spiritual gifts to enable you to meet certain needs, and He has plans for how you should use those gifts. Are you seeking His direction to know what He wants you to do? Are you sensitive to the needs of people around you? Does your life exhibit the obedient work that your heavenly Bridegroom requires? Can He trust you to fulfill your responsibilities?

Serving Natural Husbands

Just as we are to serve our spiritual Husband and family, we are to serve our natural husbands and children as well. The twelfth verse of Proverbs 31 says of the excellent wife,
"She does him good and not evil
All the days of her life."
Thus, she will endeavor to meet her natural husband's needs in every area that she can. In order to do good to her husband, the excellent wife fulfills her responsibilities in the marriage.

What kind of responsibilities? Titus 2:3-5 instructs older women to *"...encourage the young women to love their husbands, to love their children, to be sensible, pure, workers at home, kind, being subject to their own husbands, that the word of God may not be dishonored."*

Paul is telling us that if we fail to fulfill our wifely responsibilities—if we fail to love and submit to our husbands, if we fail to be kind, if we fail to work in our homes—then we bring disgrace on the Word of God! We dishonor Him. In fact, the Greek word that Paul used here was the word from which we get our word *blaspheme*, and the King James Version translates it that way. It means *to vilify, to speak impiously,* or *to speak evil of.* The apostle is telling us that when we do not choose to obey this passage, we lead people to speak evil of the Word of God. If a Christian woman does not learn to do these things, people will blaspheme and speak evil of God's Word because of her example.

We don't want to be the cause of dishonor coming to the Bible. We don't want to give people an excuse to blaspheme. Rather, we want to bring glory to His name. *"Let your light shine before men* *in such a way that they may **see your good works**, and **glorify your Father** who is in heaven."* (Matt. 5:16, emphasis mine) The idea is not that we do these things to gain praise for ourselves, but that we do them and bring glory to God.

To fail to fulfill our responsibilities to our natural husbands is to fail to keep the commandments of our heavenly Bridegroom. The Greek word that is rendered in Tit. 2:5 as *workers at home* comes from two words: one that means *a dwelling...by implication a family*, and another that means *a guard.* Paul is saying that young women must learn to work at home, to busy themselves at home caring for and guarding the well being of their families there. In other words, it's not merely a matter of staying home—of choosing not to have a career in an office somewhere—but also of fulfilling one's responsibilities in the home. All of us have known women who were at home every day, but they neglected their children, their husbands, and their houses.

Food

The most important need that husbands meet for their wives is love. Women need to be loved more than anything else. At the risk of redundancy, I say again: Love is not the most important need that your husband has; his greatest need is respect. More than anything else, he needs for you to respect him. Without your respect he will never be happy in the marriage.

Probably his needs for love and for sex alternate at different times and eventually equal out. After respect, sex, and love, food is one of the greatest needs in your husband that you can fulfill. These four (respect, sex, love, and food) are primary needs in men. If you fulfill these responsibilities well, your husband will likely overlook a legion of other things. An excellent wife will make her husband "feel like a man." That is, she will let him know that she recognizes his strength and wisdom, that she honors his leadership, that she finds him desirable—and she will prepare meals for him.

I urge you to try to prepare the foods that your husband likes and that will preserve his health. Sometimes it's hard to do both of those if he likes the wrong things, but it is good to try. (If he is absolutely not interested in eating healthful meals and only likes the wrong things, cook something for his palate. You are his wife, not his mother.) I suggest that you vary the menu, both for health and for interest. Most people tire of eating the same thing day after day.

If, however, your husband is one of those who wants the same thing every day or prefers unhealthful foods—and you don't want to eat that way—then prepare something different for yourself. That's better than complaining about his preference for eating only a few foods. Perhaps he wants chili several nights a week. Since he doesn't mind the repetition, you could prepare a double portion and serve it for the both of you the first night. Save the remainder to serve to him later. The second night, warm up some of the chili for him, but prepare chicken salad for yourself. If he wants grilled hamburgers most nights, cook up a bunch of patties over the coals and freeze them in plastic bags, separated with double layers of wax paper. When he wants a burger, you can remove one or two patties and reheat for him. You can have something else. He will be content, and you will not be resentful.

When Charles and I were first married, he was what I considered a picky eater. There were a number of foods that I was accustomed to eating that he didn't like. (From today's vantage point, I realize that I was a pretty picky eater myself in those days; but I didn't recognize it then.) Anyway, I decided to occasionally prepare for myself those foods that he didn't want to eat and cook for him a different dish that he would prefer. It wasn't long before he was trying what I was eating, although he never did learn to like beets or turnip greens. While I can't guarantee that every husband will learn to like a broader variety by this method, I *can* say that the less-picky wife will be more content.

Some husbands will not eat a certain ingredient by itself but will eat it if it's disguised in a mixture. One of the foods that the newlywed Charles didn't think he liked was chicken. If I put a chicken breast on his plate, he would eat only a few bites. I learned, however, that if I disguised it with a sauce and vegetables or other ingredients (such as in chicken divan) he would eat it. Eventually, he learned to like chicken by itself. I told this story to a friend one time, and she laughingly told me that she had to disguise the *broccoli* with chicken and sauce to get her husband to eat that vegetable.

Another trick that I have discovered is that I can put raw cauliflower through the food processor to finely mince it and then steam it in the microwave. This cooked cauliflower can then be mixed half-and-half with white rice in a casserole (such as chicken and rice) to decrease the amount of starch and increase nutrition in the meal. I have yet to have anyone notice the cauliflower since the sauce in a casserole usually adds most of its flavor.

Perhaps your husband is one who balks at eating leftovers, but you need to prepare something that will serve you for a couple of days to save time. Try this trick. The first night, serve the pot roast. Since he will not want leftover roast the second day, chop some of it and reheat it in the gravy with some mushrooms. Serve over cooked noodles and call it beef tips and noodles. Or make beef stew, beef stroganoff, barbecue beef, or some other dish with the leftover beef. If you make chili, eat it in a bowl the first night and combine it with pasta and cheese for chili-mac the second night. Another trick is to make a double batch of something (especially casseroles, chili, or spaghetti sauce) and freeze half. At a future date, you can thaw and reheat the saved portion.

The excellent wife prepares food for her family.

"She is like merchant ships;
She brings her food from afar.
She rises also while it is still night,
And gives food to her household,
And portions to her maidens." (Prov. 31:14-15)

This woman is not lazy. She doesn't sleep until noon. She rises early to provide for the needs of her husband and others in her household. She brings the food from afar. For some women in the world, that might mean that she picks it from garden plants. For most of us in this nation, it means a trip to the supermarket. The point is that she sees that there is food in the house for her family to eat.

Maybe you hate to cook. Unless your husband is one who loves to cook or you trade cooking for one of the outside chores that he hates, however, meal preparation probably should be your responsibility.

I'm not saying that you must put gourmet meals on the table seven nights a week, but you should try to prepare food that is reasonably nourishing and that your family will enjoy. For some families, meat added to a boxed or frozen casserole mix, a vegetable, and a salad will work fine. For others, it would not.

I remember one occasion when our daughter was a teenager that illustrates that point. I was preparing salmon patties for dinner, and she came into the kitchen.

"What's for dinner?" she asked.

"Salmon patties," I replied.

"I don't want salmon patties. I want *plain* food."

Now, my mother (a down-home cook) prepared salmon patties when I was growing up, so I consider them to be plain food. With my curiosity aroused, I asked my daughter, "What kind of plain food?"

"Quiche," she responded.

I dare say that most people would not consider *quiche* a "plain food." It happened, however, that *quiche* was on the table more often than salmon patties during that time in our lives. The moral of the story is that the types of food will vary from family to family.

We still had salmon patties that night, by the way.

Timing of meals is also important. Some men, particularly those who do physical labor, prefer to eat supper as soon as they come home from work. Others, especially those who do mental work, favor unwinding first. Try to meet that schedule as much as possible for your husband's needs.

When Charles and I were newlyweds, I tended to have supper ready to serve when he walked in the door. That was partly because that had been my father's preference, but it was mostly because I wanted to get the kitchen cleaned earlier. Eventually, I began to realize that Charles needed a little time to relax and "de-stress" after the day's work before he was ready to eat.

I encourage you to try to have dinner with the whole family together as often as possible. This is a time when you can communicate about your day and cement the relationships between family members.

Family meals will not only provide an opportunity for you and your spouse to strengthen your bond, but also will be beneficial to your children. Kids who have dinner with the family most nights are less likely to be on drugs, to be depressed, or to be in trouble. Moreover, they are more likely to do well in school. I suspect that these positive results would not occur if the meals were mostly eaten in front of the television set, because communication would be severely limited when the TV is the focus.

These benefits to kids probably occur even if the meals are eaten in a restaurant. Unfortunately, if you eat at a restaurant very many nights, you may fail to provide the nutrition that your family needs. It's difficult to avoid fat and to get adequate nutrients and variety at a restaurant, particularly if it's a fast-food establishment.

Furthermore, the *cost* of eating out, even in fast-food restaurants, adds up quickly. A number of years ago, Charles and I bought a house that had a gas cooking range. When we moved into the house, neither we nor the man from the gas company could find the water heater to light it. Since the previous owner of the house was out of town and was not available to direct us to the water heater, the utility man could not turn on our gas. Thus, we could not cook on the range in the house until the previous owner returned to the city. This was before microwave ovens came on the scene, so that wasn't an option either.

We thought it wouldn't be too bad to eat fast food for a few days. As we spent the money on all of those "cheap" *fast*-food meals, however, we began to realize how *fast* the cost was mounting. We did a little math and figured how much we would spend on food if we ate that way all the time and compared it to our regular grocery bill when I cooked. The difference was staggering. I'm afraid that the calories in such meals accumulate pretty *fast* too.

The Excellent Wife Cares for Her Family

Titus 2:5 instructs the older women to exhort the younger wives concerning the responsibility to work at home. One of the considerations of this book is what makes an excellent wife according to the instructions in Proverbs 31, and that passage also tells us about the work that a good wife does in the home and for the family.

We are to be trustworthy wives. Can your husband trust you to keep the house neat and to see that his clothes are clean?

Maybe housekeeping isn't one of your favorite activities, but your home needs to be at least clean enough to please your husband. It doesn't have to look like a picture in a decorating magazine; but it shouldn't be a dump, either. If the messy condition of your home is such that you are uncomfortable about inviting guests to visit you, you probably need to improve. *"Be hospitable to one another without complaint."* (1 Pet. 4:9) Furthermore, a house that is excessively untidy or dirty will likely be an embarrassment to your husband and to your children.

I'm often confused by women who assert, "Cleaning the house takes only so many hours. I would get bored if I didn't have an outside job." These same women then usually insist that their husbands share equally in the housework because the women have outside jobs!

While one wife hates and neglects housekeeping such that her husband and children are ashamed to invite anyone into their home, another woman may love a clean house so much that her family can't relax there. Balance is appropriate here.

When I was a child, I had a friend whose mother kept the house so perfectly straight and clean that few people were comfortable visiting that family. We were afraid to sit down anywhere and mess up the unwrinkled furniture! Besides, I have noticed that people who are out of balance on the clean end of the spectrum don't get invited to other people's homes very often because others fear that their own homes aren't clean enough for this person to see.

If you tend toward super-clean perfectionism, you perhaps need to work on making your home a more comfortable, cozy, "lived-in" place where your family can relax. If you are an overly casual housekeeper and your husband loves order, make yourself a "to do" list every day so that you can create a neater home for him. It's easier to keep a house tidy than to get it that way, so daily work helps.

"She looks for wool and flax,
And works with her hands in delight." (Prov. 31:13)

Sometimes the work isn't easy. The excellent wife *looks* for wool and flax. She willingly puts forth *effort* to serve her family, and she *delights* in it. She finds pleasure in it. She considers it a valuable and worthy use of her time. This is in sharp contrast to the women today who declare that they are unfulfilled in the homemaking role and who say that they must find self-esteem in their careers.

Do you find pleasure in working for your family? Does it satisfy you? Or do you grumble and complain because you have to do the laundry or clean the shower? Your service to your family is among your highest acts of service to the Lord. When you clean that toilet or dust the furniture, consider it a ministry to the heavenly Bridegroom. *"Whatever you do, do your work heartily, as if for the Lord rather than for men; knowing that from the Lord you will receive the reward of the inheritance. **It is the Lord Christ whom you serve**."* (Col. 3:23-24, emphasis mine) *"Do all things without grumbling or disputing."* (Phil. 2:14)

A friend once told me about the woman who led her family to the Lord. Rejoicing that she had been born again, my friend was very grateful to this woman. She told me, however, that the woman's own family *hated* her. This evangelistic woman was always so "busy serving the Lord" that she ignored her family's needs. Resentful of her neglect, her husband and children eventually turned away from the Lord.

I heard another woman say one time, "I don't like housework, and I do like church work; so I don't do housework, and I do church work."

Beware of falling into this trap. Jesus said that whatever we do for others, we do for Him. (Matt. 25:40) When you serve your family, you *are* ministering to the Lord.

You might be thinking, "Yeah, but the Proverbs 31 woman had servants! She had help. I don't have any servants at my house."

Is that true? Think about it. We do have *many* servants to help us today, servants that this woman in Proverbs 31 couldn't have even imagined. What about the microwave oven? What about the dishwasher? What about the laundry equipment, the vacuum cleaner, and the water faucet? Ladies, these are servants as surely as any slave is. They are in your house to do work for you.

According to Proverbs 31:17, a good wife girds herself (literally *girds her loins*) with strength and makes her arms strong. Usually when the Bible uses the phrase *"gird up your loins,"* it refers to being prepared. How do you make yourself strong and prepared to serve? Strength comes from work, because using muscles makes them stronger. Laziness deprives you of strength, since inactivity atrophies muscle. Why should you neglect your housework because it requires too much toil, and then pay out good money to exercise in a gym or to purchase exercise equipment?

The Proverbs 31 woman worked long hours, rising early and laboring late into the night to care for her family.

*"She rises also while it is still night
And gives food to her household
And portions to her maidens...
Her lamp does not go out at night."* (Verses 15 and 18)

Because we have such wonderful servants, it's much easier for us to prepare the morning meal for our families than it was for women in those days. I can usually have breakfast on the table in fifteen minutes or less, and I don't just mean cold cereal or a slice of toast.

An excellent wife clothes herself with strength and dignity. (Prov. 31:25) We too must strive to grow strong—physically (unless health prohibits it), emotionally, and spiritually—if we are to be Proverbs 31 wives. How can we meet our families' needs if we are not?

The Proverbs 31 woman was not idle. If she were alive today, she would not sit around watching soap operas.

*"She looks well to the ways of her household,
And does not eat the bread of idleness."* (Verse 27)

Solomon's mother described a wife who made certain that her family had proper clothing. She even spun the thread to weave into the fabric of which she made their attire. (Prov. 31:19) This excellent wife made garments that were beautiful and appropriate for the weather. (Prov. 31:21-22) I'm glad we don't have to spin the thread for our clothes, aren't you? For most of *us*, this primarily refers to shopping, laundering, and repairing, rather than to actually creating the apparel.

Some women do indeed have sewing abilities and love to make clothing. These ladies actually start from scratch to make some of the garments for the family.

Others hate to sew. (I confess to being in that category.) Just as ladies who hate to cook have a responsibility to provide meals, however, we who hate to sew still must see that the family's clothing is adequate, clean, and in good repair.

I'm fortunate that I don't have to make my husband's shirts, but I do need to see that missing buttons are replaced and ripped seams are repaired. When our daughter was small and money was tight, I sometimes made her clothes. I have also made garments for myself when I couldn't find or afford what I needed at the mall.

Now I don't want to get legalistic about all of this. Everyone gets behind sometimes. Please don't think that I am saying that you must always be on top of everything and never fail to do your work on time. Being a little behind on the laundry is one thing; it's quite another when your husband doesn't have clean underwear or an ironed shirt to wear to the office. I just want to encourage you to meet your family's needs.

Someone once sent me a joke in some e-mail that supposedly told the story of Eve's creation. In the joke, God noticed that Adam was lonely and offered to make a companion for him. God told Adam that the woman would always fulfill every one of her wifely responsibilities. The joke went on to say that Adam asked God what a woman like that would cost, and that God told him she would cost an arm and a leg. Then Adam asked what he could get for a rib.

Now obviously, that story is just for fun. There is, however, a lesson for us there. Don't you want your husband to think he got an arm-and-a-leg wife for the price of a rib?

Are there areas in which you need to do better in your home responsibilities? Have your family members come to think of carryout pizza as a home-cooked meal? Are they embarrassed to bring people into your home because cobwebs hang three feet from the light fixtures and there is no place to sit without landing on clutter? Does your husband have a hard time finding something to wear to work? Do you serve your family with delight, or are you doing these things with bitterness or complaints in your heart? As an older woman, I encourage you to joyfully fulfill your responsibilities in the home.

What about your service to your heavenly Bridegroom? Have you found yourself "too busy" to serve Him? Are you neglecting your responsibilities both to Him and to His children? May it be said of us that we demonstrate our love to Him by our obedient service.

It's about Time

❄❄❄

Every 24-hour period that we live, we are given 1,440 minutes, or 86,400 seconds. At the end of each day, all of the time that we have failed to put to good use is lost. We cannot save time from one day to use the next. Each day more time is given to us, but the minutes of that day can be spent only during that day. At the end of 24 hours, all of the allotted time is gone. In fact, each wasted or ill-used moment is gone as soon as another takes its place.

Lost time can never be regained. If we fail to take advantage of any moment of time, we have lost it. Furthermore, we can't take a loan from tomorrow's time. Today is the only time we have at the moment. We have no guarantee that tomorrow will even come, for we don't know how long we will live.

What is time? Is it not a measurement of the segments of our very lives?

Who gives these moments to us? The Lord created all things. He existed before time and lives outside of time. He created time for *us* to inhabit.

As Christians, to whom do our lives belong? They belong to Lord. If our lives belong to the Lord, then our time belongs to Him as well—for our lives consist of the minutes and hours that measure them. As a matter of fact, all that we are and have belong to the Lord; we are merely stewards.

The Greek word that is translated as *steward* in the New Testament comes from two Greek words: one that means *house*, and one that means *to parcel out* or *to distribute*. A steward was a manager for the owner of the house, a servant who administered the belongings of another and parceled them out according to the wishes of the owner.

Stewardship isn't a concept that's commonly discussed in America. Most of us don't have servants who serve that function for us.

Let's think of it this way: Suppose your sister's birthday is coming soon, so you go out and shop for a sweater for her birthday gift. Then you take the sweater to one of those shops that pack and ship items for their customers, giving your sister's address in another state to the woman behind the counter.

What if your sister never receives your gift? What if you return to the shipping store and find the woman who works there wearing the sweater that you had purchased for your sister? I think that you would be most upset, because you did not give the sweater to the clerk. You entrusted it to her to "parcel it out" according to *your* wishes.

Our lives belong to the Lord, and therefore our time is His as well. If we are managing our time as stewards for the heavenly Bridegroom, we may not spend it any old way that we choose. Instead, we must use it as He would have us to do. *"For we are His workmanship, created in Christ Jesus for good works, which God prepared beforehand so that we would walk in them."* (Eph. 2:10)

As Christian women, we have a responsibility to steward the time that God has put into our care. We must not to allow it to be stolen or abused. According to John 10:10, one of Satan's primary objectives is to steal from us—and our time is no exception to his list. He desires to distract us from doing what God wants us to do with our time, leading us to lose the best use of it. The devil wants to control how we use our time.

Our time doesn't belong to the enemy, however. Remember? It doesn't even belong to *us*. Since we have been bought with a price, we are stewards (not owners) of our time.

Using our time poorly means that we are abusing *God's* time. When we do that, we are much like the employee who wastes time playing computer solitaire or gossiping around the water cooler while on the company clock. We must use our time appropriately in our marriages, and indeed in our whole lives, in order to redeem the time.

Have you ever remarked, "I just don't have enough time"? Most of us have said something like that at one time or another. Everyone has the same amount of time in a day, however. Some of us have more responsibilities than others do, but a day is the same length for everyone. It's not so much a question of how much time we have, but how we *use* the time we have.

The Bible says, *"Therefore be careful how you walk, not as unwise men but as wise, making the most of your time, because the days are evil."* (Eph. 5:15-16) When Paul says that we are to be careful how we walk, he doesn't refer to merely putting one foot in front of another; he's talking about the way we live our lives.

The Greek word that is translated as *making the most of* in the NASU is rendered *redeeming* in the KJV. It literally means *to buy up* or *to ransom;* it is used figuratively to mean *to rescue from loss* or *to improve opportunity.* We are instructed to buy up the opportunities in our time each day and to keep them from being lost. In effect, life for each of us is a long series of choices. We buy up the opportunities by continually choosing to do what God wants us to do with our time.

Suppose you assigned chores to your two children one Saturday morning. One child immediately began to pick up his toys, feed the dog, and carry out the trash. The other child put off his chores for later because he wanted to play video games at the moment. A friend had invited both children to go somewhere that afternoon. When it was time to go, the first child needed only to jump into the car. The second complained that he didn't have time to do his chores or he would not be able to go with the friend. Is it true that he didn't have time, or did he simply use his time unwisely?

Satan always wants to distort the gifts that God gives to us. God gives us sex as an expression of love between husband and wife, and the tempter urges the misuse of that gift in inappropriate, sinful ways. God gives us possessions to use for His glory, and the kingdom of darkness tempts us to use them selfishly. God gives us time, and Satan desires to lead us to waste and abuse that as well.

Jesus tells us that He wants us to be wise and faithful stewards of what He gives to us. He is going to call us into account for the way we have used what is His.

*"And the Lord said, 'Who then is the faithful and sensible steward, whom his master will put in charge of his servants, to give them their rations at the proper time? Blessed is that slave whom his master finds so doing when he comes. Truly I say to you that he will put him in charge of all his possessions. But if that slave says in his heart, "My master will be a long time in coming," and begins to beat the slaves, both men and women, and to eat and drink and get drunk; the master of that slave will come on a day when he does not expect him and at an hour he does not know, and will cut him in pieces, and assign him a place with the unbelievers. And that slave who knew his master's will and did not get ready or act in accord with his will, will receive many lashes, but the one who did not know it, and committed deeds worthy of a flogging, will receive but few. From everyone who has been given much, much will be required; **and to whom they entrusted much, of him they will ask all the more.**'"* (Luke 12:42-48, emphasis mine)

The faithless steward in this parable represents the person who misuses whatever the Lord has given him to manage. That includes managing time, because our time belongs to the Lord. We have many laborsaving devices that give us more spare moments than people had in times past. Because we have been given much, He therefore requires much from us.

How then shall we use our time? What does the Lord expect us to do with the time that He has placed under our stewardship?

Caring for Our Families

What application can we make regarding the use of our time and our natural husbands? Do our husbands have a claim on our time? Can your husband trust you to use your time wisely instead of frittering it away?

Obviously, every woman needs some time for herself. We need time to relax or to visit with our friends. Your husband likely knows you need time to relax, just as the heavenly Bridegroom does.

Nevertheless, as married women, one of our first responsibilities to the Lord is to care for our families. This includes ministering to their physical, emotional, and spiritual needs. The Bible describes the excellent wife as one who is careful about the needs of the household and who works to meet those needs.

*"She watches over the affairs of her household
And does not eat the bread of idleness."* (Prov. 31:27 NIV)

Have you ever heard a woman say something like this? "I don't have time to do all that natural stuff like cleaning house and cooking meals for my family. I'm too busy serving the Lord." We must remember that the purpose of woman's creation was to serve as her husband's helper. *"Then the LORD God said, "It is not good for the man to be alone; I will make him a helper suitable for him."* (Gen. 2:18) *"Neither was man created for woman, but woman for man."* (1 Cor. 11:9 RSV)

A woman's first responsibility in serving the Lord is to care for her husband and family, and she who thinks that she is so busy serving God that she doesn't have time to serve her family is missing what God wants her to do. As we discussed in the previous chapter, a woman who serves her husband and children *is* serving the Lord.

Now, I'm not suggesting that she should not also serve others. In fact, I assert that she has a responsibility to do so in most instances. Until she cares for her family, however, it isn't time to render service to others. (Except in unusual circumstances, there is almost always opportunity to do both if she uses her time wisely and unselfishly.)

Too often, the real reason a woman doesn't want to serve her family is selfishness or laziness. She prefers idleness or pleasure to work. The Bible teaches against idleness.

"Sow your seed in the morning and do not be idle in the evening..." (Eccl. 11:6)

"For even when we were with you, we used to give you this order: if anyone is not willing to work, then he is not to eat, either. For we hear that some among you are leading an undisciplined life, doing no work at all, but acting like busybodies." (2 Thess. 3:10-11)

"Older women likewise are to...encourage the young women to love their husbands, to love their children, to be sensible, pure, workers at home..." (Tit. 2:3-5)

Our families need us not only for physical work, but also for emotional support and spiritual encouragement. We must conserve our time so that we can be available to meet those needs as well.

Serving Others

As Christians, we have the responsibility to use some of our time serving other people, both those within the body of Christ and those without. *"So then, while we have opportunity, let us do good to all people, and especially to those who are of the household of the faith."* (Gal. 6:10)

Just as our first responsibility is toward our own families before we serve those outside, Paul tells us that we should pay special attention to serving those who are our spiritual brothers and sisters.

Yet he doesn't limit us to serving Christians. In fact, he urges us to use our time wisely with unbelievers also. He said that we are to do good to *all* people. In another place, he wrote, *"Conduct yourselves wisely toward outsiders, making the most of the time."* (Col. 4:5 RSV) This is a witness to those without and will perhaps lead them to receive the Lord.

Punctuality

If I am going to discuss the wise use of time with you, I feel I must mention the importance of punctuality. It seems to me that there is an attitude today that punctuality is unnecessary. Sometimes people will even say, "Well, I was *only* an hour late!"

First of all, my sisters, this is a matter of integrity. Disregarding punctuality is a failure to do what you said that you would do.

Furthermore, it is inconsiderate to consistently keep others waiting. When you do this, you are robbing them of *their* time. You are preventing the best use of *their* time. Jesus said, *"In everything, therefore, treat people the same way you want them to treat you..."* (Matt. 7:12)

Maybe you find yourself arriving late because something frequently comes up when you should be preparing to leave. People who are habitually late often say, "It seems as if something always happens at the last minute. Just as it's time to get ready, the phone rings or something." They don't see how they can be punctual when all of these things keep delaying them.

If this describes you, I suggest that you do the most important thing first. When you have an appointment with someone else, getting ready and leaving on time is important. It is *usually* the priority for that moment. Of course, true emergencies do come up. Perhaps the phone call is about a genuine crisis. If it is not, however, you can tell the caller *immediately* that you must get ready to leave and that you will return the call later.

Occasionally a woman will say, "I didn't realize how long it would take me to drive there." Of course, we all sometimes run into unexpected traffic snarls. I try to leave a few minutes earlier than seems necessary for the trip, however. That way, I'm usually still on time even if traffic is heavy or there is some delay on the road.

Or maybe she would say, "I didn't realize until the last minute that there was a rip in the seam of my pants. I had to completely change clothes, and that made me late." One way to avoid this problem is to get ready a little early. That way, there is a little extra time in case something surprising happens while you are dressing.

Perhaps you are thinking, "Well, I can't stand to do *nothing*! If I get ready early, I couldn't bear to idly sit there until time to go. If I leave a few minutes early, I'll arrive early with nothing to do. That's *wasting* the time." I understand your feelings about this. I don't like to sit and do nothing myself!

I encourage you to make a list of things that you can do without getting dirty and that you can do in small segments without finishing the entire job at once. It's obvious that you can't scrub the floor when you are ready to go somewhere, but you could clip coupons. You could fold laundry. You could address Christmas cards or write letters. You could read your e-mail. You could make your grocery list. You could read, or pray. One warning, however: *Set the timer so that you don't become so involved with the task that you still wind up being late.* In this way, you will be able to use productively that extra ten or fifteen minutes before you leave without making yourself late. Perhaps you could carry a newspaper, book, or crossword puzzle in case you arrive at a destination before your appointment.

Punctuality sometimes pertains not to an appointment with someone but to finishing a task on time. Have you ever worked on an activity with someone who postpones everything?

Some events require a great deal of preparation and work. Perhaps you and your sisters are planning a big fiftieth-anniversary party for your parents. If you aren't in a position to get things done ahead of time, the last week before the event will be nerve-wracking. There's so much to do, and so little time to do it.

Just as it's helpful to allow a little extra time in getting ready to go somewhere so that you can deal with unexpected phone calls or scuffed shoes, starting a task early will allow plenty of time for unforeseen delays. Unexpected problems arise as you work on a project, just as they do when you are trying to go somewhere! The ink cartridge runs dry when you are ready to print the invitations. You must spend more time than you had anticipated in shopping for decorations. If you wait until the last minute to begin, you may find that you must rush to finish. That often means that you sacrifice excellence on the project, not to mention the toll it takes on your nerves and/or the nerves of others involved in the event.

Some women say that they do better work when they are pressed for time, but I think that what they really mean is that it motivates them to continue working. Running right up to the last minute while completing a project means that there isn't time to deal with the unexpected, and quality is frequently diminished.

The Time Robbers

The enemy wants us to misuse our time and become like the following women:

Obsessive women: These women waste time in doing unnecessary or less-important tasks while believing that they are doing what they should. They don't have their priorities straight; they aren't putting the most important things first.

For example, what if a woman removes the switch plates to dust behind them? It's laughable, isn't it? Doing very much of that kind of activity doesn't leave enough time for more significant tasks. Certainly such a woman would need to see that dusting the exposed surfaces and cleaning other parts of the house would be done rather than removing the switch plates!

That's a far-fetched example, of course, but some women do fill their daily routine so tightly with "good" activities that they are too exhausted and short of time for some truly important projects. I've known women who felt that if they dusted at all, they must dust every surface in the house every single time. Meanwhile, these women get three weeks behind on the laundry and their bathrooms become corrupt because they were cleaning behind every volume on the bookshelves.

Of course, we do need to clean behind the books, wipe off the tops of the door facings, and dust the figurines. If we do all of that every time we dust, however, we might not find time to do the dusting very often. The coffee table would be so fuzzy that we could write our names there. Let's do the most important things first and most often.

One of the problems that today's children face is that their parents often schedule every moment of the kids' days with organized events, and the youngsters have no time to relax and be children. A second downside of this is that the parents are over-scheduled as well.

Christian women who begin to overfill their calendars would do well to remember the story of Martha and Mary. (See Luke 10:38-42) Our schedules must include regular periods of time spent alone with the Lord. It's easy to plan so many activities that we "can't find time" to read our Bibles and pray. Our appetite for spiritual things will wane when we get too busy to sit at the Lord's feet.

The obsessive use of time also prevents our getting adequate rest. The Lord's plan for us was that we would have a day of rest each week and a night of rest each 24 hours. (See Ex. 31:15 and Psa. 104:22-23.) The evening darkness is a signal to get some rest. In our day of electric lights, many people are inclined to fill too many hours with activity and to neglect proper rest. We cannot steward our time properly if we are exhausted or ill from lack of rest.

Foolish women: These women do the necessary in a foolish or dangerous way in order to "save time." Some of these situations can result in injury or death. Climbing on unstable surfaces instead of a ladder and driving too fast to get somewhere are a couple of examples. Do you remember how I disregarded my husband's protective request and injured myself by trying to run under the garage door before it closed? I was a foolish woman who tried to save time by doing something in a dangerous manner.

Other women do everything so hurriedly that they do a poor job or break something, often requiring them to do the activity a second time. This wastes time in the long run.

Selfish women: Now we all need time for recreation and relaxation. These women, however, are going beyond that. Their problem is neglecting the necessary in order to fill their time with activities they find more pleasurable (watching TV, scrapbooking, or playing on the computer all day while the dishes pile up and dinner isn't cooked). This is really idleness: doing only that which they want to do, without fulfilling their responsibilities.

Paul warned that young widows should remarry to avoid such a lifestyle. *"Besides, they get into the habit of being idle and going about from house to house. And not only do they become idlers, but also gossips and busybodies, saying things they ought not to. So I counsel younger widows to marry, to have children, to manage their homes and to give the enemy no opportunity for slander."* (1 Tim. 5:13-14 NIV)

Notice that in this passage, Paul says that idleness gives Satan an opportunity to slander. Titus 2:5 also says that when we neglect the work in our homes, we bring dishonor to the Word of God. We don't want that. We want to bring *honor* to the Lord, don't we?

In planning our schedules, we must allow time for serving our families, for serving others, for communion with the Lord, for fellowship with those we love, and for rest.

Satan always wants to distort, so we must be diligent to keep these parts of our lives in balance. One person will be tempted more in the area of busy-ness that prevents her from enjoying time with her family and with the Lord. Another woman will be tempted to sit for so many hours in front of the computer or television that she doesn't get her work done. Each of us needs to be aware of our own weaknesses so we can resist the tempter.

Regardless of what we are doing, we are to use our time for God's glory. *"Whatever you do in word or deed, do all in the name of the Lord Jesus, giving thanks through Him to God the Father."* (Col. 3:17)

100-100 Marriage

✻✻✻

A young woman telephoned me one day to talk about a problem in her marriage. After I had advised her about how she could put some cement into her marriage by becoming a greater blessing to her husband, she asked, "Well, when will it be about *me*?"

"Love is never about the lover," I told her. "Love is always about the beloved."

Several years later, I told a shopkeeper that it was my wedding anniversary that day. We started talking about marriage, and I told her that I was working on this book. The shopkeeper said, "It takes give and take, doesn't it?"

I said, "It takes commitment…"

The shopkeeper interrupted my unfinished sentence and said, "Yes, that's right!"

"…and unselfishness," I continued. "That's what love is: unselfishness…putting the other person before oneself."

For the first time since I had entered the shop, the talkative shopkeeper was totally silent.

The attitudes of those two women are not all that unusual. We hear it all the time. Our society says that marriage should be a 50-50 proposition. Give and take. He gives half the time, and she gives half the time. It sounds reasonable, doesn't it?

There's only one problem: It doesn't work.

Well, then, why *doesn't* the 50-50 plan work?

In the first place, God has called the husband to be the leader of the family 100% of the time, not 50% of it. *"Wives, submit to your husbands as to the Lord. For the husband is the head of the wife as Christ is the head of the church, his body, of which he is the Savior. Now as the church submits to Christ, so also wives should submit to their husbands in everything."* (Eph. 5:22-24 NIV)

Beyond that, however, I would like to talk about situations that don't involve submission to a decision that the husband has made—times when a wife can *voluntarily* choose to put him before herself. Perhaps she would save the last Coke for him. Perhaps she does one of his chores for him when he's having a bad day. Maybe she goes to a football game with him—even though she hates sports—because he would like for her to go. Perhaps she makes sure that she meets him at the door with a cup of coffee every afternoon and asks about his day, even when her own day was not the greatest.

I would like to propose that a good marriage is not a 50-50 proposition, but a 100-100 situation. In a perfect scenario, the husband would see marriage as 100% for the good of his wife and 0% for himself. The wife would see it as 100% for her husband and 0% for herself. Each would see their union as an opportunity to *benefit the spouse* 100% of the time.

The reason that a 50-50 marriage doesn't work is that in any given circumstance, each spouse is inclined to think that it's his/her time to get his/her way. In a 100-100 marriage, each spouse sees any situation as an opportunity to serve the other. Obviously, someone will have to receive each time that the other one gives; but the atmosphere will be one of unselfishness, and each will feel extraordinarily blessed.

Unselfish Love

That's the point that I was trying to make to the two women at the beginning of this chapter. Doesn't *agape* mean that the lover puts the benefit of the beloved before his own good? Giving is what love is all about. *"For God so loved the world, that He **gave**..."* (John 3:16, emphasis mine) Love is about giving. Our heavenly Bridegroom gave His all for His bride. He sacrificed everything for our good. Although He is the perfect and holy Son of God, He came to earth to actually *become* our sin and to die in our place in order to redeem us.

"He made Him who knew no sin to be sin on our behalf, so that we might become the righteousness of God in Him." (2 Cor. 5:21)

"All of us like sheep have gone astray,
Each of us has turned to his own way;
But the LORD has caused the iniquity of us all
To fall on Him." (Isa. 53:6)

Jesus gave Himself fully for us, and He set the example for us to follow. Listen to His words to His disciples: *"A new commandment I give to you, that you love one another, even as I have loved you, that you also love one another."* (John 13:34)

The wife who truly understands how to love her husband is willing to give unselfishly for him. The apostle Paul wrote this exhortation: *"Do nothing from selfishness or empty conceit, but with humility of mind regard one another as more important than yourselves; do not merely look out for your own personal interests, but also for the interests of others."* (Phil. 2:3-4) Jesus had that attitude toward us, and Paul urges us, *"Have this attitude in yourselves which was also in Christ Jesus..."* (Phil. 2:5)

Did you notice that the command is that we do *nothing* from selfishness? It doesn't say that we should avoid selfishness 50% of the time. It says that we are to do *nothing* from selfish motives.

There's a big obstacle to establishing this kind of behavior in our marriages. While selfishness is perfectly natural to us, self*less* giving is absolutely contrary to our fleshly natures. We can become that kind of lover only by the power of God in our lives.

"But I say, walk by the Spirit, and you will not carry out the desire of the flesh." (Gal. 5:16)

The opposite of that is also true, however. If you do *not* walk by the Spirit, you *will* fulfill the desires of your flesh. That's because fleshly living is what comes naturally to us.

Since the fall in the Garden of Eden, the flesh is the default setting in human beings. It reminds me of a light switch. If it is not off, it's on. There are no other settings. If we are not walking by the Spirit, we *will* walk in the flesh. Sometimes we vacillate between the two; but we will walk in one or the other in any given moment, not both.

The flesh doesn't think about unselfish giving. Rather, the flesh thinks about satisfying its own pleasure. When the flesh gives, it does so to manipulate the other person into giving something else that it wants more. Or it gives because it has *been* manipulated. Or it gives because of the pleasure it receives from the giving. It does *not* give unselfishly. It does not give solely for the good of the other person, nor does it give when it does not want to do so.

*Un*selfish love gives because it will benefit the beloved, even if the lover doesn't want or like to do the thing that is needed. Isn't that why the loving mother sits up all night long with a sick baby? Isn't that why she changes dirty diapers? I've never known anyone who thought changing a dirty diaper was fun. That mother gives of herself to that baby because she loves her child and chooses to meet the infant's need.

Love is not a prerequisite for taking and demanding. Anyone can take and demand with no love at all in her heart. Nor is it true that taking or demanding will *lead* to love. Some people think that they will love those who give to them. They think, "If he would just do what I want, I would love him more."

The truth is that *giving* exhibits my love, and *giving* leads me to love more. Some people give without loving, but no one truly loves without giving. In a successful, healthy, and happy marriage, the partners are constantly choosing to benefit the other…and they don't keep a balance sheet to record who gave last.

In America today, we frequently hear people talk about "falling in love" and "falling out of love," as if love were something over which they had no control. Perhaps those people who "fell out of love" haven't been blessing the other spouse enough.

If you find yourself thinking, "I don't love him anymore," I urge you to take these two steps:
- Ask God to renew your feelings for your husband.
- Begin to give unselfishly to your husband as though you had great affection for him.

Yes, one tool for restoring loving feelings toward your husband (if they have waned) is asking God to change your heart. He will not violate your free will. If you are unwilling to have a change of heart, God will not overrule you. If your desire is to change your attitude, however, you can ask Him to do that—but you must be willing to change your behavior as well as your attitude.

With a true heart, ask the Lord to work love into your heart. It's His will for you to love your husband, so He will respond to your heartfelt request. *"This is the confidence which we have before Him, that, if we ask anything according to His will, He hears us. And if we know that He hears us in whatever we ask, we know that we have the requests which we have asked from Him."* (1 John 5:14-15)

Then choose to bless your husband. When you seek to serve your spouse, you strengthen your love for him. When you voluntarily give, you develop a caring attitude in your own heart. Isn't that why Jesus said, *"For where your treasure is, there your heart will be also"?* (Matt. 6:21 NIV) When we give (whether it's money or time or emotional support or any other gift) we develop a greater concern and interest in the benefit of the person or persons to whom we give.

I have called this chapter "100-100 Marriage," but I considered calling it "100-0 Marriage." That's really how you must view it. Ideally, both marriage partners will see the relationship as an opportunity to give 100% of the time; and then it will be 100-100. Although this cannot be your motive, a wife's giving will *usually* inspire her husband to love her more. He will *usually* begin to care more about her and to bless her more often.

You cannot, however, make your husband's choice to give; *he* must choose whether or not he will give. You *can* decide that *you* will give 100% of the time; but the moment you decide that he must also be ready to give 100% of the time, you have stopped having the 100% attitude yourself. If you show love and give to your husband only under the condition that he does the same, you will do well to remember the words of Jesus: *"If you love those who love you, what credit is that to you? For even sinners love those who love them. If you do good to those who do good to you, what credit is that to you? For even sinners do the same."* (Luke 6:32-33)

Remember the young wife at the beginning of this chapter? Too often, wives echo her attitude: "When is it *my* turn? When is he going to do what *I* want?" Not only is this sort of thought-pattern not Christ-like, it furthermore will lead to dissatisfaction with your husband and with your marriage. In fact, the young woman who wondered when it would be about her was divorced not long after that conversation.

Paul tells us, *"...I have learned to be content in whatever circumstances I am...I can do all things through Him who strengthens me."* (Phil. 4:11, 13) Notice that he said that he had *learned* to be content. It didn't come naturally to him; he had to learn it. He was talking about finances, but I believe that we can learn to be content in *all* circumstances and do *all* things that please Him by the power of His Spirit within us.

You may be thinking, "Well, if I don't look out for myself, no one else will look out for me." What you don't recognize when you say that is this: Having the look-out-for-number-one philosophy actually *blocks* your chances for true happiness and joy. Happiness is elusive when you put your efforts into receiving it; it is found when you seek to give it to others.

I will tell you something, my sisters. Happiness from getting lasts only until the person thinks of something else that she wants to get. That frequently is not a very long period of time. I have never known even one person who was both extremely selfish and very happy. Every chronically selfish person I have ever known was miserable most of the time.

Lasting contentment and joy come from giving. Paul reminded us that Jesus Himself said, *"It is more blessed to give than to receive."* (Acts 20:35 NIV)

Give Service

One of the most obvious ways to give to your husband is to serve him. Run an errand for him or do one of his chores when he is tired. Fix him a Coke. Take him water while he is mowing the grass. Massage his shoulders or feet.

You may say, "If I do that, he may take advantage of me! I can't make myself that vulnerable."

Have you ever found yourself storming through the house muttering to yourself, "Who does he think I am? His servant?" You know, we really are called to be servants. Servants to our husbands. Servants to our children. Servants to others.

Several years ago, the *Woman to Woman* group gave me a figurine of Jesus washing the feet of one of His disciples. The message of His example is a good reminder to me: Yes, indeed. We *are* called to be servants. In fact, Jesus said, *"The greatest among you will be your servant."* (Matt. 23:11 NIV) He taught us, *"If anyone wants to be first, he must be the very last, and the servant of all."* (Mark 9:35 NIV)

I remember an evening when a young man whose wife didn't view marriage this way was a guest in our home. (His wife wasn't with him.) At one point in the evening, he said to Charles, "I see what your wife does for you. My wife has *never* done those things for me." About all he had seen me do in the brief time he had been there was to notice that Charles' coffee cup was empty and refill it. I thought, "How sad! This man's wife has never done anything to serve him."

Give Concern for His Feelings

I urge you to make a conscious choice to be sensitive to your husband's feelings. In today's society, there is a tendency toward a kind of put-down humor that jokes at the expense of others. People are expected to "be a good sport," meaning that they are not supposed to be hurt by ridicule or harsh, insulting words in the guise of a joke.

I suggest that you avoid these kinds of jests, particularly in the presence of other people or concerning subjects about which your husband is vulnerable. Please don't kid about things that affect his self-esteem or manhood. For instance, shun teasing that criticizes the size of his paycheck, accuses him of physical weakness, or questions his sexual prowess. Avoid joking that he lacks intelligence or courage. How would you like it if he teased you about your physical imperfections? What if he continually teased about your being a filthy housekeeper or a lousy mother? What if he made jokes that referred to you as ugly or stupid? *"In everything, therefore, treat people the same way you want them to treat you, for this is the Law and the Prophets."* (Matt. 7:12)

Give Appreciation

One way that you can give to your husband is to show your appreciation for his actions and words that bless you.

Perhaps he has done one of your tasks for you. If his efforts merely bring a barrage of criticism about the way that he did your chore, he may well think, "Why should I bother? She won't like the way I do it anyway."

Does he faithfully fulfill his own responsibilities? Maybe he regularly carries out the trash. He goes to work every day. He's a devoted father. He calls to let you know he will be late. Sometimes a wife will think, "Why should I thank him for doing what he's *supposed* to do? That's his job!"

I'm reminded just now of an article that I read several years ago in which the author told of a conversation she had with an exchange student. He was running about the countryside exulting over the various wildflowers that grew in the area. Surprised at his excitement about mere wildflowers, the author asked if the young man didn't have wildflowers in his homeland. The young man assured her that he was indeed accustomed to wildflowers, but "only" orchids. The exchange student took the orchids for granted because they were familiar and "supposed to" grow there.

I once asked the ladies in the women's ministry group to limit criticizing their husbands during the coming month to occasions when they had first praised him on at least four different occasions. There was a place in their notebooks to keep track, because it would be hard to remember how often they had praised and criticized. Four lines for praises preceded each single line for criticism. This is good practice.

It's hard for a man (or anyone, for that matter) to receive criticism well if he feels as if that's all he hears. Unless he hears praises and honor on multiple occasions before each criticism, he will consider his wife to be the quarrelsome, contentious woman described in Prov. 19:13, who is like a constant dripping.

Never take your husband for granted. Thanking and praising him for even the little things will encourage him and create warmth in your marriage. Try thanking him when he carries out the trash or picks up the dry-cleaning. Tell him what a good job he has done when he mows the grass. Try thanking him for going to work every day. Express your gratitude for the way he manages the family finances. Thank him for being patient with the children. Thank and praise him for *anything* that you honestly appreciate about him.

I have to work at remembering to do this, but my husband is a champion at it. He is extremely appreciative of every little thing I do. His words of gratitude build me up more than I can tell you, and they inspire me to try harder to please him. Believe me, you can't overdo gratitude.

You may be thinking, "Well, it just isn't my personality to gush over people like that. I would feel uncomfortable."

That's where unselfish love comes in. Choose to do what will minister to *him,* even if it doesn't come naturally to you. Does it give you pleasure when people express appreciation for the things that you do? Of course it does! No one likes to be taken for granted, and everyone enjoys receiving praise.

In a successful marriage, each partner concentrates on the other person. When both the husband and the wife do latch onto this attitude, each begins to feel that the other spouse gives more often than he/she does. The husband feels that his wife blesses him more than he blesses her, and she feels that her spouse considers her desires more often than she considers his.

I cannot guarantee that if you begin to have an attitude of 100% for your spouse and 0% for yourself, your husband will develop the same outlook. God has given us a free will, and some people choose not to change. I *can* assure you, however, that your chances of seeing positive change in him are far better if you assume unselfishness as your role than if you continue to behave selfishly. I will suggest that if you truly begin to give *sincerely* and *unselfishly,* you will grow in *your* love for your husband and that you will find more fulfillment in your marriage.

Here Comes the Bride

Giving to the Heavenly Bridegroom

Do you remember your joyful excitement in the Lord right after you were born again? Were you filled with peace and joy? Was pleasing Him your greatest desire? Did you have an insatiable appetite for His word? Was it your greatest delight to worship Him? Did you incessantly talk about Him?

What about now? Are you still filled with that radical zeal and love for Him? Do you instead notice that your joy and peace have drastically diminished? Are you as eager to please Him now as you were then? Or is finding time to spend with Him in His Word and in prayer more a duty than a pleasure? Has that time alone with Him become a rare occurrence? Or worse, have you actually stopped finding time for Him altogether? Is the spiritual honeymoon over?

I well remember the joy of the day when at age 15 I was born again. I felt incredibly clean and happy. I rejoiced exceedingly that my sins were forgiven, and I earnestly desired to live a changed life. Unfortunately, I didn't maintain that attitude very long at all. I quickly wandered away from the Lord, and it was several years before I returned to a committed walk with Him.

Sometimes Christians have a tendency to think, "Well, I can't sustain the zeal and joy for the Lord that I had in the beginning. Life is hard. I try to do what I can, but the Lord understands when I can't continue at that level."

Is that true?

When Jesus appeared to the apostle John on the island of Patmos, He told John to send messages to certain churches in Asia. One of those churches was in the city of Ephesus. Christ first complimented the Ephesian Christians for their hard work, their perseverance through hardships, and their choice not to follow wicked, false leaders. They sound like a pretty good church, don't they?

But He then added this: *"But I have this against you, that you have left your first love. Therefore remember from where you have fallen, and repent and do the deeds you did at first; or else I am coming to you and will remove your lampstand out of its place— unless you repent."* (Rev. 2:4-5)

How easy it is to believe that leaving our first love is normal to the Christian walk! Ladies, it is not normal, although (unfortunately) it is not uncommon. "Normal" Christianity is a vibrant, Spirit-filled, love relationship with Jesus. Anything less is sub-normal.

Jesus said that if we have abandoned our first love to walk in a sub-normal, half-hearted relationship with Him, we need to repent. The Greek word that is translated as *repent* here indicates that you would change your thinking toward something. That is, you would stop having the wrong attitude toward it and begin to have the attitude that God has toward it.

The Greek says that the one who has left her first love should repent and do the "first works." The word for *first* can be used to indicate first in time, but it can also indicate first in place, order, or importance. Perhaps your experience—like mine—was a very brief honeymoon filled with first love, followed by a great lapse. Or perchance you never really felt that your works at the beginning were what they should have been. The emphasis here is on works that reflect first love (works that are first in priority) not so much that they were the works we did at first.

If you have never had a 100% giving attitude toward your husband, you cannot "return" to that attitude. You simply must go there.

In the same way, you don't want to return to the deeds that you did shortly after you came to Christ if they did not reflect first love. Rather, repentance requires that you show by your deeds that you are living in first love now. "First works" refers to the quality of the works more than chronology. "First love" has more to do with loving Him first (making Him our first priority and desiring to give Him 100% of our very selves) than it relates to the love we had at the beginning of our relationship with Him.

The church at Thyatira did not walk in first love at the beginning. Jesus told John to write this to them: *"I know your deeds, and your love and faith and service and perseverance, and that your deeds of late are greater than at first."* The works that these people had done in the beginning were not evidence of first love, but they were doing better at the time that Christ appeared to John on Patmos. To those who were doing well, He said, *"...I place no other burden on you.*

Nevertheless what you have, hold fast until I come." (Rev 2:19, 24-25) Many of them still needed further repentance, however, and the Lord gave them instructions.

There are dangers when we swallow the enemy's lie that we cannot continue in first love. First of all, it accuses God of requiring of us what we cannot fulfill. He has commanded us to walk in first love. To say that we cannot obey that command is to accuse Him of injustice. God is not an unjust Judge!

Furthermore, we begin to backslide if we abandon our first love. Listen to the message that Jesus instructed John to send to the Laodicean church:

"...I know your deeds, that you are neither cold nor hot; I wish that you were cold or hot. So because you are lukewarm, and neither hot nor cold, I will spit you out of My mouth. Because you say, 'I am rich, and have become wealthy, and have need of nothing,' and you do not know that you are wretched and miserable and poor and blind and naked, I advise you to buy from Me gold refined by fire so that you may become rich, and white garments so that you may clothe yourself, and that the shame of your nakedness will not be revealed; and eye salve to anoint your eyes so that you may see. Those whom I love, I reprove and discipline; therefore be zealous and repent. Behold, I stand at the door and knock; if anyone hears My voice and opens the door, I will come in to him and will dine with him, and he with Me. He who overcomes, I will grant to him to sit down with Me on My throne, as I also overcame and sat down with My Father on His throne. He who has an ear, let him hear what the Spirit says to the churches." (Rev. 3:14-22)

It's not uncommon to hear verse 20 quoted as an evangelistic passage, inviting unbelievers to receive Christ. I believe that He does indeed stand at the door of non-Christian hearts and knock, requesting that they invite Him into their hearts and lives. In this context, however, Jesus is speaking not of unbelievers, but of the hearts of Christians. This was written to a church! It was written to Christian people! Thus, if we are not diligent to avoid it, we may find ourselves in the same predicament as the Laodiceans who had left their first love and grown lukewarm.

Look at verses 15-16. That word *spit* is a nice, polite way of translating the Greek. The literal meaning of the word, however, is *vomit*. When we allow ourselves to backslide into lukewarmness as the Laodiceans did, we make Jesus nauseous. Oh, my sisters! We don't want to do that! He is our Bridegroom, and we want to make Him happy.

Christ furthermore instructed John to send a letter to the church at Sardis:

"...I know your deeds, that you have a name that you are alive, but you are dead. Wake up, and strengthen the things that remain, which were about to die; for I have not found your deeds completed in the sight of My God. So remember what you have received and heard; and keep it, and repent. Therefore if you do not wake up, I will come like a thief, and you will not know at what hour I will come to you..." (Rev. 3:1-3)

These are serious words of warning. We do not want to find ourselves in that condition. We do not want to drift away from first love until we are more spiritually dead than alive—until our spiritual lives are more reputation than reality.

How do you suppose a Christian gets into that predicament? Do you think that on a certain day a person who passionately loves Jesus suddenly makes a decision to move into lukewarmness? I think not. Consciously making such a decision isn't necessary to leaving our first love. Like a woman who gradually "falls out of love" with her husband, Christians often gradually drift away from the honeymoon devotion to the Lord.

When we drift away from our first love, we lose our spiritual momentum. We stop moving ahead with Christ. Some people have such a brief honeymoon period with the Lord (as I did in the beginning) that they may not even realize that they have drifted.

What are some things that could lead away from our honeymoon zeal? How do Christians leave their first love?

People are often drawn away from first love by laziness and a lack of self-discipline. They choose to do only what they want to do, what they feel like doing. (Isn't that what keeps you from giving yourself 100% to your natural husband?) Doing what you feel like doing will mean that you don't make the effort to find time for the

Lord unless you are in the mood. Far too frequently, our feelings lead us astray, and sin hardens our hearts. (See Heb. 3.)

"We want each of you to show this same diligence to the very end, in order to make your hope sure. We do not want you to become lazy, but to imitate those who through faith and patience inherit what has been promised." (Heb. 6:11-12 NIV)

Sometimes people leave their first love because they have become distracted by busy-ness. They fill their lives with so much activity that they leave no time to commune with the Lord and listen to His voice. They simply begin to neglect the Lord, the Lover of their souls. Soon they find that spiritual intimacy wanes and worship begins to be artificial and mechanical.

Maintaining our first love requires that we go on with Christ. It requires growth and progress. If we cannot have a passionate, loving relationship with our natural husbands without careful attention to maintaining the marriage, how could we neglect our first love for Jesus and expect it to flourish?

Walking in first love requires our diligence, but drifting is usually the result of carelessness and inattention. It's pretty effortless. All that is necessary to drift away is to neglect the relationship. *"For this reason we must pay much closer attention to what we have heard, so that we do not drift away from it. For if the word spoken through angels proved unalterable, and every transgression and disobedience received a just penalty, how will we escape if we neglect so great a salvation?..."* (Heb. 2:1-3)

Christ was once asked to name the most important commandment. *"Jesus replied: 'Love the Lord your God with **all** your heart and with **all** your soul and with **all** your mind. This is the first and greatest commandment.'"* (Matt. 22:37-38 NIV, emphasis mine)

Can you ever imagine that He would be pleased if you had a 50-50 attitude in your relationship with Him? Far too often, whether verbalized or not, Christians do have such an outlook. I hear women say things like these:

- The Lord understands that this is just the way I am.
- I'm only human, and I can't help myself. I don't think God expects me to control my temper [or gossip or gluttony or

self-centeredness or greed or whatever other sin has a hold on her].
- I love God, but I don't want to be a fanatic who makes that my whole life.

Remember, ladies, that the Lord is the great Giver. We cannot enrich Him with our money or possessions, and we cannot do for Him what He cannot do. We can give to Him nothing but our reverence, our love, our praises, our gratitude, our hearts, and our lives.

Don't you think that He wants us to give 100% of our hearts and lives to Him? If I truly love my heavenly Bridegroom with all my being, I will want to give what I can to Him: my life, my obedience, my praises, my love, and my worship.

Is there any part of your life that you withhold from the Lord? Jesus said, *"So then, none of you can be My disciple who does not give up all his own possessions."* (Luke 14:33) This doesn't mean that He wants us to give everything we own to the poor and move into a convent. It means that we are to regard Him as the owner of all we have and see ourselves as only stewards who use possessions as He would have us do.

He has given Himself fully for us, and He wants us to give ourselves to Him 100%.

"Only fear the LORD and serve Him in truth with all your heart; for consider what great things He has done for you." (1 Sam. 12:24)

"And this is my prayer: that your love may abound more and more in knowledge and depth of insight, so that you may be able to discern what is best and may be pure and blameless until the day of Christ, filled with the fruit of righteousness that comes through Jesus Christ—to the glory and praise of God." (Phil. 1:9-11 NIV)

Commitment

❋❋❋

Most people who remember *any* of their marriage vows will recall that they promised to remain exclusively faithful to each other until they are parted by death. In today's world, these words are often a sham. Marriages, both in the world and in the body of believers, end in divorce with appalling frequency.

Why do you think that the kingdom of darkness presents so much temptation in this particular area? Our intimate, committed relationship with the Lord is portrayed in Scripture as a marriage covenant, and the enemy of our souls hates us and abhors our love relationship with Jesus. To mar the image of this spiritual union, Satan tempts marriage partners to chase after other lovers outside the covenant that they have made with their spouses and/or to find flimsy excuses to divorce each other.

Couples don't get to the divorce courtroom with one giant step. Little steps lead their hearts astray. It's the same with apostasy. A person doesn't move from being a devout Christian disciple to becoming a reprobate in one giant step.

After many small steps, however, people who wander away from the Lord will eventually find their relationship with Him destroyed. *"For in the case of those who have once been enlightened and* **have tasted of the heavenly gift** *and have* **been made partakers of the Holy Spirit**, *and have tasted the good word of God and the powers of the age to come, and* **then have fallen away**, *it is impossible to renew them again to repentance, since they again crucify to them-*

selves the Son of God and put Him to open shame." (Heb. 6:4-6, emphasis mine) Notice that this passage refers to Christians who fall away, not to unbelievers.

*"For if we go on sinning willfully after receiving the knowledge of the truth, there no longer remains a sacrifice for sins, but a terrifying expectation of judgment and THE FURY OF A FIRE WHICH WILL CONSUME THE ADVERSARIES. Anyone who has set aside the Law of Moses dies without mercy on the testimony of two or three witnesses. How much severer punishment do you think he will deserve who has trampled under foot the Son of God, and has regarded as unclean the blood of the covenant **by which he was sanctified**, and has insulted the Spirit of grace?"* (Heb. 10:26-29, emphasis mine) Again, notice that this speaks of a person who has been made holy (sanctified) by the blood of Christ and then turned away.

Jesus said of Satan, *"...He was a murderer from the beginning, and does not stand in the truth because there is no truth in him. Whenever he speaks a lie, he speaks from his own nature, for he is a liar and the father of lies."* (John 8:44) When the devil deceived Eve with his lies, his purpose was to bring about her death. He always tempts us to turn away from our commitment to the heavenly Bridegroom for the same reason, and he relishes leading people to destroy the earthly marital image of that relationship.

I think that it will serve us well to keep in mind what we vowed before the Lord in our marriage covenants.

To Keep Him in Sickness and in Health

In my wedding, I promised to keep my husband whether sick or well. This seems pretty self-explanatory. It means that the marriage is not limited to days when we are both healthy, but is to continue when one of us is ill. It means that I made a covenant to remain with him regardless of whether he could work to support me, or was too sick to do so. Our vows stand in force if he is healthy enough to do with me the enjoyable things I want to do, or if he is not. It means that I would cling to him even if he were to become impotent, if he were to develop Alzheimer's disease, if he were to have an accident that made him a quadriplegic, or if he were to fall into a coma. I vowed to keep him in sickness and in health. Period. This promise appeared twice in my wedding, which seems to intensify it.

Forsaking All Others

God requires that His people love Him supremely. *"You shall love the LORD your God with all your heart and with all your soul and with all your might.* (Deut. 6:5)

He commands that His people forsake all other gods: *"Do not follow other gods, the gods of the peoples around you; for the LORD your God, who is among you, is a jealous God and his anger will burn against you, and he will destroy you from the face of the land."* (Deut. 6:14-15 NIV) He declares, *"You shall have no other gods before me."* (Ex. 20:3 NIV) John reminds us, *"Little children, guard yourselves from idols."* (1 John 5:21) Idolatry is the equivalent of spiritual adultery.

Sometimes we look at the stories in the Old Testament and think that the commands against idolatry are not a problem for us. We don't bow down to a golden statue or pray to a tree, so we don't realize that we are tempted with idolatry. "John must be speaking to someone else," we think. But as we consider whether we are forsaking all others, we need to remember that there are idols that are not statues.

"For this you know with certainty, that no immoral or impure person or covetous man, who is an idolater, has an inheritance in the kingdom of Christ and God." (Eph. 5:5) Paul tells us that a covetous heart is an idolatrous heart. Jesus said, *"No one can serve two masters; for either he will hate the one and love the other, or he will be devoted to one and despise the other. You cannot serve God and wealth."* (Matt. 6:24) Do possessions steal your affections from the heavenly Bridegroom's place? Do they occupy your thoughts and desires more than He does?

"For many walk, of whom I often told you, and now tell you even weeping, that they are enemies of the cross of Christ, whose end is destruction, whose god is their appetite, and whose glory is in their shame, who set their minds on earthly things." (Phil. 3:18-19) When

an appetite—for food, drink, sex, drugs, or whatever—truly controls someone, that person has allowed that appetite to become an idol.

Some women find that their families become the idol that steals their focus from the Lord. *"If anyone comes to Me, and does not hate his own father and mother and wife and children and brothers and sisters, yes, and even his own life, he cannot be My disciple."* (Luke 14:26)

Now we know from other Scriptures that Jesus wants us to love our families. *Hate* here is relative to our love for the Lord. Our love for our families must seem like hatred when compared to our love for the Lord. Ladies, we must search our hearts and be sure that we love Him before all.

Jesus said, *"Anyone who loves his father or mother more than me is not worthy of me; anyone who loves his son or daughter more than me is not worthy of me…"* (Matt. 10:37 NIV)

Do you love your family more than you love the Lord? Do you want to please your family more than you desire to please the Lord? We need not be concerned that we love our families too much. That's not the problem. It is not that we should *decrease* our love for our families, but that we must *increase* our love for the divine Bridegroom.

Frequently, it is the influence of the world that draws away the hearts of Christians from devotion to the Lord. *"You adulteresses, do you not know that friendship with the world is hostility toward God?…"* (Jas. 4:4) Does the world's view of life sway your thinking away from the teachings of the Bible? Does fitting in with your neighbors and co-workers seem more important than obeying the Lord with a whole heart?

The Lord says, *"You shall be holy, for I am holy."* (1 Pet. 1:16 RSV) To be holy is to be set apart from the world in order to be wholly His.

Just as God wants my heart to belong to Him and to no other god, I promised to forsake all others when I married my husband. I suspect that you made a similar vow when you were joined to your husband. That means that we wives are not free to dally in unholy relationships with other men, physically *or* emotionally.

I must add that it is exceedingly dangerous for a woman to cultivate a close friendship with a man unless it is a relationship involving both couples—including her husband and the other man's wife. I am aware of a number of illicit relationships that began when a man and a woman who were married to other people developed a close friendship. Beware of discussing your marriage problems with a man at work or listening to his marital difficulties. Even discussing your marital problems with your pastor without the presence of your husband and/or the pastor's wife is risky. You could be setting both yourself and your co-worker or pastor in the path of temptation.

God requires that spouses be faithful to one another. An adulteress violates not only the covenant with her husband, but also a covenant made with God. The Bible refers to this in Proverbs:

"It [wisdom] *will save you also from the adulteress,*
the wayward wife with her seductive words,
who has left the partner of her youth
and ignored **the covenant she made before God.** (2:16-17 NIV, emphasis mine)

The godly wife will wear modest, not seductive, clothing in public. She will be careful about how she sits and moves, because she will desire to keep herself only for her husband. Men are aroused by what they see, so she must not give her body to another man even in sight. Remember that Jesus said that a man who looks at a woman for the purpose of lusting after her has committed adultery with her in his heart. (Matt. 5:28) It follows, then, that the woman who has displayed her body for another man has in a sense given her body to him. I believe that is part of what is meant by the warnings against sensuality, debauchery, or lasciviousness that appear in the Bible. (For example, see Gal. 5:19 and 2 Cor. 12:21.)

When I was a teenager, girls were taught certain things about the way ladies sat and moved. I must add that I didn't really understand why we were told to sit and move properly. To tell you the truth, I pretty much considered it an etiquette thing, because I didn't understand then that men were so easily aroused by sight. I was taught only that it was ladylike to sit and move one way and unladylike to sit or move improperly. Nonetheless, I still knew what to do.

It appears that this type of training is not the norm for girls today. I have seen young women—women whom I know to be devoted to the Lord—dressing and posturing themselves in ways that present great temptation to men.

For example, I remember a situation at a Bible study one evening. A young woman across the room was wearing shorts—not even particularly short or tight ones—and the way she sat with her legs apart made the hem of her shorts form an arrow pointing to her crotch. Additionally, she was sitting in a kitchen chair and the men across from her were on a low couch. The "arrow" was just at eye level for these men.

I have seen other young women and teenage girls wear clothing to church that was so tight, short, or low-necked (or that had such a long slit up the side of the skirt) that it *must* fall into the category of indecent apparel and sensuality. (See 1 Tim. 2:9 and Gal. 5:19.) Not aroused by sight as men are, women are frequently unaware of how these things affect men. I have overheard and read words of complaint from men about the temptations that such clothing presents to them when they attempt to worship while within sight of women dressed in that manner. Be careful, then, that you don't "give your body" to the eyes of a man other than your husband.

Furthermore, the promise to forsake all others includes leaving not only other men, but also our parents. While the bride and groom should continue to love and to honor their parents, they should also "leave" them.

Sometimes parents have a hard time letting go of the way the parent-child relationship has been before and want to control the young couple's life together. We older women must be on guard so that we don't put such pressure on the younger couple.

I encourage you, young wives, to respectfully refuse to allow your parents to manipulate you (through guilt, rage, money, or any other means) to put their wishes before those of your husband. *"For this reason a man shall **leave his father and his mother**, and be joined to his wife; and they shall become one flesh."* (Gen. 2:24, Eph. 5:31, emphasis mine)

In fact, from the wedding day on, *no one* else on earth should come before the spouse. This is because marriage is a symbol for the relationship of Christ and the church.

To Have and to Hold from This Day Forward

I also promised "to have and to hold" my husband in a variety of circumstances:

For better, for worse—That is, whether in good times or bad, happy days or unhappy ones. It means that I would hold to him whether the marriage turned out to be as I imagined it would be or whether it did not. It means that the marriage would continue whether we were getting along well or we were in conflict.

Now, let me assure you that I am not asking you to remain in a house where you or your children are in danger. Certainly you must find a place of safety in such a situation. Most women who want out of their marriages, however, are not leaving for that reason.

Sometimes a woman has said something like this to me: "I don't think that God wants me to stay in an unhappy marriage." My response is this: "I don't think He does either. I think that He wants you and your husband to be filled with joy. Why don't the two of you see what you can do to make your relationship happier?"

Some will say, "I didn't know what I was doing. I was too young to get married." Others will say, "I think I married the wrong person." Perhaps you were not mature enough to get married, but you did marry. Perhaps you unwisely chose which man to marry. Nevertheless, the fact of the matter is that you vowed to your husband and to the Lord that you would be joined to this man.

I don't know how many times I've heard someone say, "Well, I think it's better for the children to have divorced parents than to have parents who fight all the time." They say this as if those are the only two options! Why can't those two unhappy parents learn to relate to each other in such an unselfish way that they put the other before themselves? Why can't they learn a good way to resolve differences? Why can't they learn to forgive? Every successful marriage is made up of people who have learned those lessons. Most problems are grounds for counseling, not divorce. The main cause of divorce is selfishness, and there is *nothing* good about divorce.

If you think that divorcing the father of your children is an escape from being around him, you are mistaken. Because you have children together, you will see him for the rest of your life. You will see him when the children are ill. You both will attend the children's sporting events, band concerts, graduations, and weddings. You will both be there for the births of your grandchildren. You will face the necessity of alternating holidays and dividing vacation time. You will still be around each other, but everything will be *far* more complicated than it is right now. Please—I beg you—work on the marriage instead of trying to run away!

For richer, for poorer—That is, you promised to continue your covenant regardless of whether or not your finances are adequate, whether or not you can buy things that you want, whether or not you like the way he handles money, and whether or not you are in debt.

I'm told that conflict over finances contributes to 90% of all divorces. (It may not be the primary cause in all of those instances, but it is said to be a contributing factor.) Ladies, it's vital that we learn to be content with our financial circumstances, to live within our means, and to communicate with our husbands about financial issues.

When Paul wrote, *"I can do all things through Christ who strengthens me,"* it was in the context of learning to live with every kind of financial circumstance. It immediately followed the words, *"...I have learned in whatever state I am, to be content: I know how to be abased, and I know how to abound. Everywhere and in all things I have learned both to be full and to be hungry, both to abound and to suffer need."* (Phil. 4:11-13 NKJV) Paul is assuring us that we too can *learn* to be content with our financial situations.

Until Death Us Do Part

This phrase in my wedding vows sets the duration of my covenant. I pledged to keep these promises as long as both of us are still alive. I vowed to set myself apart for only him as long as we both live. The Bible says, *"So then, if while her husband is living she is joined to another man, she shall be called an adulteress; but if her husband dies, she is free from the law, so that she is not an adulteress though she is joined to another man."* (Rom. 7:3)

Too many couples interpret this vow to mean, "as long as you make me happy," or, "until someone I like better comes along." What did Jesus say about that?

"Some Pharisees came to him to test him. They asked, 'Is it lawful for a man to divorce his wife for any and every reason?'

"'Haven't you read,' he replied, 'that at the beginning the Creator made them male and female, and said, "For this reason a man will leave his father and mother and be united to his wife, and the two will become one flesh"? So they are no longer two, but one. Therefore what God has joined together, let man not separate.'

"'Why then,' they asked, 'did Moses command that a man give his wife a certificate of divorce and send her away?'

"Jesus replied, 'Moses permitted you to divorce your wives because your hearts were hard. But it was not this way from the beginning. I tell you that anyone who divorces his wife, except for marital unfaithfulness, and marries another woman commits adultery.'" (Matt. 19:3-9 NIV)

Divorce is not God's plan. It causes devastation in the lives of the children, the extended family, and even friends. Moreover, if marriage pictures the relationship of Christ and the church, then divorce symbolizes apostasy. No wonder God hates divorce! (Mal. 2:16.)

The Bible gives specific commands about this. *"To the married I give this command (not I, but the Lord): A wife must not separate from her husband. But if she does, she must remain unmarried or else be reconciled to her husband. And a husband must not divorce his wife."* (1 Cor. 7:10-11 NIV)

There came a time when God was not accepting the offerings and sacrifices of the people of Israel. Consider the prophet's words to his fellow Israelites concerning this. *"This is another thing you do: you cover the altar of the LORD with tears, with weeping and with groaning, because He no longer regards the offering or accepts it with favor from your hand. Yet you say, 'For what reason?' Because the LORD has been a witness between you and the wife of your youth, against whom you have dealt treacherously, though* *she is your companion and your **wife by covenant**."* (Mal. 2:13-14, emphasis mine)

When a man and woman vow to marry each other, it is God who creates the new union. *"So they are no longer two, but one flesh. What therefore **God has joined together**, let no man separate."* (Matt. 19:6, emphasis mine) The marriage partners make the promises, but God unites the man and the woman into a couple. Then the minister merely acknowledges what has happened by pronouncing them man and wife.

Now, this chapter is not intended to bring condemnation to anyone who has already divorced a husband without Scriptural grounds and is now on a second marriage. You cannot change the past. What you *can* do is sincerely repent of anything that you did to cause the first divorce (even if you believe that your first husband was more at fault than you were) and then resolve to do all you can do to make your current marriage last until death.

Remember that the Greek word for repent means that you change your thinking to bring it into agreement with God's viewpoint. If you have repented of something, you no longer justify your sin, but rather begin to agree with God that it was wicked.

In the Old Testament, repenting carries the connotation of turning around, of changing directions. In other words, your behavior as well as your thinking must change. Consider Acts 3:19: *"Therefore repent and return, so that your sins may be wiped away, in order that times of refreshing may come from the presence of the Lord..."* The word that is rendered *repent* means *to think differently afterward*, and the word that is translated *return* means *to turn around and change directions*. Both are needed if you are to truly repent.

It's commitment that keeps a marriage together during difficult days. Don't deceive yourself. *Every* marriage has troublesome times. Romance alone will never hold a marriage together for the long haul.

No marriage is perfect, and there are at least a few occasions in every marriage when the relationship is actually pretty lousy. Money gets tight. Disagreements arise over where to live, how to rear the children, or how to divide the work. If you want to please God and to honor the vows that you made to your husband before Him, you must be committed to "hanging in there" during the tough times.

Rebuilding

❊❊❊

Well, how does your house look? Think back to the story at the beginning of this book. Does your marriage remind you of the house of the Smiths, or of the Johnsons? Or is it somewhere in between?

Does your marriage give an appropriate picture of the relationship of Christ and the church? Do you show respect to your husband? Do you meet his need for intimacy? Can it be said that the heart of your husband trusts in you, and that he has no lack of gain? Are you like a strong treasure chest that he can confidently trust with what he holds dear? Are you practicing good communication? Do you follow his leadership? Are you fulfilling your marriage vows? If you have been a "foolish wife" who has "torn down" part of your marriage, I urge you to begin to rebuild it.

As I considered this closing chapter, I thought about the experience of Nehemiah and his countrymen as they rebuilt the wall of Jerusalem. Nehemiah learned that the Holy City was in ruins and its wall had been broken down. He confessed the sins of Israel (which had led to the destruction) and sought God's assistance to restore the city and the wall. (You can read about this in Neh. 1:1-2:5.)

In answer to Nehemiah's prayer, God graciously made it possible for him to go back to Jerusalem. Nehemiah's name means *Yahweh consoles*, or *Yahweh comforts*. The city of Jerusalem was in ruins and its people in disgrace, so God sent Nehemiah to comfort them and to help them.

When Nehemiah arrived in Israel, he first inspected the wall to see what needed to be repaired. (Neh. 2:11-16.) Likewise, we wives need to periodically take inventory of what behaviors we might need to change in our marital relationships.

It was not an easy task for Nehemiah and the others to complete their work. Sanballat the Horonite, Tobiah the Ammonite official, and Geshem the Arab attempted to frighten them: *"What is this thing you are doing? Are you rebelling against the king?"* (Neh. 2:19) Hoping to bring discouragement, they ridiculed the labor and taunted the workers: *"What are those feeble Jews doing? Will they restore their wall? Will they offer sacrifices? Will they finish in a day? Can they bring the stones back to life from those heaps of rubble—burned as they are?"* (Neh. 4:2 NIV)

In the same way, the forces of darkness will whisper despair to your mind. They will say, "It's too hard to change. This is just the way you are." Or perhaps they will say, "Your marriage is hopeless. It can never be better."

I will confess to you that as I was writing this book, the enemy sought to discourage me every time I made the slightest mistake in my marriage relationship. "Who are you to write this book? Do you realize what you just said to your husband? Did you notice that you were selfish today? You yourself messed up," the accuser whispered to me. "Why should *you* write about marriage?" When the tempter speaks to us about our failures, his goal is to bring despair to our hearts.

The conviction of the Holy Spirit about a failure, however, is aimed at restoration. His desire is to lead us to repentance. *"For the sorrow that is according to the will of God produces a repentance without regret, leading to salvation, but the sorrow of the world produces death."* (2 Cor. 7:10)

Another strategy of the kingdom of darkness is to remind you of your *husband's* shortcomings: "Why should you make such an effort to rebuild your marriage? Let him first begin to do right, and *then* you can make some changes."

When the enemies of the Jews brought discouragement to those who were rebuilding the wall, the workers cried out to God as they stood guard to protect themselves from attack: *"But we prayed to our God and posted a guard day and night to meet this threat."* (Neh. 4:9 NIV)

Like Nehemiah and his companions, you can call on the God of heaven to help you resist the enemy who wants your "house" destroyed. You must stay alert and be aware of Satan's schemes to ruin your marriage.

"Put on the full armor of God, so that you will be able to stand firm against the schemes of the devil. For our struggle is not against flesh and blood, but against the rulers, against the powers, against the world forces of this darkness, against the spiritual forces of wickedness in the heavenly places. Therefore, take up the full armor of God, so that you will be able to resist in the evil day, and having done everything, to stand firm. Stand firm therefore, HAVING GIRDED YOUR LOINS WITH TRUTH, and HAVING PUT ON THE BREASTPLATE OF RIGHTEOUSNESS, and having shod YOUR FEET WITH THE PREPARATION OF THE GOSPEL OF PEACE; in addition to all, taking up the shield of faith with which you will be able to extinguish all the flaming arrows of the evil one. And take THE HELMET OF SALVATION, and the sword of the Spirit, which is the word of God. With all prayer and petition pray at all times in the Spirit..." (Eph. 6:11-18)

Resist the evil words of the enemy, *"...taking every thought captive to the obedience of Christ."* (2 Cor. 10:5)

Your enemy is persistent. You must consistently draw near to God and persevere in your resistance to Satan if you want to be victorious. *"Submit therefore to God. Resist the devil and he will flee from you."* (Jas. 4:7) Notice that the command to submit to the Lord *precedes* the promise that resisting Satan will cause him to flee.

Nehemiah and the other rebuilders continued to work in spite of the opposition because they considered their project to be worth the sacrifice and effort. Your marriage is worth it, as well.

If you have given your husband reason to lose faith in you—whether it's your family finances, his confidential conversations with you, your promises to him, your dealings with the children, your affections, your lack of respect, or any other area—it will be harder to regain his trust than it was to gain it in the first place. Begin by repenting in your heart and confessing your sin to the Lord and then to your husband. As your mate sees your daily faithfulness *over time*, you will likely be able to once again enjoy his confidence in you. Let's concentrate on being wives that the hearts of our husbands can trust!

What about your spiritual house? Is your life built on the Rock? Are you a trustworthy steward of the Lord's blessings? Can He trust you to appropriately use His gifts to you? Are you faithful with the little things, so that He can trust you with much? Are you walking in first love? Are you finding joy in His presence? How is your prayer life? Do you enjoy spiritual intimacy with the Lord? Do you walk in obedience to Christ's leadership? Is He supreme in your life? Do you trust Him to provide for you and to protect you? Do you fulfill your responsibilities to Him?

When I was teaching the *Woman to Woman* classes, I sometimes included a place in the ladies' notebooks that asked this question: "What is the Lord saying to you tonight?" In a private moment near the end of the class, each lady would write in that space what the Lord was speaking personally to her through that evening's lesson. What had she learned? What had the Lord shown her about her life that needed to change? How was she relating to her husband and to the Lord?

As I bring this book to a close, I would like to ask you a similar question: What is the Lord saying to you through this book? If there were specific areas in which He showed you the need to improve, perhaps it would be helpful to review the chapters on those subjects. You may find it beneficial to write in a notebook what the Lord is saying to you so that you can prayerfully endeavor to make the changes that He asks of you.

The writer of Hebrews says that if we hear God's voice about a matter and fail to respond, it will harden our hearts. (Heb. 3:12-15) We don't want that to happen. If our hearts harden, we will become spiritually hard of hearing or even deaf. It will be much harder for us to hear His voice in the future.

My prayer for you is *"...that you may be filled with the knowledge of His will in all spiritual wisdom and understanding, so that you will walk in a manner worthy of the Lord, to please Him in all respects, bearing fruit in every good work and increasing in the knowledge of God..."* (Col. 1:9-10)